Field Guide

Trees

of Britain, Europe and North America

Andrew Cleave

**Photographs by
Nature Photographers Ltd**

The Crowood Press

First published in 1994 by
The Crowood Press Ltd
Ramsbury, Marlborough
Wiltshire SN8 2HR

Artwork by Paul Sterry

British Library Cataloguing in Publication Data
A catalogue record for this book is available from the British Library.

ISBN 1 85223 801 1

Photograph previous page: a Rowan tree in fruit in autumn.

Acknowledgements

Many individuals and institutions have been helpful in the preparation of this book. Thanks are due to: Bedgebury National Pinetum, Forestry Authority; Bicton Gardens, Devon; Exeter University Estates Department; Sir Harold Hillier Gardens and Arboretum, Hampshire; Killerton Gardens, The National Trust; Royal Botanic Gardens, Kew; Tresco Abbey Garden; Westonbirt Arboretum, Forestry Authority; Winkworth Arboretum, The National Trust; The Wrigley Company, Plymouth, Devon.

Edited and designed by
D & N Publishing
DTP & Editorial Services
Crowood Lane, Ramsbury
Marlborough, Wiltshire SN8 2HR

Phototypeset by FIDO Imagesetting,
Witney, Oxon

Printed and bound in Great Britain by
BPC Hazell Books Ltd., Aylesbury

Typefaces used: body text, Gill Sans; headings, Gill Sans Extra Bold; folios, Gill Sans Condensed; Latin names in species headings, Sabon.

Contents

Introduction

Most of us take trees for granted and could not imagine a landscape, either urban or rural, in which trees did not play some part. It used to be said that it was not possible to stand in any street in London without being able to see a tree. This may still be true, and probably applies to most other major cities around the world. Trees are planted in our gardens, in our city streets and town squares, alongside our roads and in town and country parks, so, although not everyone can visit what remains of our once extensive natural woodlands it is still possible to study a surprising variety of trees very close to our own homes.

We are all familiar with trees as a general group, but how many different kinds of tree are there? Is it possible to identify some of the more common species? This book is an attempt to shed some light on the mysteries of tree identification.

THE IMPORTANCE OF TREES

We accept trees as a permanent part of the landscape, and only notice any changes if a tree blows down in a gale, or is damaged by disease. Trees are thought of by many people as almost static, lifeless objects in the landscape which are simply there for decoration. Few people stop to really look at a tree, and try to understand more about it. A tree is a living thing which respires, grows and reproduces, is sensitive to changes in its environment and is subject to diseases and injuries. The largest and the oldest living organisms in the world are trees. Trees are found in virtually every part of the world

Cork oak bark after harvesting; one of the many useful products derived from trees.

Opposite: a forest of firs and spruces covers many upland areas, such as this Swiss valley.

Many trees, like these White Poplars, are grown in plantations, because of their usefulness as timber producers.

where living things can exist; some can grow in salt water at the very margins of the sea, while nearly all terrestrial habitats, apart from the ice-caps and high mountain tops, have trees on them in some form.

People have many different relationships with trees. To some they are nothing more than a nuisance – as when autumn leaves have to be swept off a drive, or when the summer sun is blocked from a garden. To others they may be a blessing when an ugly view is softened by a tracery of branches and leaves. Many will look on trees as a source of food, for they can provide fruits, nuts, seeds and oils in abundance. To some they are an important source of income if felled to provide timber. Many people depend on trees as the sole source of fuel and building materials for their homes. Vast quantities of timber are required to produce the pulp which is turned into the paper that we all use in ever-increasing amounts. Trees can provide drugs and other valuable chemicals. In the natural world trees are essential for the survival of vast numbers of other plants and animals which depend on them for food and shelter. They dominate the landscape in a way in which no other plants can, and support life in more ways than we can understand.

TREES FOR EVERY CLIMATE

Trees are able to grow in a surprising variety of environmental conditions. The hardiest trees are usually the conifers, which have a slender conical shape to help them shed snow, tough needle-like evergreen leaves which can make use of the limited sunlight of a short growing season and conserve water in the drought-like conditions of a freezing winter. They have wind-pollinated flowers which help them reproduce in a hostile environment where insect polli-

A forest of spruce trees grows near the Arctic Circle at the northern limit for tree growth in Alaska.

nators may be absent. The trees growing along the northern tree-line in North America, Northern Europe and Siberia are all hardy conifers. The higher mountain slopes further south produce conditions similar to those in the far north and it is the conifers that survive here, near to the limit of the summer snow-line. In more favourable climates there will be a longer growing season and it is here that the deciduous trees can grow, for there will be time for them to grow new leaves in the spring and shed them in the autumn. This annual cycle provides leaf-mould which enriches the soil in the autumn, and fresh green leaves in the spring which are food for millions of tiny caterpillars and other herbivores. There will be many insect-pollinated trees which produce showy flowers and may also produce edible fruits. Very hot and dry conditions are unsuitable for most broadleaved trees, which cannot cope with the con-

Remnants of the once extensive Caledonian pine forests remain in Scotland; the Scot's Pine is found in many upland regions of Europe.

An open woodland of Maritime Pines, that are tolerant of hot dry conditions, grows along the shores of the Mediterranean.

Mixed broadleaved woodland is the commonest woodland type in temperate lowland areas, such as this oakwood with Silver Birch and Hazel.

stant loss of water from their leaves, so here is another harsh habitat for the conifers, looking similar to those growing in the severe northern regions.

At one time great tracts of Europe and North America were covered with forests. The nature and composition of those forests varied according to climate, altitude and soils. The far north was covered with pine and birch forests, with trees tolerant of short growing seasons and long harsh winters, while to the south broadleaved trees grew in more favourable conditions and on richer soils. The hotter and drier southern regions were clothed with woods of evergreen trees, able to resist the heat and droughts of the long, hot summers. Mountain slopes were the home of magnificent firs, spruces and larches, whilst the marshes and swamps in the valleys supported willows and alders. This rich growth of trees was gradually cleared under the advance of early peoples who needed fuel, materials for their dwellings and space to graze livestock and grow crops, until at the present time only tiny fragments of the original forest cover remain. As people became more advanced in their knowledge of agriculture, more trees were cleared to provide land for crops and livestock, but some tree species were carefully selected and planted to provide shelter, fuel or building materials. Gradually, particular tree species were introduced from one region to another to suit man's growing needs for timber and food. Explorers in more recent times have found exciting new tree species and carried these back to their homes where they now grow alongside the native trees. It is now possible, in a relatively small area like the British Isles, to study trees from almost anywhere in the world.

The Horse Chestnut is one of the most attractive of flowering trees, and is often planted in parks and gardens.

HOW TREES SPREAD

Trees are relatively slow to colonize new habitats; their life-cycles are far longer than those of annual plants, for example, but once established, trees can dominate the landscape and provide the environment for a great variety of other plants and animals. Some trees, like the Willows and Birches, produce large numbers of small seeds which are easily spread by the wind, so these are often the first colonizers of new ground. Trees with larger seeds which rely on birds or mammals to carry their seeds in some way are slower to spread, but may benefit from the cover given by the first colonizers. A bird which has been feeding on rowan berries and ingested the seeds may then fly some distance and roost on a birch tree; in due course the seeds will pass through the bird's digestive system and leave its body in its droppings.

An acorn, that may have been buried on the woodland floor as a winter food store for a bird, commences germination in the spring.

The seed will then germinate in the protection of the surrounding trees. Larger seeds like acorns or walnuts may take longer to reach new habitats as they rely on larger animals to carry them off and bury them, perhaps as a winter store of food.

Left to their own devices, trees will eventually cover large areas and those which are carried to the wrong places will die out, while those which are in a suitable habitat will flourish. Few natural woodlands will consist of a single tree species; most will be composed of a mixture of trees, some dominating the scene, like large oaks, with other, smaller species like Holly and Hazel growing in the gaps between them, perhaps in natural clearings where a large tree has fallen after a storm. Within any natural woodland there will be trees of a great variety of ages and sizes; some will be very old and dying back under attacks by fungi, while others will be young saplings, waiting to replace the older trees. 'Man-made' woods tend to be dominated by a single species of tree, all planted in organized rows and all of approximately the same age and size. Periodic thinning leads to the removal of many of the trees, including any which are diseased, and finally the whole crop will be felled and probably replaced by more of the same. There is no continuity and no chance for natural regeneration or the development of natural communities of woodland plants and animals.

TREES AND MAN

When man first came on the scene, trees were felled to provide fuel or building materials, or to make land available for agriculture. It was some time before there was sufficient knowledge to be able to plant trees in new areas. Gradually, certain trees became well known and these were planted in new areas, altering their natural distribution and the composition of woodland communities. After the retreat of the Ice Age, early settlers planted poplars and elms to give themselves fuel and shelter, and pears, plums and medlars for their fruit. Citrus trees, valued for their prolific fruits, were among the earliest to be spread across the Mediterranean region, and the Romans took many trees, such as the Walnut, the Fig and the Sweet Chestnut, with them on their conquest of Europe. These trees are so well established across Europe and in Britain that they appear to be as much at home as the native trees. During the Middle Ages, and with improvements in communications across Europe and the Middle East, various fruit-bearing trees such as the Peach and the Mulberry were introduced into northern Europe, and conifers from the Mediterranean and the Alps were grown in large plantations in other parts of Europe to provide timber.

By the end of the fifteenth century the exploration of the Americas had yielded many exciting new trees for the European explorers, and the number of species taken back to Europe increased greatly as the northern and

Many trees, like these Osiers, have their natural appearance modified as they are pruned or lopped to provide useful materials; in this case flexible shoots for basket weaving.

southern continents were explored. The east coast of North America provided Europe with the White Cedar and the Balsam Poplar as the earliest introductions, and subsequently with many other trees of great commercial importance. The explorers who first reached the west coast of this vast and unknown continent were amazed by what they found. Some of the most magnificent trees in the world, growing in stunning landscapes, provided them with ample material for introducing into Europe. Giant and Coast Redwood were sent back from California, and from further north there were Monterey Pine, Douglas Fir, Sitka Spruce and Western Hemlock. Many more were found and shipped back to Europe and now many magnificent specimens can be found growing in Europe, especially in Britain. South America produced the Chile Pine or Monkey Puzzle and many attractive ornamental trees such as the Myrtles and Eucryphias. The large Southern Beeches were relatively recent discoveries.

Parts of Asia proved much more difficult to explore and they yielded up their botanical riches far more slowly. Explorers found it difficult to gain access to China, for example, or the remoter valleys in the Himalayas. The Maidenhair Tree arrived in Britain in 1760, but it was not until the mid-nineteenth century that more fruitful explorations were made. The latter part of the nineteenth and the early part of the twentieth century provided many of our most familiar and well-loved garden trees such as the Japanese Maples and flowering Cherries. Discoveries continue to be made, but rather less frequently now, and trees are still being transplanted around the world as our knowledge of their requirements and their importance to us increases.

Today, more than ever before, we have come to recognize the vital importance of trees to the survival of life on this planet. Yet, ironically, man's main uses for trees seem to involve cutting them down. From the time of the earliest civilizations, trees have provided food, shelter, building materials, weapons, drugs and a constantly renewable source of fuel. In more recent times, trees have been seen to be of immense importance to the landscape. They help bind the soil together and prevent erosion, and often, when they are cleared in great swathes from the land, nothing remains to prevent the life-supporting top-soil from being swept away in the first heavy rain-storm. Catastrophic mud-slides, denudation of once fertile hillsides, and appalling flood disasters are the result of removing the protective blanket of trees from areas of high rainfall. Trees produce the vital oxygen essential for the respiration of all living things and they recycle the waste gas, carbon dioxide, turning it into a valuable source of food. Many trees are known to have the ability to produce valuable drugs. Primitive peoples have long had the knowledge of how to use these, and we are only just beginning to learn this for ourselves, yet before we have had the chance to fully realize the potential of many of our trees we are destroying them and the habitats they support.

Some trees have a very rapid rate of growth and are excellent producers of food and fuel if managed properly. It is possible to cultivate trees in many

Plantations of conifers are often monocultures, with no other tree species occurring amongst them.

ways without damaging the environment. Knowing as much as we do about the importance of trees in the landscape, in the support of natural life in woods and forests, and in the maintenance of the way of life of large numbers of people on earth it seems incredible that we continue to destroy more than we ever replace. An encouraging thought for the future, however, is that some people are prepared to plant trees, to protect those that are threatened, to encourage others to learn about trees and, perhaps most importantly of all, to introduce young children to the world of trees.

WHAT IS A TREE?

There is no doubt that a magnificent specimen such as a giant redwood or an old and spreading oak is a tree, but would the tiny prostrate Juniper of the Arctic, or the Least Willow, also be trees or merely shrubs? One feature common to both trees and shrubs is that their stems increase in thickness each year by the laying down of internal layers of woody tissue in the form of concentric rings. This secondary thickening builds up year by year to increase the diameter of the stem and gives a permanent record of the age of the tree or shrub. Trees are generally considered to have a single main stem of 5m or more in height with a branching crown above this, whereas shrubs may have numerous stems arising at ground level and may not normally reach the height of a tree. The species described in this book are all considered to be trees, although some of them may have the habit of shrubs under certain conditions. Hazel, for example, is frequently seen as a multi-stemmed shrub in woodlands as a result of regular coppicing, or cutting back to the root-stock; each time this is done, new shoots arise from the root-stock and the hazel regenerates. If this cutting back does not take place, the hazel can grow as a medium-sized tree on a single stem.

Trees do not belong to a single family of plants; many plant families are represented, and some, like the Leguminosae and Rosaceae, also include many herbaceous plants and shrubs as well as large trees. The plant kingdom is divided up into two main classes, the Gymnosperms and the Angiosperms. The most primitive of the two classes is the Gymnosperms, the name meaning 'naked seeds'; the ovule is borne on a bract and not enclosed in a seed-pod or case. This class includes the Maidenhair Tree, a very primitive tree, and all the conifers, or cone-bearing trees. The name 'Angiosperms' means 'hidden seeds' and refers to the way the seeds are contained inside an ovary, a structure which may later develop into a seed-pod or fruit. This large class includes many well-known plant families, some of which are mostly made up of herbaceous plants, and some of which are mostly composed of trees. The Limes (Tiliaceae) and Elms (Ulmaceae), for example, are mostly trees, whilst the Foxglove family (Scrophulariaceae) has only a single tree. All of our garden and wild flowers, bulbs, palms and the grasses and cereals are Angiosperms.

Woody Tissue
The principal way in which a tree or shrub differs from other members of its family which are herbaceous plants is in its ability to produce woody tissue; this serves to conduct materials around the plant, and leads to the production of permanent shoots. In the case of perennial herbaceous plants the shoots die back at the end of each growing season, or in the case of annuals, the whole plant dies and the new generation arises from seeds formed by the previous generation.

Trees and shrubs have an important layer of cells enclosing shoots, buds and roots, called the cambium layer. This is an active layer which is constantly producing new cells on its inner and outer surfaces. The cells which grow on the inside of the cambium develop into the woody tissue or xylem which conducts water from the roots up to the shoots, buds and leaves. This eventually forms the bulk of the trunk and branches of the tree as a new layer is laid down each year. The cells which grow on the outside of the cambium form the conductive tissue which carries sugars from the leaves down to the roots. This vital layer must not be damaged. If a complete ring of this tissue is cut away from the trunk of a tree the roots will be deprived of nourishment from the leaves and the tree will eventually die.

Annual Rings

When the tree begins to grow vigorously in the spring it forms large conductive cells which allow the sap to flow freely through the trunk. As the season advances the cells produced by the cambium layer are smaller, with thicker walls for support, so they give a more dense appearance. In winter, cell production slows down and then ceases for a while, until there is a sudden burst of cell-production again in the spring when the large cells are produced once more. The new growth of large cells immediately next to the thinner layer of dense cells gives the appearance of the ring. In poor seasons fewer cells will be produced so the final ring will not be as thick as one for a

The concentric rings inside the trunk of a tree indicate its age.

good growing season. By examining a cut stump it is possible to count the rings and therefore discover the age of the tree, and also to find out which were the best growing seasons. This is a surprisingly accurate test of environmental conditions, as years in which there was known to be a summer drought, for example, can be shown to have narrower rings than warm and wet summers.

Bark

The bark is an important part of a tree, protecting the vital growing layers of cells below from varying environmental conditions. It is produced by a layer of cambium cells and grows to accommodate the increasing girth of the tree. It may be thin and papery, smooth and shiny, or thick and deeply furrowed (see illustrations). Each type of bark is matched to the tree's environment, so trees which are subject to heat and strong sunlight have a thicker bark than those that grow in cooler, humid conditions.

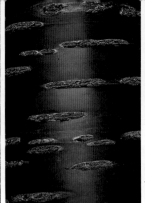

Smooth bark. The bark of *Eucalyptus johnstonii* is very smooth and sometimes peels away in thin strips.

Smooth bark. The smooth red bark of Tibetan Cherry is ringed with thick lenticels.

Peeling bark. The thin bark of London Plane peels away in irregular patches.

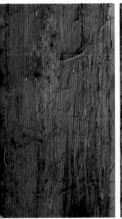

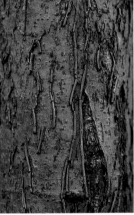

Peeling bark. The King William Pine has thick red bark which peels off vertically in long shreds.

Peeling bark. Hazel has a thin bark that peels vertically in tiny strips.

Furrowed bark. Bark, such as this mature Elder, may support colonies of simple plants like algae and mosses, giving the tree a greenish appearance.

REPRODUCTION

Trees normally produce flowers when they are several years old. The Common Beech, for example, will produce its first flowers at the age of 30 years, and will then continue to produce flowers each spring, followed in the autumn by its shiny brown seeds, for the next 200 years if it remains healthy. Some trees, such as Apples or Oaks, have years in which they produce a large crop of fruits or seeds, followed by other years with hardly any, whilst other species, such as some Maples, produce a good seed crop year after year.

The John Downie Crab Apple is often planted for its showy flowers. These are an attraction to pollinating insects like honey bees.

Some trees produce conspicuous flowers which attract pollinating insects. The Horse Chestnut is a magnificent sight in early summer as its abundant white pyramids of flowers cover the rich green foliage. Cherries and Apples also bear showy and attractive flowers which make them popular ornamental trees in gardens. Honey bees are particularly important pollinators, but numerous other insects visit the flowers for nectar and pollen. Many flowering trees produce an attractive scent in addition to their showy blooms and have long been prized by gardeners.

A larger number of trees are pollinated by the wind, and produce less conspicuous flowers. Their flowers are often in the form of catkins, which are pendulous and usually open before the leaves so that nothing impedes the free movement of the pollen grains. The flowers are normally of separate sexes and the male flowers are usually the largest and most abundant. Hornbeams produce yellowish-green male catkins which release clouds of pollen in the spring. Each catkin consists of numerous small flowers, lacking the bright petals of the insect-pollinated trees, but usually containing several yellow stamens protected by overlapping bracts. Together the flowers form the 'lamb's-tail' or catkin which moves freely in the wind, allowing the pollen to be shaken out. The female flowers of Hornbeam are also in the form of catkins, looking like leafy buds. After pollination they form pendulous clusters of winged seeds. Many wind-pollinated trees are such prolific producers of pollen that on warm breezy days in the spring clouds of pollen can sometimes be seen blowing from the trees.

The flowers of conifers will be either male or female, and borne on the same or different trees. There are no petals, but some of the flowers are still quite colourful and decorative. Male flowers are short-lived, falling off after they have released clouds of pollen, but the female flowers, often covered with brightly coloured scales, remain on the tree after pollination and develop into cones containing the seeds. They rely on the wind for pollination and also for seed dispersal. Some may take up to 3 years to develop and ripen fully, and at the end of this time they will be tough woody structures with tightly packed scales which open to release the seeds. A few close relatives of the conifers, such as the Yews, produce fleshy fruits instead of cones.

The flowers of broadleaved trees are usually hermaphrodite, containing both male and female parts, but there are a number of exceptions. They may occur on the same or different plants. Both will probably have petals in some form or other and they may also be scented. Small flowers are often grouped together in larger clusters to help attract pollinating insects. Some are wind-pollinated and open early in the year before the leaves, but insect-pollinated flowers usually open in the summer when more insects are active. Their fruits are much more varied than the cones of the conifers. They range from tiny papery seeds with wings, through nuts and berries, to large succulent fruits in a variety of shapes and colours. Many are edible and of great economic importance.

THE STRUCTURE OF A TREE

Each part of a tree has some important function to perform. The showy flowers of a cherry tree help attract pollinating insects, the spongy bark of a redwood protects it from fires, the spreading roots of a beech anchor it in shallow soils. The leaves, growing in an immense variety of shapes and sizes, are all part of the tree's food-production system. Nothing is wasted and there are no unnecessary structures.

Root Systems

The first part of a tree to emerge from a seed is a tiny root whose first function is to draw up water and dissolved minerals from the soil. From this simple start the tiny root will grow and divide, eventually forming a large network of powerful roots, side-branches and fine root hairs which spread out in all

Root systems are often extensive and spread out through the top soil. The roots of these Beech trees have been unable to penetrate the chalky bedrock.

directions around the base of the trunk. The main roots will be woody and very strong, but their many branches terminate in fine root hairs which are only a few cells long; they have thin, permeable walls through which will pass all the water and minerals needed for the survival and growth of the tree. Although the sturdy roots strengthened with woody tissue help anchor the tree in the ground, it is the millions of fine root hairs which keep the tree alive by supplying it with water and nutrients. These fine root hairs are very short-lived, being constantly replaced as the main roots grow through the soil.

The root system of a large, mature tree does not penetrate far down into the soil. Although many species have a tap root, it is usually very short in relation to the height of the tree. The most useful supply of dissolved nutrients for the tree, in the form of nitrates, phosphates and potassium, will lie in the shallow layer of top soil and the adjacent sub-soil, so it is more beneficial if the roots spread outwards through this layer rather than penetrate to a great depth into a rather sterile and hostile layer. Many soils are shallow and lie over a bedrock through which roots could not penetrate in any case, so illustrations in text books of very long tap roots are usually wildly inaccurate. A 50m-tall tree will probably only have a 2m depth of tap root beneath it, but it will have a great spread of smaller branching roots all around the bole. The extent of the spread of the roots is approximately equal to the spread of the branches, or sometimes, to the height of the tree. The proximity of other trees, the nature of the soil, and the presence of obstacles like rocks or river-banks will all influence the final extent of the root system, however. This knowledge of the spread of the roots is useful when planning where to plant large trees which may damage drains or the foundations of buildings when they reach maturity, and it should also be borne in mind when digging ditches or ponds near large trees.

In order to be able to function at all, roots require a supply of nutrients from the leaves, so within the root system there is a two-way traffic of water and minerals up from the soil to the leaves, and dissolved sugars and other nutrients down from the leaves.

The root hairs are living cells which require oxygen in order to be able to carry out respiration. They give off carbon dioxide as a waste gas, so they need access to air in the soil to allow these gases to circulate. Most trees, and most land plants, cannot grow in completely waterlogged soils where there are no air spaces and where oxygen is lacking. The ideal conditions are soils which retain moisture but have minute air spaces between the particles. Some trees, such as the Swamp Cypress, which grows in completely wet conditions in swamps and on riverbanks, have special adaptations to cope with the lack of oxygen. It produces strange woody 'knees' which emerge from the water around the bole and help the roots obtain oxygen.

A number of trees, especially members of the Leguminosae, such as the Honey Locust, have many rounded nodules on the roots which contain colonies of nitrogen-fixing bacteria. These are able to use gaseous nitrogen and turn it into compounds vital to the growth of the plants.

Leaves – The Tree's Food Producers

Leaves are among the most conspicuous and distinctive features of any tree. They grow in a bewildering variety of shapes, sizes, colours and combinations. They are usually the best feature for identifying the tree because of their unique structure. Although leaves are incredibly varied from one species to another, they all perform the same vital function as the principal producers of food for the tree.

The first pair of leaves to emerge from the seed are simple, and bear no resemblance to the true leaves of the tree. They are derived from the cotyledons which contain the seed's food store. They are green, however, and supply the tiny seedling with its first food made from sunlight energy. Soon the

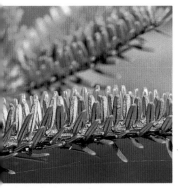

Needles. **The leaves of conifers are normally in the form of needles which may be short and densely packed, or much longer and thinner. Needles help the tree conserve water and cope with harsh environmental conditions.**

Simple leaf. **The simplest form of leaf consists of a leaf blade and short leaf stalk or petiole.**

Serrated leaf. **Simple leaves, like these from an Italian Alder, may have a serrated edge. This is often an important feature for identification.**

Lobed leaf. **Many leaves, like those of the English Oak, have lobed margins. The number, depth and shape of the lobes varies between species.**

Lobed, toothed leaf. The leaves of the Wild Service Tree have pointed lobes and a toothed margin.

Compound leaf. Such leaves consist of numerous leaflets, sometimes arranged in pinnate form, like the leaf of the Wingnut tree.

seedling will start to produce leaves which are scaled-down versions of the true leaves. Once these have been formed growth can begin very rapidly. Tiny seedlings are vulnerable to grazing, trampling, drought, scorching and competition from other seedlings, so very few survive.

Leaves are basically thin layers of living tissue with the ability to trap light energy and use this to convert the raw materials of water and carbon dioxide into a simple sugar. This reaction, known as photosynthesis, must be one of the most important chemical reactions in the world, for it is the basis of all other food production. Animals do not have the ability to convert these simple materials into food; they have to rely on plants to do it for them. The simple sugar produced in the leaves is glucose, and this can be formed into a variety of other important materials, particularly starch, which many plants store, or pack into their seeds. A vital by-product of this reaction is oxygen, the gas essential for the respiration of all members of the animal kingdom. This explains the vital role of trees in the ecosystem: they are major consumers of carbon dioxide, one of the so-called 'greenhouse gases', and they are major producers of oxygen, the gas we need for our respiration. They are also major producers of food for much of the animal kingdom.

Contained within a leaf are numerous specialized cells. Some are concerned with the transport of materials in and out of the leaf, some are the vital energy-trapping cells which utilize sunlight, and others are concerned with the regulation of water movements. The cells that trap light-energy contain a light-absorbing pigment called chlorophyll, which gives the leaves their green colour. Other pigments of different colours may be present in varying amounts, and it is this variety which gives leaves of different trees their own subtle shade of green. Without the green chlorophyll or other light-absorbing pigments, the leaves would be unable to perform their important function, and also, if deprived of light, they would be unable to manufacture the tree's food. The leaves arrange themselves in such a way as to be able to absorb the maximum amount of sunlight, so spreading canopies, or trees growing taller than their neighbours, are both ways in which trees maximize the light-gathering power of their leaves. Some leaves have paler patches lacking the green chlorophyll; these are known as variegated leaves and certain trees, such as the Highclere Hollies, regularly produce green-and-yellow leaves. If the leaves were completely lacking in chlorophyll they would be unable to manufacture food for the tree; the small areas of green tissue in the leaf produce all the food needed by the whole leaf.

All leaves have tiny pores in their surfaces (normally just the lower surfaces) called stomata. These allow water to evaporate into the atmosphere. To some extent the tree can regulate the opening and closing of these stomata, but during daylight hours, when the tree is trapping sunlight, they will be open, allowing water out and also allowing the circulation of the gases involved in photosynthesis. This can lead to problems for trees growing in hot, dry areas, or in well-drained soils where little ground water is available. In order to allow the essential gases to circulate, while minimizing water loss, many leaves have become reduced in size, such as the needles of Firs and Pines, or have thick waxy upper surfaces such as the glossy-green leaves of Hollies and Magnolias. This reduces water loss to a minimum without impeding photosynthesis.

The great variety of shapes and sizes of leaves is an indication of the variety of ways in which trees can cope with environmental conditions. Some

Semi-natural woodlands, like this oakwood, often remain in steep valleys where it has been impossible to clear the land for agriculture. Woodlands such as this are rich in wildlife and often contain many rare species of native trees and shrubs.

Deciduous trees shed their leaves in autumn to cope with harsh winter conditions.

trees grow in areas where water is at a premium, so they have leaves which are small, to cut down on water loss through their thin skins. Some grow in shady conditions, possibly below other trees, so they may have larger leaves which can trap the maximum amount of light energy. Some trees are subject to grazing by animals, so their leaves are spiny or prickly, or protected on tough thorny stems.

Evergreen trees do not lose all their leaves at the end of every growing season; most leaves remain on the tree through the winter, although there is always some loss and some replacement. In many of the Pines, for example, the needles will remain on the tree for about 3 years. As the shoot grows longer each year, a new set of needles grows on the tip of the lengthening shoot. The older needles, finding themselves further and further away from the tip, gradually fall off. Small leaf scars remain, and these are quite distinctive in some species and may be a useful aid to identification. Broadleaved trees such as Holly also replace their leaves gradually so there is always some leaf-fall, but plenty of green foliage remains on the tree.

Deciduous trees generally shed all of their leaves at the end of the growing season, before the onset of winter. Many of them produce spectacular displays of colour before the leaves finally fall. These colour changes are the result of the gradual withdrawal back into the tree of all the useful materials in the leaf; as the various pigments are removed the leaf itself changes colour until finally a corky layer, called the abscission layer, grows at the base of the petiole or leaf stalk. This seals off the shoot and when the leaf finally falls, a scar is left through which mould spores and other harmful materials are unable to pass. The Horse Chestnut has very distinctive leaf scars on its twigs which look like tiny horse-shoes. If these are examined carefully through a hand-lens, the sealed-off ends of the vessels which conducted materials in and out of the leaves can clearly be seen.

There may be as many as 250,000 leaves on a mature oak tree, whilst a large spruce probably has 10 times as many, in the form of needles. The oak's leaves will be shed at the end of the growing season, adding to the rich accumulation on the ground beneath it, whilst the spruce's needles will be shed and replaced gradually, each individual needle remaining on the tree for about 4 years.

HOW TREES ARE NAMED

The tree species described in this book are arranged in systematic order in botanical families. Coniferous trees will be found before broadleaved trees. Both coniferous and broadleaved trees are further subdivided into families, such as the Cypresses (Cupressaceae), the Pines (Pinaceae), the Beech family (Fagaceae) or the Elm family (Ulmaceae). Each family contains one or more genera, and may be a very large group, such as the Fagaceae (the family name is always written in roman type). A genus is a smaller group, containing one or more species, such as the genus *Quercus* (the name is always written in italics and starts with a capital letter). A species is a single item, and adding the specific name narrows the reference down to just one plant, such as *Quercus robur* (the specific name is always written in italics and begins with a lower-case letter). Thus the English Oak belongs to the family Fagaceae, the genus *Quercus* and the species *robur* and is known as *Quercus robur*. This name is unique to this tree alone and means the same thing all over the world. Although a species may have many other local names in Britain and differing common names in other languages, the scientific name can be understood in any country. Specific names are also descriptive and usually refer to some important feature of the tree. In the case of the Silver Birch *Betula pendula*, the name *pendula* actually refers to the pendulous or weeping shoots, and in the Paper-bark Birch *Betula papyrifera*, *papyrifera* refers to the peeling papery bark. In some cases the specific name honours an individual who may have discovered the tree, so *Betula ermanii* refers to Erman, who brought the tree to Europe from Asia.

There may be sub-divisions of the species in some cases, when certain very similar sub-species occur. In this case the sub-species name is added to the specific name, written in italics after the abbreviation 'ssp'. If different colour forms, or growth forms of the same species occur they are listed as either a variety (var.) or a forma (f), with the names written in italics after the full species name. Finally, garden cultivars of certain trees have been bred and maintained for some useful attractive feature. Their names are written in roman type in quotation marks. The bright-yellow leaves of one cultivar of the English Oak have led to it being cultivated and given the name *Quercus robur* 'Concordia', while the Cypress Oak is known as *Quercus robur* 'Fastigiata'.

Hybrids are trees that have arisen as a result of cross-pollination between 2 different species of the genus. In order for a hybrid to be successful, the 2 parents should be as closely related as possible. The Lucombe Oak *Quercus* x *hispanica* 'Lucombeana') is a hybrid between the Turkey Oak (*Quercus cerris*) and the Cork Oak (*Quercus suber*) which was raised in Lucombe's Nursery, Exeter. The name *hispanica* reflects the origins of the tree, and the name 'Lucombeana' honours the nurseryman who raised it. The multiplication sign (x) between the first 2 names indicates that the tree is a hybrid.

A mixed woodland of Ash and Bird Cherry has grown on a limestone hillside where the soil is too thin to support other tree species.

How to Use this Book

Family and Genus Descriptions

Trees belonging to the same family are listed together in this book, and before each family (and in some cases before each genus within a family) there is a brief description of the important features of that family or genus. Thus all members of the Pine family (Pinaceae) are grouped together, and the relevant section of the book opens with a brief description of the common features, such as similarities in their cones and needles. Within the family, genera such as the Firs (*Abies*) are introduced in the same way, and points such as their symmetrical growth and upright cones are covered.

Species Names

Each entry begins with the commonly accepted English name of the species, printed in bold roman type. Any frequently used alternative common names are also given. Some species have vernacular or local names which have been omitted unless they are of particular interest.

The scientific name follows, in italics. This consists of the Latin name of the genus, followed by the specific name and, in some cases, the name of the sub-species, variety or cultivar (see 'How trees are named', above).

Height

The names of each tree are followed by its height in metres. This is the height that should be attained by a tree growing in normal conditions, usually in its native habitat. Following this there may be a second, higher figure in brackets. This is the height sometimes attained by the tree in exceptional circumstances, but not normally seen for trees growing in difficult situations or out of their natural range. It should be borne in mind that many trees are very long-lived, so may not have reached their full height even though they look like large mature specimens. Environmental factors may have influenced the growth of the tree, or it may have lost its leading shoots in a storm, so the height of a tree can be misleading as a guide to its identification.

Description

The first section of each description describes the vegetative features of the tree which are unique to that species and will help in its identification. The general shape and form of a tree are helpful, especially if it is growing in the open with plenty of room to spread out. Some trees have a most distinctive outline, often clear enough to make a good start with identification. The Serbian Spruce has a striking upright shape unlike that of any other conifer, so this is very helpful in arriving at the correct identification. The massive bole, level branches and dense plates of foliage of the Cedar of Lebanon give it a silhouette unlike that of any other tree. By looking at the tree from afar it is possible to make a start on narrowing down its identity. The thickness of the

Conical tree. Conifers, such as these spruces in Alaska, have slender conical shapes in order to shed snow that could damage more spreading branches.

Domed tree. Many broad-leaved trees, such as this Lime, grow very tall and have a domed crown, especially if they grow close to other trees.

Spreading tree. When given plenty of space in which to grow, some trees, like this oak, will form a broad spreading shape.

bole, and the colour and texture of the bark, are also of great help as these are easily examined and often very distinctive. The Tibetan Cherry has a rich shiny-red bark, for which it is often planted in gardens. This is quite different from the spongy red bark of the Giant Redwood, or the peeling grey-and-white bark of the Snow Gum.

Shoots and buds should be examined carefully, as these are quite distinctive in many species. They can vary in size and shape, colour, position on the shoot and the degree of hairiness or stickiness. The shoots and twigs themselves can also be smooth or hairy, or sometimes pitted with lenticels, tiny 'breathing holes' in the bark. The Common Ash has flattened tips to the shoots which terminate in opposite sooty-black buds, contrasting strikingly with the greenish-grey bark. This feature alone is enough to separate this tree from other Ash species. The sticky, resinous buds of the Western Balsam Poplar are also quite distinctive and make this tree easy to identify, even in winter, if a few low branches can be reached. Buds may occur in pairs opposite each other on the shoot or may be alternate, sometimes arranged in a zigzag pattern.

The leaves are a very important identification feature for nearly all trees. The size is often given, but leaves are very variable and when they first open they will not be the full size. The measurement given is normally the length of the leaf from the tip to the point where the leaf stalk (petiole) joins the leaf blade. Different leaves from the same tree will show some variation, so the figure given for their size is an average figure for an average leaf. The shape of the leaves is important, and probably more useful for identification than the size. The margin may be toothed, lobed or entire, and this feature is normally constant for any species. The petiole is also distinctive: its length, shape, colour and degree of hairiness can all be helpful identification features. Using a hand-lens it should be possible to see the tiny tufts of hairs which are sometimes present on the undersides of leaves amongst the veins. The arrangement of these hairs, their shapes and colours are all variable between species.

Simple leaves are much as their name suggests; they consist of a single leaf blade with or without a petiole. They may have entire margins or lobes or teeth. Compound leaves consist of a number of leaflets on a petiole. The compound leaf may be pinnate, such as an ash or hickory leaf, with several leaflets arising from a central leaf stalk (rachis), or it may be palmate, like a horse chestnut leaf, with several leaflets radiating from a single point on the petiole, rather like the fingers on a hand.

Reproductive Parts
The flowers and fruits of many trees are often very conspicuous features, and are often the reason for them being cultivated. Although they are usually not present on the tree throughout the year, they can be invaluable as aids to identification when they are present. A hand-lens will be needed to check small features like the numbers of stamens or styles inside a flower, or the

Many trees provide valuable fruits and seeds for human consumption. The Lemon is one of the most important fruit-bearing trees of the Mediterranean region.

numbers of seeds in tiny capsules. The text includes details of the number and arrangements of the floral parts, the approximate times of year for flowering, and the appearance of the fruits and seeds.

Habitat and Distribution

For each species a brief description is included of its normal habitat, that is, the type of environment in which it would normally be found growing. This may be a mountain woodland, lowland, wetland or other broad habitat type. Its native range is also included where known. Some species have been in cultivation for so long that their natural habitat is unknown; the Maidenhair Tree was first discovered in monastery gardens in Japan, but is believed to have originated in China. However, it has never been found growing in the wild. Where trees are cultivated, or planted outside their normal range, this is also indicated.

Comments

At the end of some of the species descriptions there are additional comments of interest regarding that species. These comments may concern the tree's history or its usefulness to man, for example, rather than features that will help in identification.

Similar Species

Some of the species descriptions in the book are followed by a subsection covering trees that are very similar to the main species, differing only in minor details. The full description is not repeated, but any differences helpful in identification are mentioned.

Identifying Trees in the Field

EQUIPMENT

Very little equipment is required to identify trees, but a few simple items are helpful. The first essential is a notebook in which to record observations in the field. The traditional botanists' rule of 'Take the book to the plant and not the plant to the book' applies to trees in that snapping off twigs, fruits or flowers should be avoided where possible; this may be prohibited, or simply be bad manners if the tree in question is growing in a garden or park, for example. Some arboreta and botanical gardens are very firm in prohibiting the removal of living materials and may take action against a person who damages a tree. It is best if detailed notes can be made in the field, and if there are some fallen leaves or fruits beneath the tree, and it is certain that they are from the tree in question and not any nearby trees, then these can be taken for help in identification.

Photographs are a very useful way of keeping records and will be of great help in identification. A record of the same tree in different seasons of the year would be helpful to show the changes in foliage colours and the appearance of the flowers.

A hand-lens, capable of magnifying up to x10, is very helpful. Many features of trees, even very large specimens, are easier to see in close-up. Coniferous trees often have lines of tiny pores (stomata) on their needles, and the number and arrangement of these can be crucial to correct identification. The degree of hairiness of the leaves and petioles is often very important; some species have hairs in the form of tiny stars, others may have fine hairs of a particular colour and these features can only be reliably seen in close-up. The arrangement of the parts of the flowers is often a help in tracing a tree to a particular family and these parts are usually quite small.

A small ruler with a scale marked in millimetres is also very useful as the measurements of needles, leaves, petioles and floral parts can be very important, although it should be stressed that these are often variable. A longer tape-measure is also helpful for measuring the circumference of trees; this information can be used to estimate the age of most trees (see 'Estimating the age of a tree', below).

ESTIMATING THE HEIGHT OF A TREE

Although the height of a tree should not be used as a definitive guide to identification, it is helpful to know this measurement when deciding on the identity of a species. There are a number of simple methods which can be used with reasonable accuracy.

Find a stick which is the same length as your outstretched arm. Hold this vertically at arm's length and then, looking along the arm at the stick, with the tree directly behind it, walk backwards or forwards until the stick appears to be the same height as the tree, with the top of the stick matching the top of the tree and the bottom of the stick matching the base of the tree. You will now be standing at the point where the top of the tree would be if it were to fall down in your direction. The distance along the ground from you to the tree will be the same as the tree's height, and can easily be measured by pacing it out or using a tape-measure.

If a helper is available, ask this person to stand at the base of the tree, and then line the tree up with the stick as before. This time turn the stick through 90° to the left or right so that it is lined up with the ground. Ask the helper to walk away from the tree along the line of the stick as far as the position shown by the end of the stick. The distance walked will correspond to the height of the tree.

Some people who have flexible lower spines can bend down and look between their knees at a tree behind them. The point at which the top of the tree can be seen from this position should be noted; the distance from this point back to the base of the tree is approximately equal to the height of the tree.

One of the tallest of all trees is the Giant Redwood. Its height can be estimated by a number of simple methods.

ESTIMATING THE AGE OF A TREE

For each year of its life a tree adds an internal ring of woody tissue to its trunk (see 'Annual rings', page 14). This leaves a permanent record of its age, but this record can be examined only if the tree is felled, or in some cases, if a fine core can be extracted from the bole, removing a radial section of woody tissue. (This is extremely difficult to do and is certainly not a task for the average naturalist. A dendrochronologist, specializing in this technique, will be able to extract useful samples from the bole of a tree without causing it any permanent damage.)

Examining cut stumps after forestry operations, measuring the circumference and counting the annual growth rings will give an idea of the age of trees of the same species of similar circumference. Other clues may help you to arrive at a reasonably accurate estimate of the tree's age. Many conifers, like the Larches, for example, produce a new set of shoots around the crown each year, while lower down, the oldest branches die off and fall away, leaving stumps around the bole. Each year's growth produces a new ring of shoots around the main bole with a gap between them and the preceding year's shoots. If the number of rings of old branch stumps low down is added to the number of rings of growing branches higher up, the sum will give a rough guide to the age of the tree.

The circumference of the bole does give a good guide to the tree's age, however, as for every species there is a point at which it reaches its optimum size. After that, it increases very slowly, if at all, gradually declining into old age. During the period of its maturity, however, it is fairly safe to assume that each 2.5cm of circumference represents one year of the tree's life. This applies to normal healthy trees growing in places where they are free to attain their natural spread and height, unimpeded by other, neighbouring trees. It applies to most species of

Towards the end of its long life an oak tree begins to lose its upper branches and growing shoots. Its age can be estimated by measuring its girth.

broadleaves and conifers growing in the open. Trees growing in woodland, with many other trees close by, will grow at only about half this rate, so before ageing a tree in this way, look at its surroundings, and at the crown and spread of the tree. Does it have a good-sized crown, or does it appear to be restricted in any way by other trees? If it appears to be growing normally with a good, healthy crown, then the 2.5cm-per-year rule can be applied.

Some trees are very slow-growing, so this rule cannot be applied to them. Yew, for example, is slow-growing but long-lived, and in its old age it is so slow-growing that it hardly appears to increase in circumference at all. When using the circumference method for ageing a tree it is important to look for a vigorous and healthy tree in natural surroundings.

GINKGO FAMILY, Ginkgoaceae

An ancient family, representing the pre-cursors of our modern conifers and broadleaves. Only a single species has survived, all the others being known only from fossils dating from at least 200 million years ago.

Maidenhair Tree
Ginkgo biloba 28m (30m)

A tall, slender to slightly conical deciduous tree with one main trunk, sometimes divided higher up. The grey-brown bark has a corky texture and in mature trees is ridged, with each ridge separated by a wide fissure. The spreading branches bear long, greenish-brown shoots which in turn bear shorter brown shoots. Leaves on the long shoots are widely separated, but those on the short shoots are much closer together. Yellowish-green to dark-green leaves are fan-shaped and divided at least once; radiating veins reach the margins, and leaves may attain a size of 10 × 12cm.

Reproductive parts Male catkins are yellow and grow in small upright clusters; female flowers grow singly on a 5cm-long pedicel. Fruits are up to 3cm long and usually ovoid, and contain a single seed inside a harder shell. They are green at first, yellowing with age and becoming foul-smelling, although considered edible in China. Fruits are not often seen.

Habitat and distribution A native of the Chekiang province of China, although first found by Europeans in Japan.

Comments The only representative of a family of trees dominant 200 million years ago. Neither a broadleaf nor a conifer, but in its own genus which was thriving before the present tree families had evolved. No longer occurs in the wild, and is known only from cultivation. Rarely produces flowers in Britain or colder parts of Europe; only a small number of older trees flower and these are mostly males. A very hardy tree, surviving in city centres, but does best in warmer areas. Does not tolerate pruning or lopping and quickly dies back if the trunk is damaged.

Maidenhair Tree, leaf and fruit

Maidenhair Tree, autumn

Maidenhair Tree

Maidenhair Tree

YEW FAMILY, Taxaceae

A small family of primitive conifers, some being little more than shrubs, restricted to the northern hemisphere. They have poisonous seeds and foliage. The male and female flowers are produced on separate trees and the seeds are surrounded by a fleshy cup called an aril. They can be propagated by seeds and cuttings.

Common Yew
Taxus baccata 25m (28m)

A dense-foliaged, broadly conical conifer with flattened, needle-like leaves up to 4cm long and 3mm wide and narrowing to a sharp point. Leaves dark glossy green above and paler below with 2 pale yellowish bands. Leaves arise spirally around the twig but are flattened to lie in a row on either side of the twig. The bole of a mature tree may be long and twisted, with reddish bark peeling to reveal reddish-brown patches beneath. Branches may be level or ascending, with an irregular pattern of slightly pendulous twigs growing from them.

Reproductive parts Male and female flowers are borne on separate trees. Male flowers are solitary, consisting of clusters of yellowish anthers which release a fine dust of pollen. Female flowers are mostly solitary, greenish and give rise to hard fruits each surrounded by a bright-red fleshy aril with a depression at the tip.

Habitat and distribution A native of much of Europe, NW Africa and SW Asia, usually preferring drier lime-rich soils and rarely forming dense woodlands.

Comments A very poisonous tree, dangerous to humans and livestock. Widely planted for ornament in its many cultivated forms. The subject of myths and superstitions. Very long-lived: many specimens more than 1,000 years old thrive in country churchyards. Quite tolerant of exposure to harsh weather and atmospheric pollution in towns, and can also grow in shady places.

Similar species
Irish Yew *T. baccata* 'Fastigiata'. Differs from Common Yew in having a more columnar, upright form with ascending branches. Leaves, flowers and fruits are almost identical to those of Common Yew. **Comments** Present-day plants of this variant are survivors of one of a pair of trees found in County Fermanagh, Ireland, in the mid-eighteenth century.

Japanese Yew *T. cuspidata* 10m Similar to Common Yew, but leaves are more erect on the twigs, and yellow beneath. Fruits are produced in clusters. Thrives where sheltered by other trees.

California Nutmeg
Torreya californica 20m

A broadly conical tree with a fine, stout bole in mature specimens producing a high-quality timber. The long branches are almost horizontal in mature trees and support descending lines of greenish shoots. Needle-like leaves, with two pale greyish bands on the underside, grow in a row on each side of the shoot, and smell of sage if crushed.

Reproductive parts Trees are either male or female, but in some specimens branches bearing flowers of opposite sex can be found on the same tree. Male flowers resemble small yellowish catkins, borne on the undersides of shoots. Fruits are ovoid, 5cm long, and green with purplish streaks; they resemble nutmegs and contain a single seed, but are not edible.

Habitat and distribution A native of mountain woodlands in California, but often planted in mature gardens in Britain and Europe where it can attain a good size if given some shelter.

Similar species
Japanese Nutmeg *T. nucifera* 12m (see photograph on page 37) A slender, conical tree with sparse foliage, often looking yellow and apparently not thriving. The needle-like leaves, when crushed, have a sage scent. Shoots develop a reddish-brown colour after 2 years.

Yew, aril

Yew

Yew, ancient tree

Yew, var. *fastigiata* 'Aurea'

California Nutmeg

California Nutmeg

COWTAIL PINE FAMILY, Cephalotaxaceae

Once a widely distributed family, according to fossil remains, but now restricted to the Far East. The leaves are large, flattened needles, the male and female flowers are borne on separate plants and the fruits are plum-like.

Japanese Cowtail Pine
Cephalotaxus harringtonia 6m

A small, bushy, yew-like evergreen tree with dense clusters of leathery, spineless leaves on slightly down-curved twigs.

C. harringtonia var. *drupacea* is a more frequently seen variant with shorter leaves growing almost vertically on the gracefully curving shoots and showing their silvery-green lower surfaces.

C. harringtonia 'Fastigiata' is an upright form with much darker foliage; leaves reach 7cm in length, although they are shorter near the tip of the current year's growth. This is the form more likely to be seen in formal gardens.

Reproductive parts The creamy-white male flowers are borne in small clusters on the underside of twigs, female flowers on very short stalks, on separate trees, later giving rise to small greenish plum-like fruits.

Habitat and distribution Known only as a garden plant, originally from Japan, and never seen growing in the wild.

Chinese Cowtail Pine or Chinese Plum Yew
Cephalotaxus fortunei 10m

A small densely foliaged tree when growing in favourable conditions. It may have a single bole with reddish, peeling bark, or sometimes 2 or 3 boles. Dense foliage can sometimes become so heavy that the branches sag under the weight and the tree leans over. The flattened, greenish needles lie on either side of bright-green shoots and may be up to 10cm long. They are glossy above and have 2 pale bands on the underside.

Chinese Cowtail Pine

Reproductive parts The creamy-white or yellowish male and female flowers are produced on separate plants, opening in spring. Fruits are up to 2.5cm long, oval and with a fleshy, purple-brown skin.

Habitat and distribution A native of mountain forests in central and E China, and occasionally seen elsewhere as an ornamental garden tree.

Comments Seed was brought to Britain by Robert Fortune (hence *fortunei*) in 1849, and some trees originating from this time are still growing in gardens in parts of England.

Japanese Nutmeg   **Chinese Cowtail Pine**

Japanese Cowtail Pine, *fruit*

Chinese Cowtail Pine

YELLOW-WOOD FAMILY, Podocarpaceae

A family of yew-like trees with fruits borne on fleshy stalks which are edible. Mainly confined to the tropics and the southern hemisphere, but some occur in Japan and India.

Plum-fruited Yew
Podocarpus andinus 20m
Not a yew, but resembles it in having dense shoots of flattened, needle-like leaves up to 2.5cm long which are a deep bluish-green on the upper surface and have 2 pale bands on the underside. The leaves are much softer than true yew leaves, except in young trees when they are more leathery and bear small spines. They may be arranged in 2 ranks on either side of the shoot or spread all round it. The bark is dark grey and smooth with occasional scars and ridges. Trees can grow with a single upright bole and horizontal branches, or sometimes with several boles and more upright branches.
Reproductive parts Male catkins are yellow and borne in branched clusters near the ends of shoots. Female flowers are greenish and produced in small spikes at the tips of the shoots. The flowers occur on different plants, opening in the spring. Fruits resemble small green plums at first, containing a single seed, and may ripen to become blackened and covered with a fine bloom like sloes.
Habitat and distribution A native of the mountains of Argentina and Chile.

Plum-fruited Yew

Comments A fairly hardy tree which is tolerant of clipping and severe pruning to form hedges.
Similar species
Totara *P. totara* 18m A large tree in its native New Zealand, but in Britain thrives only in sheltered gardens in the west, if protected from frequent frosts. The flattened leaves are tough and leathery, with noticeable spines, and look yellowish-green. The greyish-brown bark peels off in mature specimens.
Willow Podocarp *P. salignus* 20m Sometimes grows as an attractive multi-stemmed bush, but in favourable conditions may grow as a larger tree on a stronger bole with dark orange-brown bark which peels off in strips from mature specimens. The willow-like leaves may grow to 12cm. They have a leathery appearance but a softer, more pliable texture. A native of Chile, growing in loose stands, it attains a size suitable for yielding a useful timber, often used for building.

Prince Albert's Yew
Saxegothaea conspicua 18m
Often resembles a large yew, with a strong ribbed bole covered with a reddish or purple-brown bark which peels off in rounded scales. The leaves are flattened needles up to 3cm long, which show a distinct curve and are arranged untidily on the shoot. When they first appear they have a hint of purple, but become greener later. There are 2 pale bands on the underside. Crushed leaves have a smell of grass.
Reproductive parts Male flowers are purplish, growing in the leaf axils on the undersides of the shoots. The female flowers are small and blue-grey, and give rise to tiny greenish conelets which are borne at the tips of the shoots.
Habitat and distribution A native of the forests of S Chile and Argentina, preferring damper areas where there is some shelter from cold winds. The best specimens outside the native area are to be found in Ireland and SW England.

Plum-fruited Yew

Plum-fruited Yew

Totara

Totara
Prince Albert's Yew

Willow Podocarp
Prince Albert's Yew

MONKEY-PUZZLE FAMILY, Araucariaceae

A family of large evergreen trees, some important timber-producers, found mainly in S America and Australasia. Sexes are separate and trees are raised from seed.

Monkey Puzzle or Chile Pine
Araucaria araucana 29m (50m)
An evergreen, conical or, more usually, domed tree with a tall cylindrical trunk. The bark is greyish and tough, and heavily ridged and wrinkled, showing numerous rings of old stem scars. Branches may be horizontal, or more often slightly drooping, evenly distributed around the trunk. Shoots are densely covered with spirally arranged, scale-like, bright glossy green leaves. Each leaf is 3–5cm long, oval, with a triangular tip, and with a sharp brownish spine at the tip, and the base overlaps the shoot and the next leaf.

Monkey Puzzle, female cone

Reproductive parts Male cones, up to 10cm long, are borne in clusters at the shoot-tips, and release pollen in June–July. Female cones are rounded, up to 17cm long and green for the first 2 years, growing on the upper surface of the shoots. The large scales taper towards a slender outwardly curved point, and conceal 4cm-long, edible brown seeds. Trees are either male or female; both sexes must grow close together in order to produce fertile seed.

Habitat and distribution A native of the mountains of Chile and Argentina, first brought to Europe in 1795 when it remained a scarcity until a large consignment of seed arrived in 1844; now very common as an ornamental tree in parks and gardens of W Europe, producing some very fine specimens in the far west. Will grow well in towns, but prefers well-drained soils.

Norfolk Island Pine
Araucaria heterophylla 15m (20m)
A curiously palm-like evergreen tree with horizontally arranged branches bearing upswept shoots growing up the full extent of the trunk. Young plants have more open, spreading leaves, showing the shoot they are growing on, but older trees have closely packed incurved leaves which hide the shoot.

Reproductive parts Trees are either male or female, and it is not possible to determine which is which until they flower.

Habitat and distribution A native only of Norfolk Island, to the north of New Zealand, but now a familiar tree of many Mediterranean gardens, and sheltered sites elsewhere. Thrives out of doors only in the extreme SW of Britain. Also occurs as a magnificent pot plant in large buildings.

Monkey Puzzle

Monkey Puzzle

Monkey Puzzle

Norfolk Island Pine

Norfolk Island Pine

CYPRESS FAMILY, Cupressaceae

A large group of coniferous trees widely spread around the world. Most have very small, scale-like leaves and tiny buds. The cones are small and tough, often rounded and woody, or fleshy in the case of Junipers. Most are slow-growing and long-lived, giving strong, scented timber, and were mistakenly called cedars by early explorers.

Lawson Cypress
Chamaecyparis lawsoniana
40m (45m)
An erect, narrowly conical evergreen tree with dense foliage. Sometimes grows as a single slender trunk, but often on a repeatedly forked trunk. The bark cracks vertically into long greyish plates. The trunk bears many small branches, each in turn bearing numerous smaller shoots which are usually flattened and pendulous. Leaves are small and scale-like, up to 2mm long and flattened along the shoot, growing in opposite pairs, and showing paler colours on the underside of the shoot. Crushed leaves smell of parsley.

Many cultivars of this species exist, showing a wide range of leaf colours ranging from blue-grey through various greens to a rich gold. Most are narrowly conical with the lower branches arising at ground level, and all show the flattened scale-like leaves along the shoots. Most are raised easily from cuttings and many form vigorous large trees.

Reproductive parts Male flowers, borne at the tip of the twig, are small reddish cones, up to 4mm long, shedding pollen in March. Female cones, found on the same tree, are up to 8mm in diameter when young, greenish-blue at first, and becoming yellowish-brown with age. Each cone has 4 pairs of scales which have a depression in the centre; they gradually open up to reveal the winged seeds inside the cone.

Habitat and distribution A native of the western USA, introduced into Britain in 1854, and now one of the commonest park and garden trees in its many cultivars.

Comments Many of the earliest Lawson Cypresses planted in Britain are still growing so that the maximum height attainable here is not yet known. In its native Oregon and NW California, this species can reach heights of over 60m, but so far in Britain no tree has greatly exceeded 40m.

Hinoki Cypress
Chamaecyparis obtusa 25m (40m)
An evergreen with a similar form to Lawson Cypress, but the leaves are blunt-pointed and bright green with delicate white lines on the underside which smell slightly of eucalyptus when crushed. They grow in dense, flattened sprays on the end of mostly level branches.

Several cultivars exist, including a golden form, 'Crippsii', and several very dense-foliaged, smaller forms such as the Club-moss Cypress 'Lycopodioides'. There are numerous dwarf forms which are very slow-growing and are popular for small gardens.

Reproductive parts Rounded female cones are blue-green at first, becoming yellowish with age, and are borne in small clusters at the tips of the shoots. Male cones are small and reddish-yellow, releasing pollen in spring.

Habitat and distribution A native of Japan and Taiwan, introduced to Britain in 1861. Grows best in wetter areas with reliable summer rainfall, so the finest specimens in Britain are seen in the west.

Comments In its native Japan and Taiwan, the Hinoki Cypress can grow to become one of the largest trees and attain a great age, but it is a very slow grower.

Lawson Cypress

Lawson Cypress 'Wissellii', male and female flowers

Lawson Cypress

Lawson Cypress, golden form

Hinoki Cypress 'Aurea'

Lawson Cypress 'Wissellii'

Sawara Cypress

Chamaecyparis pisifera 24m (50m)

An evergreen similar in appearance to Lawson Cypress and sometimes mistaken for it, but with finer foliage, usually paler in colour and with incurved tips. The scale-like leaves have white marks on the undersides, and have a distinct resinous scent when crushed. The crown is more open than that of Lawson Cypress and the branches are mostly level. The bark is reddish-brown, often peeling off in vertical strips.

Many cultivars are planted, and these are usually easier to find than the type, the favourites being 'Plumosa' and the attractive golden-leaved 'Plumosa Aurea'. Both are broadly conical, eventually forming impressive tall, columnar trees with a stout bole dividing about 2m above ground level into 3 or 4 stems. Can attain heights of 24m in the west of Britain.

Reproductive parts Male flowers are small brownish cones, female flowers are paler brown and grow in clusters at the tips of shoots. Both open in spring. The small wrinkled, pea-like cones are about 8mm in diameter and are hidden among the foliage.

Habitat and distribution A native of mountain woodlands in Japan, often growing on the banks of streams.

Similar Species

C. pisifera 'Squarrosa' is a smaller, more conical tree, with a single, sometimes drooping leading shoot, and softer blue-green foliage. A popular garden variety.

Alaska Cedar or Nootka Cypress

Chamaecyparis nootkatensis
30m (40m)

An evergreen sometimes known to foresters as the 'Stinking Cedar' because of the strong and unpleasant smell (reminiscent of turpentine) of the crushed leaves. It forms an elegant conical tree with slightly upturned branches and pendulous shoots bearing tough scale-like leaves.

Reproductive parts Cones are distinctly blue in their first year, ripening through green to brown; each scale bears a beak in the centre. Male flowers are yellow, shedding pollen in spring.

Habitat and distribution First discovered near Nootka, on Vancouver Island, but also occurs further north in Alaska, and south to Oregon, growing at high altitudes just below the snow-line. Tolerant of a wide range of conditions, but not happy on lime-rich soils.

Comments A hardy tree in Britain, often planted for ornament, especially the cultivar 'Pendula' which has graceful upswept branches and longer pendulous shoots. This form may reach a height of 25m. The cultivar 'Variegata' has bright-golden foliage.

Sawara Cypress

Sawara Cypress 'Plumosa Aurea'

Sawara Cypress

Sawara Cypress 'Squarrosa'

Alaska Cedar   **Sawara Cypress 'Squarrosa'**

Formosan Cypress

Chamaecyparis formosensis 16m

An evergreen distinctive for its upturned branches, which form a U-shaped pattern. The dense greenish-bronze foliage lacks white markings on the underside, distinguishing it from the similar Sawara Cypress. Crushed leaves smell vaguely of seaweed.

Reproductive parts Female flowers are small and green, lying along the shoots partly hidden by the leaves. After pollination they develop into tiny conelets.

Formosan Cypress

Habitat and distribution A native of Taiwan, but a rare tree there, though some very large specimens still exist. Thought to reach an age of 3,000 years. Has been planted in gardens in Britain since around 1910, and in the west is beginning to form some sizeable specimens.

Leyland Cypress

× *Cupressocyparis leylandii* 35m

An evergreen hybrid between the Monterey and Nootka Cypresses, first raised in 1888. Normally a tall, narrowly conical tree; densely foliaged, fast-growing and hardy. Branches arise along the whole length of the trunk, and are almost vertical, with a dense growth of green shoots covered in pointed scale-like leaves about 2mm long. The bark, normally hidden by the dense branches, is reddish-brown with thin vertical ridges.

Grows even in town centres and is often clipped into hedges, suffering mutilations because of proximity to buildings or too vigorous growth. Two forms are commonly planted 'Haggerston Grey', which has leaf sprays arising at all angles, and 'Leighton Green', which has thicker shoots and leaves in longer, flatter sprays. Attractive golden forms, such as 'Robinson's Gold', are also quite widely planted. **Habitat and distribution** Not found anywhere as a native tree, due to its hybrid origins, but very widespread in parks and gardens, including urban sites. Tolerant of most soil types.

Reproductive parts Male and female cones are infrequently produced, but occur on the same tree. Male cones are small and yellow, growing at the tips of the shoots, and release their pollen in March. Female cones are up to 3cm in diameter, rounded and formed of 8 scales bearing pointed processes. They are green at first, then become brown and shiny.

Leyland Cypress 'Haggerston Grey'

Leyland Cypress 'Haggerston Grey'

Leyland Cypress

Leyland Cypress, clipped hedge

Monterey Cypress
Cupressus macrocarpa 36m

A large evergreen conifer, growing into a broadly domed, spreading tree, although more pyramidal when younger. Branches are crowded, growing fairly upright on younger trees, but becoming more horizontal and spreading in older specimens. Small scale-like leaves are borne on stiff, forward-pointing shoots, arranged haphazardly around the leading shoot. Leaves smell of lemon when crushed. Bark is reddish-brown, forming ridges and scales in older trees. A golden-foliaged form 'Lutea' is more spreading and better at tolerating sea winds.

Reproductive parts Male cones are yellow, up to 5mm in diameter and produced on the tips of shoots behind the female cones, shedding pollen in June. Female cones are 2–4cm in diameter, rounded and bright green at first, becoming purplish-green with maturity. The scales each bear a sharp central point and hide up to 20 brown papery-winged seeds.

Habitat and distribution A native of a small area near Monterey, California, where it is now rare and never attains the size it can in W Britain and Ireland. Formerly widely planted as a hedgerow and shelter-belt tree, it has now been superceded by the Leyland Cypress.

Similar species

Cedar of Goa or **Mexican Cypress** *C. lusitanicus* 25m An evergreen with spreading branches, slightly pendulous at the tips. Leaves bear spreading sharp points,

and have no characteristic smell when crushed. Bark is brown and peels in vertical strips. Female cones are up to 1.5cm in diameter and shiny brown when mature. A native of Mexico and Guatemala, introduced first into Portugal and later Goa. Not hardy in very severe winters, so common only near southern and western coasts of Britain, and in S Europe where it is sometimes grown as a timber tree.

Italian Cypress
Cupressus sempervirens 22m (50m)

A distinctive slender, upright evergreen with dense dark-green foliage. Usually columnar in form, but occasionally forms a broader pyramid. Branches are strongly upright and crowded, bearing clusters of shoots. Numerous young shoots arise from the leading shoots and they all bear closely adpressed dark-green scale-like leaves, no more than 1mm long. No distinctive scent can be detected in crushed foliage.

Reproductive parts Small greenish-yellow male cones up to 8mm in diameter grow on the tips of side-shoots. Elliptical female cones, up to 4cm in diameter,

Italian Cypress,
female cone

grow near the ends of the shoots, their yellowish-grey colour contrasting with the dark foliage. When ripe they are brown, and have overlapping scales.

Habitat and distribution A native of stony hillsides and mountain slopes in S Europe and the Balkans, occurring as far east as Iran. Truly wild trees have a more spreading form, but the elegant columnar form is the one most widely planted elsewhere, and is a familiar and conspicuous feature of many Mediterranean landscapes.

Cedar of Goa

Monterey Cypress, cones

Monterey Cypress
Italian Cypress 'Green Pencil'

Monterey Cypress 'Aurea'
Monterey Cypress

Italian Cypress, cone

Smooth Arizona Cypress
Cupressus glabra 22m

The form seen in Britain grows into a neat, almost egg-shaped tree with a pleasing blue-grey foliage often showing white tips. In its wild state in Arizona it has a more spreading habit with raised tips to the branches. The greyish-green leaves often have a central white spot and smell of grapefruit when crushed. The bark of older specimens falls away in rounded flakes, revealing yellow or reddish patches. The bark is difficult to see through the dense foliage, but is reddish-brown or purple-tinged.

Bhutan Cypress

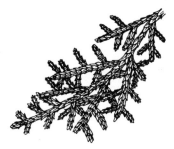

Smooth Arizona Cypress

Reproductive parts Male cones are small and yellow and grow at the tips of shoots, sometimes appearing in winter. Female cones are oval, up to 2.5cm in diameter when mature, and greenish-brown; each scale has a central blunt projection.

Habitat and distribution A native tree of Arizona, but planted in Britain and Europe as an ornamental tree, and sometimes as a hedging species when it will tolerate clipping while still retaining its neat habit.

Similar species
Bhutan Cypress *C. torulosa* 27m Forms an ovoid crown like the Arizona Cypress but has a more open appearance with raised branches and descending sprays of looser foliage. The green shoots are long and narrow, smelling of new-mown grass when crushed. The bark of older trees is spirally ridged. Generally a slow-growing species except in the most favourable conditions.

Gowen Cypress *C. goveniana* 24m An evergreen conifer forming a compact column when growing in Europe, but more sparse and spreading in its native California where it is now extremely rare. Numerous short shoots, often growing out of the lead-

Gowen Cypress

ing shoot at right-angles, are covered with small, rounded leaves smelling of lemon and herbs when crushed. Cones are shiny red-brown and grow in small clusters.

Smooth Arizona Cypress

Bhutan Cypress, cones

Bhutan Cypress

Patagonian Cypress

Fitzroya cupressoides 22m (50m)

A densely foliaged evergreen conifer with ascending branches bearing descending masses of shoots. The bark is reddish-brown, peeling away in vertical strips. Thick branches grow from low down on the bole and curve upwards to grow almost vertically. The leaves are hard, blunt-ended scales, curving outwards away from the shoot and bearing white stripes on both surfaces.

Patagonian Cypress

Reproductive parts Sometimes a prolific producer of cones, which are small, rounded and brown, and up to 8mm in diameter.

Habitat and distribution A native of the mountains of Chile and Argentina, growing to a great size and attaining a great age. Named in honour of Captain Fitzroy of HMS *Beagle* which conveyed Charles Darwin on his explorations of S America in the 1830s.

Incense Cedar

Calocedrus decurrens 35m (40m)

An elegant columnar evergreen, with numerous short upright branches running all the way up the trunk from near ground level, terminating in a narrowly rounded crown. The shoots are hidden by the closely adpressed scale-leaves which grow in whorls of 4, each bearing a short, incurved, pointed tip. Crushed foliage smells of turpentine. The bark is dark and cracked into large reddish-brown flakes.

Incense Cedar, female cone

Reproductive parts Male cones are up to 6mm in diameter, ovoid and a deep yellow, and are borne at the tips of lateral shoots; pollen is often shed as early as January. Female cones are 2–3 cm in diameter when mature, oblong to ovoid and pointed, with 6 scales; the 2 large fertile scales have outwardly pointed tips.

Habitat and distribution A native of California and Oregon, but very popular as an ornamental tree in Britain and W Europe. In its native habitat it can be a broader tree with more level branches.

Comments An easy tree to propagate from cuttings, and also easy to grow from the fertile seed which is produced freely in most years.

Similar species

Chilean Incense Cedar *Austrocedrus chilensis* 15m A similar tree to the Incense Cedar, but less regular in its outline with occasional forks. Sprays of foliage are very flattened and do not always show the white stripes seen in the Incense Cedar. More tender and shorter-lived than the Incense Cedar, so only seen thriving in gardens in the west of Britain and Ireland.

Chilean Incense Cedar

Patagonian Cypress

Patagonian Cypress

Incense Cedar

Incense Cedar

Incense Cedar

Incense Cedar

JUNIPERS *Juniperus* A very widespread group across most of the northern hemisphere from the Arctic to the desert regions nearer the equator. Seeds are borne in cones in which the scales become fleshy and merge to look berry-like. All junipers are slow-growing, and none reaches a great size. Many are aromatic.

Common Juniper
Juniperus communis 6m (9m)
Often no more than a small aromatic evergreen shrub, but occasionally grows into a small bushy tree. Three-angled, ridged twigs bear small, pointed, needle-like leaves in whorls of 3, emerging at right-angles. Leaves may be up to 2cm long and 2mm wide, with a pale white band on the upper surface. The lower surface has a thin keel, and the leaf is stalkless. When crushed, the foliage has a smell reminiscent of gin to some people, of apples to others. The bark is reddish-brown, peeling off in thin sheets on older trees.
Reproductive parts Male cones are small, yellow and globular, borne singly in the leaf axils, and produce pollen in March. Female cones are rounded, up to 9mm long, and green at first, ripening through blue-green to black in the second year when fully ripened. Cones usually contain 3 seeds. Male and female flowers are normally produced on separate trees.
Habitat and distribution Possibly the most widespread tree in the world, occurring all round the northern hemisphere from the Arctic tree-line to the drier regions of the Mediterranean, and growing high on mountains, beneath pines and on limestone grassland. Sometimes exists only in a prostrate form or as an undershrub, especially in extreme conditions, but can grow to a larger tree in the open. Popular in gardens in a variety of cultivated forms.
Comments The ripe cones are collected to provide the flavouring for gin and in cooking, and are also eaten by birds. The aromatic wood is used for wood-carving.

Prickly Juniper or Cade
Juniperus oxycedrus 14m
A spreading evergreen shrub or small untidy tree with sharply pointed needles arranged in whorls of 3. The upper leaf surface has 2 pale bands separated by a slightly raised midrib, and the lower surface has a pronounced midrib. The bark is brown, sometimes tinged with purple, and peels away in vertical strips.

Prickly Juniper, female cones

Reproductive parts Female cones are rounded or pear-shaped, and mature to a reddish colour.
Habitat and distribution A native of S Europe, generally preferring drier habitats. Very variable, with 3 subspecies recorded: ssp *oxycedrus* has leaves 2mm wide and cones no more than 1cm in diameter, and is present in dry mountains and stony areas; ssp *macrocarpa* has leaves 2.5mm wide and cones 1.5cm in diameter, and is commoner in rocky areas and maritime habitats across S Europe; ssp *transtagana* has narrower leaves no more than 1.5mm wide and cones less than 1cm in diameter, and is restricted to maritime sands of S Portugal.
Comments A medicinal oil, used to treat skin problems, can be extracted from the wood. The berries can also be used to flavour gin.

Juniper, berries

Prickly Juniper, berries

Juniper

Prickly Juniper

Prickly Juniper

Phoenician Juniper

Juniperus phoenicia 8m

A small evergreen tree, or a spreading shrub, with rounded, scaly twigs bearing 2 types of leaves. Young leaves are up to 1.5cm long and 1mm wide, sharply pointed, showing pale bands on both surfaces, and borne in bunches of 3 spreading at right-angles. Mature leaves are only 1mm long, looking like tiny green scales clasping the twig.

Grecian Juniper, female cone

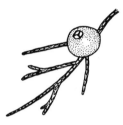

Phoenician Juniper, female cone

Reproductive parts Male cones are inconspicuous and borne at the ends of the shoots, female cones are up to 1.4cm long, rounded and changing from black through yellowish-green to a deep red when fully ripe in the second year.

Habitat and distribution A native of the Mediterranean coastline and the Atlantic shores of Portugal.

Grecian Juniper

Juniperus excelsa 20m

An evergreen tree, conical in shape at first, but broadening out into a flatter pyramidal shape when mature. Scaly, narrow twigs, 8mm wide, bear 2 sorts of leaves: young leaves are needle-like and pointed, about 6mm long with 2 pale bands on the lower surface, and mature leaves are scale-like, oval and usually closely clasped to the stem.

Reproductive parts Male cones grow on the ends of the shoots, female cones

are rounded, up to 8mm long and a dark purple-brown colour with a slight bloom when mature in the second year.

Habitat and distribution A native of the Balkan regions and the Crimea, although sometimes planted elsewhere in dry habitats.

Similar species

Stinking Juniper *J. foetidissima* Sometimes confused with Grecian Juniper, but grows into a neater, more upright and columnar tree. Shoots are sharply 4-angled, scaly and strong-smelling when crushed. Female cones are dark reddish-brown or black when ripe with small protuberances. A native of the mountains of the Balkans and Crimea.

Stinking Juniper,
female cone

Spanish Juniper *J. thurifera* Very similar to Stinking Juniper, but has twigs neatly arranged in 2 ranks, and adult leaves up to 2mm long with slightly toothed margins and a furrowed gland on the back. Cones are 8mm long and dark purple when mature. A native of the French Alps and the mountains of Spain.

Phoenician Juniper

Phoenician Juniper, female cones

Stinking Juniper, female cones

Temple Juniper
Juniperus rigida 15m

A broadly conical evergreen tree with a strong main trunk, and widely spaced ascending branches bearing slightly pendent soft foliage. The specific name *rigida* seems inappropriate for this species as the shoots and leaves are less rigid than those of other Juniper species. At a distance the foliage has a yellowish-green tinge and trees growing in the open look rather sparse. The greyish bark peels off in strips leaving darker-brown patches exposed.

Temple Juniper,
female cone

Reproductive parts Female trees bear bluish-green cones which become a darker purple-brown when fully ripe. The stalkless cones are carried in lines along the fine hanging shoots.

Habitat and distribution A native of Japan, Manchuria and Korea, but found in warmer regions of Britain and Europe, usually in well-established large gardens and collections.

Syrian Juniper
Juniperus drupacea 18m

A shapely evergreen, forming a slender, tall column of compact, bright-green foliage. Occasionally the trunk and crown divide to make a more conical tree. Leaves are needle-like, pointed with a spine and 2 pale bands on the underside, and are longer than any other Juniper at 2.5cm. The needles grow in bunches of 3. The bark is orange-brown and peels away in thin shreds.

Reproductive parts Male trees produce tiny, bright yellowish-green, oval flowers. Female trees produce tiny green flowers in

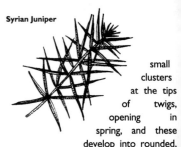

Syrian Juniper

small clusters at the tips of twigs, opening in spring, and these develop into rounded, woody cones, about 2cm in diameter, which turn purple-brown when mature.

Habitat and distribution A native of mountain forests in W Asia, but just extends into Greece. Occasionally planted in gardens where it makes a fine specimen tree, tolerating a wide range of soils but rarely producing cones.

Pencil Cedar or
Eastern Red Cedar
Juniperus virginiana 17m (30m)

A slender pyramidal or sometimes narrowly columnar evergreen tree, usually growing on a single trunk, with numerous small ascending branches bearing fine, rounded, scaly twigs. Young leaves, found in pairs at the ends of shoots, are needle-like, finely pointed and up to 6mm long; the upper surface has a bluish band and the lower surface is green. Mature leaves are only 1.5mm long, rounded and scale-like, and usually grow close to the shoot. May be found in a variety of shades of green. Crushed foliage has a curious smell reminiscent of paint. The reddish-brown bark peels away in vertical strips.

Reproductive parts Male cones are small and yellow, and found at the tips of the shoots. Female cones are oval, up to 6mm long and ripen in the first year, changing from bluish-green to violet-brown when mature.

Habitat and distribution A common native of woodlands and stony hillsides in the eastern USA in a variety of habitats, including roadsides. Infrequently planted in Britain and Europe.

Syrian Juniper

Syrian Juniper   **Pencil Cedar**

Chinese Juniper

Juniperus chinensis 18m (20m)

A large evergreen with dark-green foliage and a rather sparse habit when mature. Young leaves are needle-like, 8mm long with sharply pointed tips and 2 bluish stripes on the upper surface. They are usually carried in clusters of 3 at the base of adult shoots, radiating at right-angles. Adult leaves are small and scale-like, closely adpressed to the shoot. Crushed leaves have an unpleasant 'catty' smell. The bark is reddish-brown and peels away in vertical strips.

Reproductive parts Male cones are small and yellow and grow on the tips of the shoots. Female cones are rounded, up to 7mm long, and bluish-white at first, ripening to purplish-brown in the second year.

Habitat and distribution A native of the hills and mountains of Japan and China, now fairly common in parks, gardens and churchyards, although more usually seen in the form of some of the more attractive cultivars such as the golden-leaved 'Aurea' which forms a neat column of golden-green foliage.

Similar species

Meyer's Blue Juniper *J. squamata* 'Meyeri' 11m A small conical evergreen with striking blue-grey foliage when young. The needle-like leaves have a paler stripe on the underside. The bark of mature trees peels in thin pinkish-brown scales. Very tolerant of poor soils and tough growing conditions, so a popular small tree for town gardens and municipal plantings.

Drooping Juniper

Juniperus recurva 14m

A small evergreen tree with ascending branches but drooping foliage, forming a broadly conical outline which may become very irregular in old specimens. Tough, needle-like leaves clasp the shoots and give off a paint-like smell when crushed. Bark is greyish-brown and peels off in long untidy shreds. Several cultivars exist which show varying degrees of drooping in the foliage.

Drooping Juniper

Reproductive parts Male cones are yellow, growing in small clusters at the tips of shoots. Female cones are produced at the ends of shoots and become oval and black when mature, growing to 8mm in diameter and resembling berries rather than cones.

Habitat and distribution A native of the higher mountains of SW China and the Himalayas and introduced to Britain and Europe for ornament.

Alerce

Tetraclinis articulata 15m

A juniper-like evergreen tree with dense, flattened sprays of dark-green foliage. The scale-like leaves are arranged in whorls of 4, 2 of them larger than the other 2, and with 2 pointed and 2 blunt. The trunk is quite thick and covered with reddish-brown bark.

Reproductive parts Solitary female cones up to 1.3cm long are borne at the tips of branches. They split into 4 to release the seeds. The male cones shed their pollen in February and March.

Habitat and distribution A species restricted to very dry habitats in S Spain, Malta and N Africa.

Comments A resin called sandarac can be extracted from this tree, and the timber is prized for fine woodwork such as cabinet-making.

Alerce,
female cone

Chinese Juniper

Chinese Juniper

Chinese Juniper 'Aurea'

Chinese Juniper
Meyer's Blue Juniper

Chinese Juniper 'Aurea', male cones
Drooping Juniper

Meyer's Blue Juniper
Drooping Juniper

THUJAS *Thuja* Some of the thujas are called cedars, but they are closely related to the cypresses. There are 6 species, found in N America and E Asia.

Western Red Cedar
Thuja plicata 45m (65m)

A large evergreen growing rapidly to form a tall, shapely conical tree supported by a large buttressed trunk. The tiny leaves are scale-like and clasp the shoots in alternate, opposite pairs. They are a glossy, dark green above, but paler below with some whitish markings. Crushed leaves are strongly scented of pineapple. The bark is reddish-brown, strongly ridged in large trees, and divided into soft, fibrous plates. This tree may at first be confused with Lawson Cypress, but the upright, not drooping, leading shoot is distinctive.

Reproductive parts Male and female cones are borne on separate trees. The small yellow or brownish male cones grow at the tips of shoots, releasing their pollen early in spring. The female cones are roughly ovoid, up to 1.2cm long, covered by about 10 scales bearing very small terminal spines, which open to release the small winged seeds.

Habitat and distribution A native of hills and mountains in the western USA, but now widely planted in Britain and Europe for timber, for shelter, or as a fine ornamental tree.

Comments A useful timber tree, producing a strong but lightweight timber, used in its native N America for building and for canoes and totem poles.

Northern White Cedar or
American Arbor-vitae
Thuja occidentalis 20m

A less shapely, but still broadly conical tree, similar to Western Red Cedar. The flattened, fern-like sprays of foliage show white, waxy bands on the underside. When crushed, the leaves smell of apple and cloves. The orange-brown bark peels away in vertical strips. Numerous cultivated forms with varying foliage and dwarf habits exist.

Reproductive parts The male cones are very similar to those of Western Red Cedar, but the female cones have smooth, rounded tips to the cone scales.

Habitat and distribution A native of E Canada, the Great Lakes states and the Appalachian Mountains. Usually found on stony mountain slopes, especially on limestone, and sometimes in swampy areas. Probably introduced into Europe as early as 1539. Can cope with wet conditions, but generally does not thrive in Britain.

Comments A very useful timber tree when able to grow well, producing high-quality lightweight timber used for both indoor and outdoor work, such as fence-posts and greenhouses.

Japanese Thuja or
Japanese Arbor-vitae
Thuja standishii 22m

A slow-growing evergreen forming a fine, broadly conical tree with a fairly open crown showing U-shaped branches and slightly pendent shoot-tips of grey-green or silvery-green foliage. Leaves are very small and scale-like on flattened sprays, smelling of lemon when crushed. The bark is reddish-brown and peels away in strips or broader flakes.

Reproductive parts Male flowers are borne at the tips of shoots, dark red at first, becoming yellower when open. Female flowers are greenish, in separate clusters on the tips of different shoots on the same tree, ripening to form a red-brown cone covered with scales.

Habitat and distribution A native of rocky mountains and uplands in Japan, but widely planted for ornament in Britain and Europe.

Comments Arboriculturalists often refer to the thujas as 'Arbor-vitae', meaning 'tree of life', because the evergreen foliage seems to grow without any obvious buds.

Western Red Cedar

Western Red Cedar

Northern White Cedar, cones

Chinese Thuja
Thuja orientalis 16m

An evergreen which holds its foliage in flat vertical sprays, showing both surfaces to be the same shade of green. The shoots are similar to those of other thujas in being covered with small scale-like leaves, but there is no noticeable scent when the leaves are crushed. The form 'Elegantissima' is smaller and produces a compact, neatly conical tree with bright yellowish-green foliage which shows bright shoot-tips in summer.

Reproductive parts Male flowers are small, yellow-orange and borne on the ends of shoots. Female flowers are greenish and produce cones with prominent hooked scales.

Habitat and distribution A native of China, introduced into Europe in 1752, and now a popular tree in parks and gardens.

Korean Thuja or
Korean Arbor-vitae
Thuja koraiensis 11m

The only evergreen tree with flat fern-like sprays of foliage whose undersides are almost completely silvery or white. The upper side of the shoot is bright green and the leaves are typically small and scale-like. The foliage is strongly and pleasantly aromatic when crushed, releasing a rich fruity aroma. Usually grows to form a neat conical tree, but may be a less symmetrical dense shrub.

Reproductive parts The male cones are small and green with very dark tips, and the immature female cones are green, growing in separate groups at the tips of the shoots on the same plant, opening in spring. The brown, mature 1cm-long cones have 8 outer scales.

Habitat and distribution A native of mountain woodlands in NE China and Korea. Planted in gardens mainly for its attractive silvery foliage but also for its pleasant scent.

Hiba
Thujopsis dolabrata 20m (30m)

An evergreen tree variable in size and shape, but always showing the same scale-like leaves clasping the shoots, in opposite pairs and on flattened sprays of foliage. Leaves are glossy green on the upper surface, marked with white bands on the lower surface, and end in a pointed, curved tip. Hiba may grow into a fine conical tree on a single bole, but can also be found as a broader shrub on a much divided-trunk.

Reproductive parts Small blackish male cones are produced at the tips of shoots and the rounded female cones are also produced singly on the ends of shoots on the same tree. Mature cones are about 1.2cm long and are brown with a slight bloom.

Habitat and distribution A native of humid mountain forests in Japan, but widely planted in Europe and elsewhere, mainly for ornament. Prefers wetter regions with damp soils.

Chinese Thuja

Chinese Thuja 'Sibbaldii', cones

Hiba

REDWOOD FAMILY, Taxodiaceae

An ancient family, once with many more representatives than the 15 species that exist today. Four species are deciduous, the others all evergreen and mostly with hard, spine-tipped leaves. The globular cones are relatively small. The bark in all species is fibrous and a rich red-brown. Some redwoods are the largest living organisms in the world.

Giant Redwood or Wellingtonia
Sequoiadendron giganteum 50m (87m)

An outstandingly large evergreen in its native California, and even in Britain has grown to become the tallest tree in many areas. Forms a striking, narrowly conical tree with a huge tapering bole, ridged and fluted at the base and covered with a deep, spongy, rich-red bark. The lower branches, which may not start for several metres above the ground, are pendulous, but the upper branches are more level. Scale-like green leaves, up to 1cm long, clasp the shoots, and smell of aniseed when crushed.

Reproductive parts The small yellow male cones can be abundant and grow at the tips of the shoots, releasing their pollen in spring. Female cones are solitary, sometimes paired, and ovoid, up to 8cm long and 5cm in diameter when ripe, with a deep brown colour and a corky texture.

Habitat and distribution A native of the Sierra Nevada in California, where it grows in groves on the western slopes of the mountains. First discovered in 1852, it was soon introduced into Britain, where it thrives best in the west. It only grows slowly in polluted air.

Comments The thick, spongy bark often develops deep holes which are used by roosting birds, particularly treecreepers.

Coast Redwood or California Redwood
Sequoia sempervirens 50m (110m)

An impressively large evergreen, growing to be the tallest tree in the world in its native California and Oregon. A conical to columnar tree with a tapering trunk arising from a broader, buttressed base. The thick reddish-brown bark becomes spongy, eventually deeply fissured and peeling. Branches mostly arise horizontally or are slightly pendulous. Green twigs support a unique combination of 2 types of leaves arranged in spirals; leading shoots have scale-like leaves, up to 8mm long, clasping the stem, and side-shoots have longer, flattened, needle-like leaves up to 2cm long, lying in 2 rows. Crushed foliage smells of grapefruit.

Reproductive parts Male and female cones are produced on the same tree.

Coast Redwood, female cone

The small yellow male cones grow on the tips of main shoots, releasing pollen in early spring. The pale-brown female cones grow singly on the tips of shoots, becoming 2cm long and ovoid.

Habitat and distribution A native of California and Oregon, growing best in the hills where the permanent sea-mists keep the trees supplied with moisture. The biggest European specimens are in the west and north of Britain.

Giant Redwood

Coast Redwood

Giant Redwood

Coast Redwood

Giant Redwood

Japanese Red Cedar
Cryptomeria japonica 35m (50m)

A tall, narrowly conical evergreen on a rapidly tapering bole covered with a thin, hard bark which peels off in thin shreds. The distinctive foliage, consisting of narrow, claw-like, yellowish-green leaves pointing towards the shoot-tip, distinguishes this species from the Coast Redwood, as does the thin bark.

Reproductive parts Male and female cones are produced on the same tree but on different shoots. The small yellow male cones are borne in clusters at the tips of shoots and release their pollen in early spring. The mature female cones are covered with feathery scales, unique to this tree, giving the appearance of brownish globular flowers.

Habitat and distribution A native of China and Japan, where it is an important timber tree. Present in Britain and Europe since 1842, and commonest in the west, where the finest specimens are found.

Swamp Cypress or Bald Cypress
Taxodium distichum 35m (40m)

A deciduous conifer, conical at first, but becoming broader and domed with maturity. When growing in or near water the fluted trunk is surrounded by emergent 'breathing roots' (likened by some to knobbly knees) characteristic of this species. The pale reddish-brown bark peels away in thin fibrous strips. The branches are upright or spreading in older trees, carrying 2 types of shoots: long shoots bear spirally arranged leaves, and alternate side-shoots bear flattened leaves set in 2 ranks. Leaves are alternate, up to 2cm long, and pale green; a greyish band on the underside has a fine midrib. A mature tree colours well in autumn before shedding its needles.

Reproductive parts Male cones are produced in slender, branching clusters up to 15cm long on the end of 1-year-old shoots. Female cones are globose and woody, on short stalks, ripening to a purplish-brown colour in the first year. Each scale has a small curved spine in the centre.

Habitat and distribution A native of swamps in the SE and S of the USA, but frequently planted for ornament in parks and gardens elsewhere. Will also grow on drier ground, but does not then produce the breathing roots around the bole. Prefers regions with warm summers.

Comments The timber is not particularly strong, but is water-tolerant, so is used for outdoor structures like greenhouses.

Pond Cypress
Taxodium ascendens 18m (30m)

A slender, conical to columnar deciduous tree with horizontal branches which curve down sharply at the ends, and fine shoots with small clasping leaves which give a knotted-cord appearance. The deciduous shoots are shed in the autumn. There is a fine display of autumn colours, starting orange and turning brown. The bark is grey and ridged in older specimens.

Reproductive parts Male flowers are yellowish-green, in the form of hanging catkins up to 20cm long. Female flowers are produced on the same tree at the base of the male catkins, first appearing in the autumn, but not opening until spring. Rounded cones up to 3cm long are green at first but ripen to brown.

Habitat and distribution A native of the south-eastern USA, growing in wet ground by ponds and swampy ground. Introduced into Britain, where it succeeds only in warmer parts of the south.

Japanese Red Cedar

Japanese Red Cedar

Swamp Cypress

Pond Cypress

Pond Cypress

Pond Cypress

Dawn Redwood
Metasequoia glyptostroboides
35m (40m)

A neatly conical deciduous conifer with shoots and leaves arranged in opposite pairs. Leaves are 2.5cm long, flattened and needle-like, pale green at first, becoming darker green later. They are produced on short, lateral shoots which are shed in the autumn. Leaves emerge early in the spring, and turn yellow, pink or red before falling. The bark is a rich orange or reddish-brown, peeling in vertical strips. The attractive trunk is tapering and buttressed at the base, becoming more ridged in older trees.

Reproductive parts Male and female flowers are produced on young shoots in separate clusters on the same tree in spring. Males are yellow, females greenish, producing rounded green, then brown cones about 2.5cm in diameter.

Habitat and distribution A native of SW China, known only from fossil records, and unknown as a living tree until 1941. Now a popular garden tree in Europe.

Summit Cedar
Athrotaxis laxifolia 10m (17m)

A broadly conical evergreen with upcurved branches. Leaves are small and scale-like, up to 6mm long, and have sharp tips pointing away from the shoot. Young leaves and shoots are bright yellow-green, older shoots and leaves dark green. The reddish-brown fibrous bark peels vertically, leaving orange or grey-brown patches.

Reproductive parts Male and female

Summit Cedar, cones

flowers are yellowish-brown, in different clusters, on the same plant. Cones are rounded, 2cm in diameter, starting green but ripening to red-brown, with conspicuously spiny scales.

Habitat and distribution A native of the mountains of Tasmania.

Japanese Umbrella Pine
Sciadopitys verticillata 23m (25m)

A broadly conical evergreen, often with a finely tapering crown, but may sometimes be bushy. Leaves are needle-like, up to 12cm long and borne in umbrella-like clusters. Needles are deeply grooved on both sides, dark green above, but more yellow below. The red-brown bark peels off in long vertical strips.

Reproductive parts Male flowers are yellow and produced in clusters; female flowers are green, and grow at the tips of the shoots, ripening into ovoid, 7.5cm-long, red-brown cones after 2 years.

Habitat and distribution A native of the mountains of Japan, but grows well in many parts of Britain and Europe.

Chinese Fir
Cunninghamia lanceolata 25m

A broadly conical evergreen conifer with foliage superficially resembling the Monkey Puzzle, although it is a brighter and more pleasing green. The leaves are up to 6cm long, narrowly strap-shaped and pointed, glossy green with 2 white bands on the underside. The bark is reddish-brown and ridged in old specimens, and there may be more than one trunk. Dead foliage persists inside the crown, looking bright orange in sunlight.

Reproductive parts Both male and female flowers are yellowish, produced in clusters at the tips of shoots. Cones are rounded and scaly, up to 4cm in diameter, green at first and then brown.

Habitat and distribution A native of evergreen forests of China, and fairly common in large gardens in Britain, thriving best in the south and west.

Dawn Redwood

Japanese Umbrella Pine

Dawn Redwood
Japanese Umbrella Pine

Japanese Umbrella Pine
Chinese Fir, male cones

Chinese Fir, young branch bark

PINE FAMILY, Pinaceae

A large family of 200 species, all originating in the northern hemisphere. Their cones are woody and composed of a spiral arrangement of scales, each with two seeds. The leaves are needle-like. The arrangement of the needles, such as being grouped in pairs or threes, or growing on short pegs, is a great help in the identification of these trees.

FIRS *Abies* About 50 species, often tall and imposing trees with a pleasing, symmetrical, conical shape on a strong single bole. Cones are erect and leathery leaves are attached to the shoot by sucker-like structures at the base.

Common Silver Fir
Abies alba 47m (50m)
A fast-growing fir, reaching a great size, and until relatively recently (1960s) holding the record for the tallest tree in Britain. The bark of the trunk and branches of mature trees are white, but on younger trees the bark is greyer and smoother. The thick needles are up to 3cm long, notched at the tip and arranged in 2 rows on the twigs, which are covered with pale brown hairs.
Reproductive parts The erect cones are green at first, becoming orange-brown when mature and reaching a length of up to 20cm. They finally disintegrate into fan-like scales and toothed bracts, leaving a central woody axis protruding from the twig. The cones normally grow high up on the tree so are difficult to examine intact.
Habitat and distribution A native of the mountains of Europe, forming dense forests from 800 to 1,900m, occurring eastwards from the Pyrenees as far as Bulgaria, but at one time also widely planted in Britain as an important timber tree. Its susceptibility to aphid attack, vul-

nerability to late frosts, and the superiority of species like the Noble Fir have led to it becoming much more scarce in Britain, and large trees are now mainly confined to Scotland and Ireland.
Comments Small specimens of the Common Silver Fir are popular as Christmas trees in many parts of Europe.
Similar species
Delavay's Silver Fir *A. delavayi* 25m Similar to Common Silver Fir, but buds are resinous and young twigs are smoother, or downy, reddish-brown. Cones are dark purplish-green, shorter, at 10cm, and more rounded, and scales have a long projecting, sometimes bent spine. A native of China, and a popular tree in large parks and gardens.

Caucasian Fir
Abies nordmanniana 42m (50m)
A large and shapely fir when mature, with thick foliage giving the crown a pleasing appearance. The tough, green, forward-pointing needles are arranged in dense rows around the brownish twigs. The needles are 1.5–3.5cm long, slightly notched at the tip and grooved on the upper surface. On mature trees the bark is dull grey and fissured, forming numerous small square plates.
Reproductive parts Male flowers are reddish and grow on the underside of the shoot, releasing their pollen in spring. Female flowers are greener and upright, growing in separate clusters on the same tree. Cones are borne high up on mature trees (30m) and are dark brown and resinous with projecting, downcurved scales, reaching a length of 12–18cm. They break up on the tree, so are rarely found in good condition at ground level.
Habitat and distribution A native of Turkey and regions further east but widely planted in central Europe as a timber tree, and in Britain as an ornamental tree to replace Common Silver Firs lost through disease.

Silver Fir

Delavay's Silver Fir, male and female cones

Caucasian Fir

Noble Fir
Abies procera 50m (80m)

One of the largest conifers when mature, recognized by its pleasing, narrowly conical shape, densely crowded blue-grey needles and large cones, up to 25cm long, held erect on the upper side of the branches. The heavy cones disintegrate in winter, but may be so abundant at times that branches are damaged by their weight. The silver-grey or purplish trunk develops shallow fissures as the tree matures. The bluntly pointed needles reach 3cm long and are grooved on the upper surface; their blue-grey coloration is marked by paler bands on both surfaces. The youngest twigs are reddish-brown and hairy, with resinous buds at the tip.

Noble Fir, cone

Reproductive parts Male flowers are reddish and supported below the shoot. The cylindrical female flowers, resembling small cones, are red or green and upright, growing on the upper side of the shoot. A green spine emerges beneath each scale on the female cone.

Habitat and distribution Native to the Cascades and coastal mountains of Washington and Oregon, preferring west-facing mountainsides, and widely planted in Britain and Europe since 1850, reaching its greatest size in Scotland.

Comments Fallen trees provide nurseries for seedlings, which are often found growing in dense lines along lengths of decayed trunk in damp woodlands.

Grecian Fir
Abies cephalonica 36m

A more spreading tree than the Common Silver Fir. The rigid, prickly needles arise from all round the hairless red-brown twigs and are not borne in rows, unlike most other firs; they reach a length of 3cm and have 2 white bands on the underside. The bark of young trees is slightly scaly and mostly grey with a hint of orange, but in mature trees it is a deeper grey and fissured to form squarish plates.

Grecian Fir, cone

Reproductive parts The upright cones are a rich golden-brown colour, reaching a length of 16cm. Like the needles, they have a prickly appearance because of the downcurved triangular bracts which protrude from between the scales. Mature trees are often heavily loaded with cones to the extent that branches can be broken under their weight.

Habitat and distribution Replaces Common Silver Fir in the high mountains of Greece where it forms forests from 750 to 1,700m. This may be one of the first conifers to produce new buds in spring, so it is especially vulnerable to late frosts when planted away from its normal range. It grows well in dry areas of Britain, but also thrives in wet regions, where it reaches the greatest size.

Noble Fir, cones

Grecian Fir

Noble Fir, male cones

Noble Fir

Grand Fir or Giant Fir

Abies grandis 55m (100m)

A magnificent fir when mature and one of the fastest-growing conifers, reaching a height of 40m in as many years. Best recognized by its comb-like arrangement of needles; the soft, shining-green needles are borne in 2 rows on either side of the downy olive-green twigs and have a curious scent of oranges when crushed. The needles reach a length of 5cm and have a notched tip; there are 2 pale bands on the underside.

Reproductive parts The small, smooth cones rarely exceed 10cm in length and are produced high up on trees which are at least 50 years old; they break up on the tree to release the seeds, so they are not often seen closely by observers on the ground.

Habitat and distribution A native of the mountains of N California to Vancouver Island and reaching inland as far as Montana. Planted in Britain and Europe as an ornamental tree and sometimes commercially. Specimens around 100m tall have been recorded in the tree's native habitat, and many trees in Europe are still growing, especially those in Scotland, so it may not yet have reached its greatest height in Britain.

Similar species

Colorado White Fir *A. concolor* 55m
Similar to Grand Fir, but not normally attaining the same height. The bark is dark grey, becoming deeply fissured, and the buds are highly resinous on smooth, yellowish-green twigs. The bluish-grey needles grow in 2 ranks curving upwards almost vertically. They have 2 pale blue bands on the underside, and are up to 6cm long. The cones are cylindrical and upright, 10cm long, green at first, ripening through purple to brown. A native of the Rocky Mountains, USA.

Alpine Fir

Abies lasiocarpa 16m (30m)

A narrowly conical evergreen with densely packed needles growing on the upper side of the shoot, the central ones pointing forwards. Each needle is up to 4cm long, notched at the tip, greyish-green above, and with 2 white bands beneath. The bark is greyish-white and smooth with resinous blisters bursting out in places. The variety 'Arizonica' has bluer leaves and a corky bark, hence its alternative name of Corkbark Fir, from its native Arizona.

Reproductive parts The small male flowers are yellow tinged with red, growing on the underside of the shoot. Female flowers are purple and upright, growing in clusters on the same plant in the spring. Cylindrical cones, up to 10cm long, are purple at first, becoming brown when ripe.

Habitat and distribution A native of the mountain slopes of the western USA from sea-level to high altitudes.

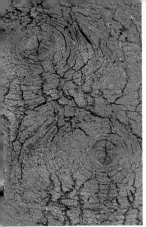

Grand Fir

Grand Fir

Colorado White Fir

Alpine Fir 'Arizonica'

Spanish Fir or Hedgehog Fir
Abies pinsapo 25m

The short, usually blunt, bluish-grey needles, no more than 1.5cm long, are densely arranged all around the twig, as in the Grecian Fir, but unlike any other fir. This explains the alternative name 'Hedgehog' Fir. Young trees have a pleasing shape, but older trees (100 years) can become more open-crowned and straggly before dying back.

Reproductive parts The small male flowers are red at first, becoming yellow as they open beneath the shoot; female flowers are green, growing in small upright clusters above the shoot. Both open in spring. The cylindrical cones taper to a fine point and are borne upright on the twigs. They have a smooth texture as the bracts do not project beyond the scales.

Habitat and distribution A native tree of the Sierra Nevada in S Spain, but not abundant even there. Has been planted in drier parts of central Europe and will tolerate limestone soils. Sometimes found as an ornamental tree in parks and gardens in Britain.

Similar species

A. × insignis A hybrid between the Spanish Fir and the Caucasian Fir, frequently planted in parks and gardens for ornament. Blunt needles up to 3.3cm long and 2.5mm wide are arranged all round the shoot, but sometimes with a parting on the underside. Twigs are hairy. Female cones are up to 20cm long and 5cm in diameter, with bracts pointing away from the lower few scales.

Beautiful Fir
Abies amabilis 32m

An attractive tree with silvery bark and a thick tapering crown. In suitable wet climates in Britain it grows rapidly to form luxuriant foliage and a good strong trunk, but in drier areas it may be rather sparse. The crushed needles release a scent of oranges, and are densely packed around the twigs.

Reproductive parts The smooth oval cones have a purplish tinge and grow on the upper surface of the twigs.

Habitat and distribution A native of Washington State, USA, where it may grow to a height of 60m. It is widely planted as an ornamental tree in suitable areas elsewhere.

Veitch's Silver Fir
Abies veitchii 28m

Most easily recognized by the fluted and ribbed silvery-grey trunk and the silvery undersides of the 3cm-long notched needles which show well on the outermost shoots, which usually curve upwards. The bark is grey and smooth in younger trees, becoming more scaly as the tree ages.

Reproductive parts The small male flowers are reddish, looking yellow as they open in the spring. The female flowers are red with a greenish tinge, and grow in upright clusters on the top of the shoot. The bluish-purple cylindrical cones are smooth and erect, up to 7.5cm long and are brown when fully ripe.

Habitat and distribution A native of the evergreen forests of Japan, discovered by John Veitch and introduced into Britain in 1879. Not a very vigorous tree in S Britain, where it may not live for long. It thrives only in N Scotland.

Spanish Fir, developing cones

Spanish Fir, in flower

Spanish Fir

Beautiful Fir, cones

Siberian Fir
Abies sibirica 12m (30m)

A pyramidal or conical tree growing on a slender trunk with greyish-brown bark and numerous resinous blisters. Young twigs are pale grey and finely downy, and buds are sometimes covered with a pale-grey resin. Needles grow all round the shoot, but spread horizontally to leave a gap below. Needles are 3cm long, curved, thin and flexible, mostly blunt-tipped, and pale yellowish-green, with pale lines below.

Siberian Fir, cone

Santa Lucia Fir or Bristle-cone Fir
Abies bracteata 38m

A tall, narrowly conical evergreen with a finely tapering crown and strong foliage. Needles are up to 5cm long, tough and sharply spined, dark green above and marked with 2 light bands below. Buds are pointed. Bark is black and marked with scars of fallen branches.

Santa Lucia Fir, cone

Reproductive parts Male flowers are small and yellowish, female cones are tapering cylinders, 8cm long and 3cm in diameter, bluish at first, but becoming brown later.

Habitat and distribution A common species forming forests in N and E Russia, and planted for timber in parts of Europe. Not common in Britain.

Similar species

Sakhalin Fir *A. sachalinensis* 20m From the Russian island of Sakhalin, off Japan, and Hokkaido. Smooth purplish-brown bark with horizontal lines and reddish resin blisters, dense sprays of narrow green needles which are sticky and smell of cedarwood when crushed.

Reproductive parts The most distinctive feature is the bright-green cones, up to 10cm long, with their long projecting hair-like bracts, which persist on the tree throughout the summer. The flowers are small and insignificant; males are yellowish and grow on the underside of the shoot, and females are green, growing on top of the shoot.

Habitat and distribution A rare native of the evergreen forests on the coastal mountains of S California where the climate is fairly dry. Does well in rainier parts of Britain.

Santa Lucia Fir

Santa Lucia Fir

CEDARS *Cedrus* A small genus with just 4 species, found only in Europe and Asia. Cedars flower in the autumn, produce large woody cones and have strong, aromatic timber. A simple tip for remembering which cedar is which is to look at the angle of the branches and think of the first letter of the tree's name: **D**eodar = **D**rooping; **L**ebanon = **L**evel; **A**tlas = **A**scending.

Deodar or Himalayan Cedar
Cedrus deodara 36m (70m)

A broadly conical evergreen characterized by the drooping tips to the branches and the drooping leading shoot on the tapering crown. Leaves grow in whorls of 15–20 on short lateral shoots, or in a spiral on larger twigs. Needles are 2–5cm long, shortest on the lateral shoots, dark green with pale-grey lines on either side. The bark on old trees is dark, almost black, and fissured into small plates. Young trees are usually paler and more graceful than long-established trees.

Reproductive parts Male flowers are up to 12cm long and purplish, turning yellow when releasing pollen in the autumn. Mature female cones are solid and barrel-shaped, up to 14cm long and 8cm in diameter, growing only on older trees.

Habitat and distribution A native of the mountain forests of the western Himalayas. Introduced into Britain in 1831 and widely planted in parks and gardens, where it can form a stately and imposing tree if well placed.

Atlas Cedar or Atlantic Cedar
Cedrus atlantica 40m

A broadly conical or sometimes pyramidal evergreen tree, with a domed outline when mature. The leading shoot can usually be seen above the domed top, and the tips of the branches are angled upwards. Shoots are short and ascending, bearing clusters of up to 45 needles, which are 1–3cm long and shiny deep green. Bark is dark grey, cracking into large plates and forming deep fissures.

Reproductive parts Male cones are 3–5cm long, pinkish-yellow, and open in the autumn to release their pollen. Ripe female cones are up to 8cm long and 5cm in diameter, squat, with a sunken tip and small central boss.

Atlas Cedar, cone

Habitat and distribution A native of the forests of the Atlas Mountains of N Africa, and widely planted in Europe for timber or, more frequently, ornament. The most frequent cultivar is the Blue Atlas Cedar *C. atlantica* var. *glauca*, with attractive bright bluish-grey foliage. It is hardy, tolerant of atmospheric pollution and widely planted in town gardens, often in sites where it soon outgrows its allotted space.

Deodar, male flowers

Deodar

Deodar

Deodar

Atlas Cedar

Atlas Cedar 'Atlantica', cones

Cedar of Lebanon
Cedrus libani 40m

When mature, this is a characteristically flat-topped tree with massive ascending main branches and smaller, level, lateral branches supporting flat plates of foliage. Needles similar to those of other *Cedrus* species, up to 3cm long, but usually in clusters of only 10–15 on short shoots or singly if growing on long shoots. The bark is dark grey, fissured and ridged, becoming dark brown in very old trees. The trunk can be immense in very old trees.

Reproductive parts Male cones are up to 7.5cm long, greyish or blue-green and erect, opening to release pollen in the autumn. Mature female cones are solid, ovoid and up to 12cm long and 7cm in diameter, ripening from purple-green to brown.

Habitat and distribution A native of the mountain forests of the eastern Mediterranean, but very widely planted in parks and gardens as an ornamental tree. Known since 1640 in Britain, where it is a familiar feature of old and well-established gardens, often dominating the lawns of large houses with its sweeping branches.

Similar species
Cyprus Cedar *C. brevifolia* 21m Dark-green needles are much shorter than those of any other cedar (2cm), and the crown is more open. New shoots grow very slowly. Female cones are up to 7cm long, ripening from purple-green to brown. A native of the Troodos Mountains on Cyprus, and sometimes planted in collections elsewhere.

Common Larch

LARCHES *Larix* A genus containing 10 species, some very widespread around the northern tree-lines of Asia, Europe and N America. Larches are coniferous, but all of them are deciduous, some producing fine autumn colours. The leaves are produced in short spirals on new shoots, and in whorls on tiny spurs produced on older wood. The cones are small, woody and persistent. Freshly cut foliage has a pleasant scent of new-mown hay. Many are commercially important timber species.

Common Larch
Larix decidua 35m (50m)

A deciduous conifer, forming a tall, narrowly conical tree if growing alone, but more often seen in close rows in plantations. Branches mostly horizontal, but lower ones on old trees slightly drooping. Leaves grow in tight bunches of up to 40 needles, up to 3cm long, fresh green when first open, becoming darker, with 2 pale bands below in summer, and then changing through red to yellow before falling in autumn. Bark is rough and greyish-brown in young trees, becoming fissured with age.

Reproductive parts Male flowers are small, soft yellow cones, releasing pollen in spring. Female cones are conspicuously red in spring, maturing to become woody, brown and ovoid. Cones ripen in the first year but persist on the twigs after releasing their seeds.

Habitat and distribution A native of the mountains of central and E Europe but long established elsewhere as a timber species, or as an ornamental tree in gardens.

Common Larch, cones

Cedar of Lebanon

Cyprus Cedar

Cyprus Cedar

Larch, autumn colours

Larch, early spring　　　　**Larch**　　　**Larch**, cones and flowers

Japanese Larch
Larix kaempferi 40m

A deciduous conifer resembling Common Larch, but lacking the drooping shoots, and having a more twiggy appearance with a dense crown. Needles grow in tufts of about 40, and are slightly broader, and greyer in colour than those of Common Larch. Bark is reddish-brown, flaking off in scales.

Reproductive parts Male cones are similar to those of Common Larch, but female cones are pink or cream in spring, becoming brown and woody in autumn, and differing from those of Common Larch in having turned-out tips to the scales, looking like woody rose-buds.

Habitat and distribution A native of Japan, but now very common in forestry plantations, replacing the Common Larch because of its more vigorous growth. Of less value to wildlife, because of the dense needle-litter that accumulates beneath it, and the later leaf-fall.

Dunkeld Larch or Hybrid Larch
Larix × eurolepis 32m

A vigorous deciduous conifer, with a conical outline when mature. Shares characteristics with both parents (Common Larch and Japanese Larch), with most features intermediate between the 2; can be rather variable.

Reproductive parts Female cones are pinkish at first, but ripen to yellow-brown and have slightly reflexed scales with projecting bracts.

Dunkeld Larch, cones

Habitat and distribution A more vigorous tree than either of the parents, and better able to cope with harsh conditions and poor soils, so is quite widely planted mostly for timber but occasionally as a specimen tree.

Similar species

Tamarack *L. laricina* 20m The N American counterpart of Common Larch, found in woods and swamps from the north-eastern USA, through Canada and Alaska to the Arctic tree-line. A very slender upright tree with the smallest cones and flowers of any larch.

Tamarack, cone

Japanese Larch

Japanese Larch

Japanese Larch, cones

Dunkeld Larch

Dunkeld Larch   **Tamarack**, cones and flowers

Dahurian Larch
Larix gmelinii 30m

A slender, conical deciduous tree with level branches sometimes forming flattish areas of foliage, and supporting long, yellowish or red-brown, slightly hairy shoots. Leaves grow in clusters of 25, up to 4cm long, blunt-tipped, bright green above and with 2 paler bands below. Bark is reddish-brown and scaly.

Reproductive parts Female cones similar to those of other larches, with pinkish or greenish, slightly projecting bracts, becoming brown when ripe, with square-ended scales.

Habitat and distribution A native of E Asia, and sometimes planted for timber or as a specimen tree in N Europe. Prince Rupert's Larch is a variant with larger cones which is most widely seen in Britain.

Western Larch
Larix occidentalis 30m (65m)

The largest of all the larches, although it rarely reaches its maximum height away from its native range. A tall, slender, conical tree with slightly ascending, short branches and red-brown shoots. Leaves are soft needles up to 4cm long, borne in tufts on side-shoots. The bark is grey and scaly, forming deep fissures low down.

Reproductive parts Male flowers are yellow, and pendent below the shoots; female flowers are red and upright above the shoot on the same tree. Both open in spring. Cones are ovoid, 4cm long, with long bracts protruding from between the scales, distinguishing this from all other larches.

Habitat and distribution A native of the mountains of British Columbia, south to Oregon. Introduced in 1881 into Britain, where there are now some very fine specimens in mature collections.

Golden Larch
Pseudolarix amabilis 25m (40m)

A deciduous conical tree very similar to other larches in its foliage, but differing in its cones. Branches are level and produce flattened sprays of foliage, supporting long reddish, hairless shoots on which leaves grow in a scattered spiral. The short shoots support bunches of up to 30 pointed needle-like leaves, up to 6.5cm long and 0.3cm wide. Leaves are bright yellow-green above and marked with greyish bands below.

Reproductive parts Female cones are ovoid, green through the summer, but

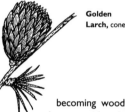

Golden Larch, cone

becoming woody and brown, with triangular scales, which eventually break up on the tree.

Habitat and distribution A native of China, introduced into Europe as an ornamental tree, mainly for its prolonged display of fine autumn colour. Not an easy tree to propagate.

Dahurian Larch

Western Larch

Dahurian Larch, spring growth

SPRUCES *Picea* About 50 species occur in the northern hemisphere, found high on mountains in the south, but coming down to lower levels further north. All have a pleasing conical shape, rough, scaly bark which does not form ridges, tiny pegs left behind on the shoots after the needles have fallen and tough, often spined leaves. The long cones are pendulous when ripening and normally fall from the tree intact. Many are commercially important timber trees and are planted widely across the temperate and cooler regions of the northern hemisphere.

Norway Spruce
Picea abies 44m (65m)
One of the most familiar evergreens, commonly used in its early years as the Christmas tree. A narrowly conical tree on a slender, unbranching trunk, with numerous almost level branches. Needles are stiff and short, 4-angled and borne on short pegs (a characteristic of all spruces), spreading to expose the undersurface of the twig. Bark is brownish, scaly and with resinous patches on older trees.

Reproductive parts Male cones are small, yellowish and clustered near the tips of shoots, female cones are up to 18cm long, narrowly oval and pendulous, like all spruces.

Norway Spruce, female cones

Habitat and distribution A native of the mountains of Europe, and lower altitudes further north. Widely planted elsewhere for commercial reasons, especially for Christmas trees, shelter-belts, and occasionally for ornament.

Similar species
Siberian Spruce *P. obovata* 18m Replaces the Norway Spruce from Finland eastwards to Siberia. A brighter green, more conical tree with smaller neater cones. The name *obovata* refers to the oval shape of the cone scales. Rarely planted outside its native range.

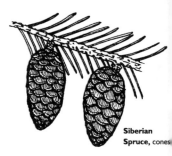

Siberian Spruce, cones

Colorado Spruce
Picea pungens 30m (50m)
A slender conical evergreen with smooth yellowish-brown twigs. Leaves grow all round the shoot, but the upper surface has more and some curve upwards to make the top surface look more dense. Sharply pointed stiff needles are about 3cm long and usually dark green, but some cultivars are markedly blue-green. Colorado Blue Spruce, *P. pungens* var *glauca* (23m), is the most commonly seen cultivar, favoured for its attractive bluish foliage.

Reproductive parts Male and female flowers are borne in small, separate clusters on the same tree; males are red-tinged, females greener. Mature female cones are pendent, narrowly oval and up to 12cm long, sometimes with a slight curve, and the scales have irregularly toothed tips.

Habitat and distribution A native of the south-western USA, growing on dry stony mountain slopes and streamsides but commonly planted for ornament and timber throughout much of N Europe.

Norway Spruce

Colorado Spruce

Norway Spruce

Colorado Spruce

Brewer's Weeping Spruce or Brewer Spruce
Picea breweriana 20m (40m)

An evergreen, markedly conical tree with a slender bole and grey-purple scaly bark. Twigs pale brownish or pink and downy. The most striking feature is the 'weeping' habit of the shoots along the branches. Leaves grow all round the shoot and often curve forwards. They are flattened, needle-like, up to 3cm long and sharply pointed, green above and with white bands below.

Reproductive parts Male flowers are large for a spruce, up to 2cm in diameter and reddish; female cones are pendent, cylindrical and up to 12cm long, starting purplish but ripening to brown. Overlapping scales have blunt, rounded tips.

Brewer's Weeping Spruce, female cones

Habitat and distribution Native to the mountains of the California–Oregon boundary, but a popular tree in large parks and gardens in Britain and Europe where it does well, growing gracefully if not crowded by other trees.

Oriental Spruce
Picea orientalis 40m (50m)

A dense-foliaged evergreen growing into a strongly conical tree on a short, stout bole. Branches slender with numerous hairy twigs. Very short, blunt needles, less than 1cm long, arise all round the shoots, but leave more open area on the lower surface. Needles are dark green and glossy above and square in cross-section. Bark is pale brown and scaly.

Reproductive parts Small male flowers are red then yellow. Female cones are up to 8cm long, ovoid and often curved and green with purple or grey tinges when still growing, but ripening to shiny brown, and hanging below the shoot.

Habitat and distribution A native of the mountain forests of the Caucasus and NE Turkey, widely planted in Britain and Europe as an ornamental tree, and occasionally for commercial forestry. The variety 'Aurea', with bright yellow young foliage, is a popular arboretum tree.

White Spruce
Picea glauca 24m (30m)

A narrowly conical evergreen, but broadening out with maturity to become more rounded. Branches turn upwards at the tips, bearing hairless, greyish twigs and blunt buds. Needles are pointed, 4-angled and up to 1.3 cm long, pale green (sometimes bluish), and smelling unpleasantly to some when crushed. Bark is purple-grey with roughly circular scales.

Reproductive parts Female cones are about 6cm long and 2cm in diameter, cylindrical, pendent and orange-brown when ripe, with rounded margins to the scales.

Habitat and distribution A native of evergreen woodlands of Canada and the northern USA, widely planted for timber and ornament in Britain and N Europe, especially Denmark.

Brewer's Weeping Spruce

Oriental Spruce
Brewer's Weeping Spruce

White Spruce
Oriental Spruce, cones

Oriental Spruce

Black Spruce
Picea mariana 19m (30m)

A slender, conical evergreen with the shortest needles and cones of any spruce apart from the Oriental Spruce, whose needles are darker green and blunt. Bluntly pointed needles are blue-green above and pale blue beneath, up to 1.5cm long, 4-angled, growing all round the hairy, yellowish shoots. Bark is greyish-brown and scaly, and only in its native Canada does it look very black.

Reproductive parts Cones are ovoid, reddish and pendent, up to 4cm long, usually growing near the top of the tree.

Habitat and distribution A native of mountains and boggy areas in Canada and the Great Lakes regions, but planted in Britain and Europe as an ornamental species for its neat habit and bluish foliage.

Engelmann's Spruce
Picea engelmannii 30m (50m)

A slender, conical evergreen growing on a narrowly tapering, thin trunk. Branches are ascending or turn upwards at the tips, with slightly pendulous young shoots. Pointed needles spread out to show lower surface of twig and hide upper surface, are up to 2.5cm long, 4-angled, bluish-green and smell unpleasant when crushed.

Reproductive parts Cones are up to 7cm long, narrowly oval, and taper to a pointed tip, becoming brownish when ripe, with squarish toothed scales.

Habitat and distribution A native of the Rocky Mountains from Canada south to Mexico, including the hills of Washington and Oregon. Introduced to Britain and Europe, although scarce. The form usually seen in parks and gardens is the ornamental variety 'Glauca' which resembles the Colorado Blue Spruce with its bluish foliage, except that the leaves are softer, smelling pleasantly of menthol, the bark is orange-brown with thin papery scales and the cones are small and shiny brown.

Sitka Spruce
Picea sitchensis 52m (60m)

A large conical evergreen tapering finely to a spire-like crown. The trunk is stout and buttressed in the largest specimens, with greyish-brown bark, becoming purplish and scaly in older specimens. Branches are ascending with slightly pendent, hairless side-shoots. Needles are up to 3cm long, stiff and flattened with a distinct keel, bright green above and with 2 pale-blue bands below. Needles appear crowded on the upper surface of the shoot, with the lower surface more exposed. The general impression is of tough, sharply spined, blue-green foliage on a sturdy tree.

Reproductive parts Female cones are yellowish and small at first, growing to about 9cm, and becoming cylindrical and shiny pale brown, covered with papery toothed scales.

Sitka Spruce, cones

Habitat and distribution A native of high-rainfall areas on the coast from Kodiak Island, Alaska, to mid-California, and named after Sitka Island, Alaska. It is the largest spruce and some specimens, guarded in National Parks, have reached heights of 80m. Introduced into Britain and Europe and widely planted for commercial forestry and sometimes for ornament.

Comments A fast-growing species in good conditions, increasing in height by1m a year when young, even in the poorest soils, so a popular tree for commercial forestry and often planted in vast plantations, providing lightweight but strong timber.

Black Spruce

Black Spruce, female cones

Engelmann's Spruce

Sitka Spruce

Sitka Spruce

Sitka Spruce, new growth

Serbian Spruce
Picea omorika 30m

A narrowly conical to columnar tree, with a slender form unlike all other spruces. The lower branches are slightly descending with raised tips, the higher branches being mostly level or ascending. All branches are short. The flattened and keeled needles, up to 2cm long, may be blunt or barely pointed, dark blue-green above with 2 pale bands below. Bark is orange-brown and scaly in older trees.

Reproductive parts Male cones are large and red, becoming yellow when releasing pollen. Female cones grow on curving stalks and are up to 6cm long, ovoid and blue-green at first, ripening to brown. Cone scales are rounded with finely toothed margins.

Habitat and distribution A native of limestone rocks of the Drina basin of Serbia, unknown until 1875, and now a popular ornamental tree because of its pleasing shape, tolerance of a wide range of soil types, ability to grow in polluted air near towns, and resistance to frost damage. Also planted for timber in Scandinavia.

Sargent Spruce
Picea brachytyla 26m

A broadly conical spruce with a tapering crown and a fairly open habit with ascending branches and pendulous side-shoots. The pointed needles are crowded, and have a green upper surface and a pale to silvery-white lower surface.

Reproductive parts Male flowers are small and reddish-yellow, female cones are narrowly ovoid with triangular-tipped scales.

Habitat and distribution Introduced into Britain from China in the early twentieth century, and now mostly confined to gardens and collections.

HEMLOCKS *Tsuga* About 10 species occur, and there is one hybrid. Closely related to the spruces, but lacking the small pegs on the shoots. Widespread across N America and Asia. Important commercially for the paper-pulp industry. The cones are small, woody and usually pendent.

Western Hemlock
Tsuga heterophylla 45m (70m+)

A large, narrowly conical or almost columnar evergreen tree with dense dark-green foliage, topped by a spire-like crown and a drooping leading shoot. The most distinctive feature is the shoot bearing 2 different sizes of leaf (hence *heterophylla*): some needles are up to 6mm long and others up to 2cm long, both having rounded but blunt tips and very finely toothed margins. All needles are dark glossy green above and marked with 2 pale bands below, and lie in 2 flattened rows on either side of the shoot.

Reproductive parts Male flowers can be abundant, reddish at first, but yellowing when releasing pollen. Female cones are solitary and pendent, growing on the ends of shoots, ovoid and up to 3cm long with a few blunt scales.

Habitat and distribution A native of the forests of western N America from Alaska to N California, reaching a great size in central parts of its range, such as Washington State. Widely planted in Britain and W Europe where it also reaches a great size, but not yet as great as in its native habitat. Grows well on most soil types apart from chalk, preferring areas of high rainfall. Often grown for commercial forestry purposes, but also makes a splendid specimen tree.

Comments Despite its great size, the timber from this and other hemlocks is mainly used for paper pulp.

Serbian Spruce, male and female flowers, and cones

Serbian Spruce

Serbian Spruce

Sargent Spruce

Western Hemlock

Western Hemlock

Eastern Hemlock
Tsuga canadensis 30m (45m)

Away from its native Appalachian Mountains this evergreen grows into a rather shapeless, untidy-looking tree with heavy branches, a forked trunk with blackish bark and dark foliage. Leaves are similar to those of Western Hemlock, sometimes with a further row of leaves along the middle of the shoot, twisted around to show their white undersides. Individual needles are more tapering, with a narrower tip than those of Western Hemlock.

Reproductive parts Male flowers are small and yellowish-green, clustered along the underside of shoots. Female cones are similar to those of Western Hemlock but noticeably smaller at only 1.5cm long. The cone scales have slightly thickened edges.

Habitat and distribution A native of woodlands in hilly and rocky areas in eastern N America, where it can grow into a slender, more shapely tree, but widespread as an introduction in Britain and parts of Europe where it is not as attractive, but is still planted for ornament.

Comments This was the first species of hemlock to be discovered by Europeans, who thought that the crushed leaves smelt of the poisonous herb hemlock and named the genus after it. There is no other connection between the two plants.

DOUGLAS FIRS *Pseudotsuga* The scientific name means 'false hemlock'; the foliage is soft and the bark is deeply fissured in large trees. The cones are distinctive in having projecting 3-pointed bracts between the scales; they are pendent and shed whole when ripe.

Douglas Fir or Oregon Fir
Pseudotsuga menziesii 60m (100m+)

A very tall, slender, conical evergreen, with conspicuous whorls of branches supporting pendulous masses of dense aromatic foliage. Leaves grow on either side of the shoot; needles are up to 3.5cm long, blunt or slightly pointed, dark green above with a groove and marked with white bands below. Bark is greyish-green and smooth with some resinous blisters in younger trees, but becomes reddish-brown, and fissured in more mature trees revealing colourful patches. Resin blisters release a pleasant aroma if broken.

Reproductive parts Male flowers are small, yellow and pendulous, growing

Douglas Fir, cone

near the tips of twigs. Female flowers grow at the tips of twigs and resemble tiny pinkish shaving-brushes. When ripe they are ovoid, pendulous and brown with unique 3-tailed bracts lying between the scales.

Habitat and distribution A native of western N America where it can grow to an immense size: one tree, felled on Vancouver Island in 1895, was 133m tall, but most trees surviving today are around 80m tall. Widely planted in Britain and Europe for timber and for ornament, growing especially well in Scotland. The English name is given in honour of the Scottish explorer David Douglas.

Comments Annual rings are easy to count in this tree as the wood laid down in summer is very dark. The heartwood is red-brown, and the sapwood is pale brown, resembling pine.

Eastern Hemlock

Douglas Fir

Douglas Fir

Douglas Fir

PINES *Pinus* The largest genus of conifers, with over 100 species occurring in most climatic regions of the northern hemisphere. They are commercially very important, many of them providing good softwood timber. Cones are generally large, woody and pendent, and the long needles grow in bunches of 2, 3 or 5. Most of the northern species are 2-needle pines.

(a) Two-needle Pines Needles grow in bunches of 2.

Scots Pine
Pinus sylvestris 36m (50m)
A conical evergreen when young and growing vigorously, but becoming much more open, and flat-topped with a long bole when an older tree. Branches irregular, with broken-off stumps of old branches remaining on the trunk lower down. Needles are borne in bunches of 2, grey-green or blue-green, up to 7cm long, usually twisted with a short point at the tip. Bark is reddish- or grey-brown low down on the trunk, but is markedly red or orange higher up the trunk in mature trees. The lower trunk is scaly, and higher up it becomes more papery.
Reproductive parts Male flowers are yellow and borne in clusters at the ends of the previous year's shoots, shedding pollen in late spring. Female flowers grow at the tips of new shoots; they are usually solitary, and are crimson at first, ripening to brown by the end of the summer and persisting through the winter. In the second summer they enlarge and become green and bluntly conical, ripening to grey-brown in the autumn; they do not open their scales and shed seeds until the following spring. Each cone scale has a blunt projection in the centre.
Habitat and distribution A tree native to Scotland, and originally much of Britain, and a wide swathe of Europe from Spain to Siberia and Turkey. Introduced to the USA where it is often used as a Christmas tree.
Comments A useful timber tree, producing 'deal', used for pit-props, telegraph poles, building, furniture, chipboard and paper pulp. The native pinewoods in Scotland support many species of wildlife unique to the area and not able to survive in plantations of alien species.
Similar species
Japanese Red Pine *P. densiflora* 15m Young trees are the most attractive, with a neat conical shape and bright green shoots showing clearly between the rather sparse, slender, paired needles. Older trees are less shapely and have a flatter, more twiggy crown. The bark is distinctly red and flaky and the pointed cones are also reddish. Flowers and cones are produced on quite young trees. A native of China, Japan and Korea.
Red Pine *P. resinosa* 20m Very similar to Scots Pine, with an attractive reddish bark, but with longer, more slender and widely spaced needles which have the unique characteristic of snapping easily when bent in a curve. A native of the Great Lakes area of the USA and Canada.
Japanese Black Pine *P. thunbergii* Bark is very dark and deeply fissured in older trees. The tree has a rather sparse appearance with straggling branches and whorls of leaves. Cones often grow in dense clusters.

Scots Pine, new growth

Scots Pine

Scots Pine

Scots Pine, cone

Japanese Red Pine

Japanese Red Pine

Japanese Black Pine

Japanese Black Pine, cones

Beach Pine, Shore Pine or Lodgepole Pine
Pinus contorta 30m

A small to medium-sized evergreen which occurs in 2 different subspecies. The type species is var. *contorta* which grows near the shore from Alaska to California, and gained its scientific name from the twisted appearance of branches contorted by the wind. Needles are paired, up to 7cm long, with sharp points and are usually twisted and densely packed on young shoots, but sparser on older shoots.

The Lodgepole Pine, *P. contorta* var. *latifolia*, is very similar, but more columnar with a less dense crown, and usually growing on a much straighter, but sometimes divided trunk. The needles are broader than those of *P.c.contorta*, and more spread apart. It grows in the mountains well inland away from the sea. The straight poles were used for supporting Native Americans' lodges. Sometimes planted for timber in Britain and Europe, but does not thrive.

Beach Pine, cone

Reproductive parts Male flowers occur in dense clusters near the tips of shoots. Female flowers grow in groups of up to 4 close to the tip of the shoot. Cones are rounded to ovoid, up to 6cm long and 3cm in diameter, and usually a shiny yellow-brown. Each cone scale has a slender, sharp tip, which easily breaks off.
Habitat and distribution A very variable species, native to the western coasts of N America, and widely planted in Britain and N Europe for timber on poor soils and exposed sites.
Similar species
Jack Pine *P. banksiana* 30m A variable, usually untidy-looking, loosely conical tree becoming domed with age. Paired needles are up to 4cm long, yellowish-green and stiffly twisted. Female cones are distinctive: cylindrical, knobbly and usually twisted, with spineless scales, pointed forwards along the branch. Native to eastern

Jack Pine, cone

Canada, near the Arctic tree-line. Very hardy, so planted elsewhere in very severe climates, but not common.

Bosnian Pine
Pinus leucodermis 24m (30m)

A broadly pyramidal tree with a strong tapering bole and grey bark, breaking up into irregular plates. Whitish patches are revealed on older trees, hence *leucodermis*. Paired needles are up to 9cm long, densely packed on the shoots, stiff and projecting at right-angles, and are pungent when crushed.
Reproductive parts Cones are up to 8cm long and 2.5cm in diameter, narrowly ovoid and ripening to brown, with a recurved prickle on each scale. Second-year cones are an attractive deep blue, relieving the monotony of the dull foliage.
Habitat and distribution A native of the Balkans and SW Italy, occurring mainly in mountains on dry limestone. Thought by some to be the mountain form of *P. nigra*. Planted infrequently for ornament, growing well on any free-draining soil.

Beach Pine

Bosnian Pine

Bosnian Pine

Bosnian Pine

Bosnian PIne, cone

Austrian Pine
Pinus nigra var. *nigra* 35m

A broadly conical, heavily branched evergreen usually growing on a single bole, and with a narrow crown. Paired needles up to 15cm long, stiff and flattened with finely toothed margins, lasting for up to 4 years on the twigs before falling, and giving the tree a dense appearance. The greyish-brown bark is very rough in older trees.

Austrian Pine, cone

Reproductive parts Mature cones are woody, up to 8cm long and 3cm in diameter, with keeled scales bearing a spine; sometimes solitary, or in small clusters.
Habitat and distribution A native of the hills and mountains of central Europe, very variable across its range. Planted elsewhere mainly for shelter or ornament, and tolerant of a range of soils and climates, but the timber is too coarse and full of knots to be of much use.

Similar species
Corsican Pine *P. nigra* var. *maritima* 43m A more shapely tree with soft, narrow needles, paler green, up to 15cm long, and sometimes twisted in younger trees. Branches shorter and level giving a more slender, columnar appearance to younger trees. Cones similar to var. *nigra*. A native of the mountains and coasts of Corsica, S Italy and Sicily, and widely planted elsewhere near the coast on dunes, lowland heaths and poor soils. Resistant to pollution, and provides a useful timber crop.
Crimean Pine *P. nigra* var. *carmanica* 40m Distinguished by the strong bole which divides into several vertical stems, growing upright close to each other. A native of the Crimea and Asia Minor. Sometimes seen in parks and gardens.

Mountain Pine
Pinus mugo and *Pinus uncinata* 20m

Two forms have been named, the dwarf, shrub-like *P. mugo*, and the larger, tree-sized *P. uncinata*. Both have a greyish-black scaly bark and paired needles. Bright-green needles grow densely around the shoot giving a whorled appearance; each needle is up to 8cm long, curved and rather stiff.
Reproductive parts Male flowers grow in clusters near the ends of shoots; female flowers are reddish, growing at the ends of twigs in the first year, in groups of 1–3. Cones ripen to become ovoid, pale brown and woody, up to 5cm long and 2.5cm long, giving a smooth appearance, but the scales have a small prickle.
Habitat and distribution A native of the mountains of central Europe – the Alps, Pyrenees and Balkans. The dwarf forms are found in more exposed situations at high altitudes. *P. uncinata* is planted for forestry, shelter, stabilizing sand etc, in N Europe. The dwarf form is favoured for ornamental plantings, especially in polluted city centres, in Britain, Europe and the USA.

Corsican Pine

Corsican Pine

Crimean Pine

Mountain Pine

Crimean Pine

Mountain Pine

Mountain Pine, cone

Stone Pine or Umbrella Pine
Pinus pinea 30m
A broad umbrella-shaped tree with a dense mass of foliage on spreading branches on top of a tall bole. Paired needles are up to 20cm long and 2mm wide, and slightly twisted. Through a hand-lens 12 lines of stomata can be seen on the outer surface and 6 on the inner surface. The bark is reddish-grey on old trees and fissured, flaking away to leave deep orange patches.

Reproductive parts Cones are rounded to ovoid, up to 14cm long and 10cm in diameter, and ripen to a rich glossy brown after 3 years. The closely packed scales have a slightly pyramidal surface and conceal large, slightly winged seeds.

Habitat and distribution A native of light sandy soils near the Mediterranean coasts. Planted in the USA, S Africa and N Europe, where its resistance to salt winds makes it a useful species near coasts.

Comments The large, edible seeds, the size of small peas, have a dark mottled black and brown husk, and are harvested commercially and sold as 'pine kernels' to the confectionery trade. These seeds give the tree its 'Stone Pine' name.

Maritime Pine
Pinus pinaster 32m
The needles of this tree are the longest and thickest of any of the 2-needle pines. The bole is sturdy and slightly tapering, often with a curve in exposed coastal areas and the crown is usually shapeless and fairly open, reflecting the curve of the bole. The bark is yellowish-brown and breaks up into rectangular flakes.

Reproductive parts Male flowers are yellow and ovoid, and grow in clusters near the tips of the shoots. Female cones are ovoid and red at first in small clusters, ripening to become conical and woody with a greenish-brown gloss.

Habitat and distribution A native of the coastal hills and lowlands of the SW Atlantic coasts of Europe, and the Mediterranean region. Grows well on poor sandy soils so is often planted on heathlands and in coastal areas elsewhere.

Comments A resin can be obtained by cutting grooves into the bark and allowing it to ooze out into a receptacle.

Aleppo Pine
Pinus halepensis 20m
A small pine, often growing in a gnarled and deformed manner, but sometimes maturing to form a broad, shapeless crown on a stout bole. Twigs are characteristically pale grey, or even white, and this, together with the long, fine needles and shining red-brown cones, make it an easy tree to recognize. The paired needles are slender (0.7mm) and up to 15cm long, sometimes slightly twisted and with very finely toothed margins. Young trees have an almost shiny, smooth, silvery-grey bark, but it becomes scaly and fissured, and redder with age.

Reproductive parts Cones are up to 12cm long and 4cm in diameter, oval or conical and borne singly on short stalks, or in groups of 2–3, and sometimes deflexed. Cone scales are shiny reddish-brown, and hide winged seeds up to 2cm long.

Aleppo Pine, cone

Habitat and distribution A widespread and common tree around the Mediterranean, and planted elsewhere to stabilize dunes or provide a windbreak.

Similar species
Calabrian Pine *P. brutia* Closely related to Aleppo Pine, but leaves are broader (1–1.5mm), darker green and stiffer. Twigs are reddish-yellow or greenish. Cones spread out from the twig and are never deflexed. Occurs in similar places, but further east, in Calabria, Crete, Cyprus and Turkey, where it can form open forests on coastal hills.

Stone Pine

Stone PIne

Maritime Pine

Maritime Pine
Calabrian Pine

Aleppo Pine

Calabrian Pine

Canary Island Pine *Pinus canariensis* is very similar to *P. halepensis* (see previous page), but leaves are up to 30cm long and occur in threes on yellow shoots. Cones are very large.

(b) Three-needle Pines Needles grow in bunches of 3.

Monterey Pine
Pinus radiata 45m

A large pine of variable shape; slender and conical when growing vigorously, and becoming more domed and flat-topped on a long bole with age. Main branches sometimes hang low enough to touch the

Monterey Pine, cone

ground. Bright-green needles grow in bunches of 3. Each needle is thin and straight, up to 15cm long, with a finely toothed margin and a sharp-pointed tip. **Reproductive parts** Male flowers grow in dense clusters near the ends of twigs, releasing pollen in spring. Female cones grow in clusters of 3–5 around the tips of shoots, ripening to form large, solid woody cones, up to 15cm long and 9cm in diameter, with a characteristically asymmetrical shape. Cone scales are thick and woody with rounded outer edges, and conceal black, winged seeds.

Habitat and distribution A native of only a small area around Monterey, California, Guadalupe Island and Baja California, Mexico. Widely planted in western Europe as a shelter-belt tree and occasionally as a specimen tree, growing well next to the sea. A vigorous species when young.

Comments A species adapted to live in areas subject to bush fires. The cones open to release seeds only when heated by fire; the seeds germinate and grow rapidly in the ash, so that the young trees are well ahead of the competing scrub species after a severe bush fire. Cones can be encouraged to release seeds by heating them in an oven, and seedlings are easy to grow.

Similar species

Northern Pitch Pine *P. rigida* 20m (25m) A narrowly conical tree with stiff, tough needles in clusters of 3, and small cylindrical or rounded cones with thin-

Northern Pitch Pine, cone

ner, but stiff (hence *rigida*) scales. The most noticeable feature, unique to this species of pine, is sprouting foliage on the bole. Native to the eastern coasts of N America, occasionally planted for timber in Europe.

Canary Island Pine

Monterey Pine

Monterey Pine

Monterey Pine

Northern Pitch Pine

Ponderosa Pine or
Western Yellow Pine
Pinus ponderosa 40m (50m)
A large, slender, conical pine with a sturdy, straight bole and scaly pinkish-brown bark. Needles are up to 30cm long, narrow (3mm) and stiffly curved with finely toothed edges and a sharp, pointed tip. They are clustered densely on the shoots and persist for 3 years.

Reproductive parts Cones are ovoid, up to 15cm long and 5cm in diameter, growing on short stalks or directly on the twigs, and sometimes leaving a few scales

Ponderosa Pine, cone

behind when they fall off. Occasionally solitary but sometimes growing in small clusters. Cone scales are oblong with swollen, exposed, ridged tips hiding 5cm-long, oval, winged seeds.

Habitat and distribution A common tree in the western USA, planted over a wide range in Europe, but in small plantings, sometimes for timber, but mostly for ornament.

Similar species
Jeffrey Pine *P. jeffreyi* (40m) The upland counterpart of the Ponderosa Pine, found mostly above 2,000m in the mountains of the western USA. It has bluer foliage and larger cones, up to 30cm long, with scales

bearing slender, curved spines, and the bark is blacker. Grows well in Britain and Europe, where it is found mainly as an ornamental tree.

Digger Pine *P. sabiniana* 25m A more slender tree with sparser foliage and more glaucous needles.

(c) Five-needle Pines Needles grow in bunches of 5.

Arolla Pine or **Swiss Stone Pine**
Pinus cembra 29m
A large, densely crowned tree, forming a columnar or slender cone shape with a strong bole when mature. Needles, borne in bundles of 5, are up to 8cm long and held almost upright on the shoots, and look densely crowded. The leaf margins are faintly toothed and there are 2 central resin canals just detectable on the inner surface of the leaf. The bark is usually covered with resinous blisters, reddish-grey and peeling to leave thin scaly patches.

Reproductive parts Cones are rather squat-looking, up to 8cm long and 5cm in diameter, growing on very short stalks. At first they are a deep violet-blue, but they ripen to a rich brown. Cone scales are rounded and slightly downy, hiding wing-less seeds. They usually fall from the tree intact, releasing the seeds only when the scales have started to decay, but many are eaten by rodents before this happens.

Habitat and distribution A native of the Alps and Carpathians, from 1,700m and above, and often planted in dense stands to minimize the risk from avalanches. Planted elsewhere in N Europe as a timber tree, and often as an ornamental tree in town parks and gardens where it is quite hardy.

Ponderosa Pine

Jeffrey Pine

Arolla Pine
Arolla Pine

Arolla Pine

Bhutan Pine

Pinus wallichiana 35m (50m)

A narrowly columnar pine at first, with spreading lower branches and ascending upper branches, but becoming more shapeless with increasing age and size. Needles grow in bundles of 5, growing erect on the younger shoots but becoming more spreading or pendulous on older shoots. Some needles may be up to 20cm long, but only 7mm wide, supple and with a finely toothed margin. Bark is normally greyish-brown, thin and fairly smooth, with resinous patches, but becoming slightly fissured in older trees.

Bhutan Pine, cone

Reproductive parts Cones are long and cylindrical to tapering, up to 25cm long and 3cm in diameter, growing below the shoot, light-brown in colour and resiniferous. Cone scales are up to 3.5cm long, wedge-shaped and grooved, becoming thickened at the tip. Basal scales are sometimes turned back. Winged seeds are up to 2cm long and are shed freely, often leaving empty cones still on the tree.

Habitat and distribution A native of the Himalayas, between 2,000m and 4,200m, but occasionally planted for timber in parts of Europe, and sometimes as an ornamental.

Similar species

White Pine or **Weymouth Pine** *P. strobus* 32m (50m) A large tree when mature, with a tapering trunk and similar slender, slightly curved cones. Old trees have a rounded crown with blue-green foliage held in horizontal masses. A distinctive feature is the tuft of hairs below each 10cm-long bunch of 5 needles. A native of the Great Lakes area of the USA and Canada, and of mountains further south. Widely planted in Europe, mainly for timber. Subject to a rust disease which wiped out many fine specimen trees in some gardens. Timber quality is excellent, making it a popular wood for intricate work like carvings and musical instruments. *P. strobus contorta* is a variant with twisted needles and a smaller habit.

Japanese White Pine *P. parviflora* The needles are slightly twisted and up to 6cm long, blue-green outside and blue-white inside. The cones are up to 7cm long, ovoid, with tough scales. Native of the mountains in Japan.

White Pine

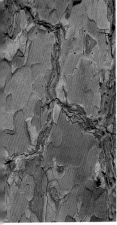

White Pine

Bhutan Pine

White Pine 'Contorta'

Macedonian Pine
Pinus peuce 30m

A narrowly conical pine on a slender, tapering trunk with a dense, pointed crown. The slender, supple needles are up to 12cm long and about 7mm wide, with finely toothed margins and a pointed tip, in bunches of 5, lasting for 3 years before falling. Shoots are green with a slight bloom. Young trees have a smooth greyish-green bark, but it becomes browner and fissured in older trees.

Reproductive parts Cones are up to 20cm long and 4cm in diameter, mostly cylindrical and sometimes slightly curved near the tip. They grow on the underside of the shoots and are green at first, ripening to brown, and slightly resinous. Wedge-shaped scales have greyish tips curving inwards, and are slightly concave. Seeds are 8mm long with a 2.5cm papery wing.

Habitat and distribution A rare native of the mountains of the Balkans, growing at altitudes from 600m to 2000m. Planted elsewhere at high altitudes where its hardiness makes it a successful timber tree. Sometimes seen as an ornamental.

Similar species

Mexican White Pine *P. ayacahuite* 25m (35m) A broadly conical tree when mature with elegant, slender, 15cm-long needles hanging from finely downy shoots. The heavy, tough cones are up to 40cm long and cylindrical, usually straight, with spreading basal scales. A native of Mexico and Guatemala, planted elsewhere mainly as an ornamental tree.

Holford Pine *P. × holfordiana* 29m A variable hybrid between the Mexican White Pine and the Bhutan Pine, raised by Sir George Holford of Westonbirt. It shares features of both parents such as orange-brown bark and downy shoots. Needles are up to 18cm long, bright green on the outer surface, blue-green on the inner surface. Cones may be larger than those of either parent, becoming dark, resinous and blunt-tipped. Planted in gardens as an ornamental tree.

Bristle-cone Pine or
Rocky Mountain Pine
Pinus aristata 10m

A small and slow-growing tree, rarely attaining a great height, especially when not in its native Rocky Mountains. Short needles are usually 2–4cm long, dark green and sometimes flecked with white resin specks, and remarkably long-lived, persisting for up to 14 years on the twigs. Twigs are mostly unbranched and densely clothed with needles, and release a turpentine scent when crushed.

Reproductive parts Cones may be 6cm long with a noticeable 6mm-long spine on each scale (hence the English name).

Habitat and distribution A rare tree outside of its native range, normally found in specialist collections and mature gardens, but sometimes grown on a small scale for its timber.

Comments *P. aristata* var. *longaeva* is possibly the longest-lived tree in the world, with specimens from California and Nevada known to be at least 5,000 years old. It is an unspotted form of the Bristle-cone Pine.

Bristle-cone Pine

Macedonian Pine, cone

Macedonian Pine

Japanese White Pine

WILLOWS AND POPLARS, Salicaceae

A very widespread group of trees and shrubs, numbering well over 300 species, with many more hybrids that are often difficult to place. Male and female flowers are found on separate trees and usually take the form of catkins. Leaves are alternate, and usually long and pointed. Most species, apart from Goat Willow and Grey Willow, propagate easily from cuttings. Many grow in wet habitats such as streamsides, and small shrubby species are often found in upland regions. Wind-dispersed seeds make them rapid colonizers of new habitats. Most members of this family are vigorous, fast-growing trees and tolerant of much bad treatment from both man and natural disasters like storms. Many are of great importance for wildlife, supporting large numbers of insect larvae. A number are grown for ornament, having a weeping habit, bright foliage or colourful winter twigs.

WILLOWS *Salix* About 300 species exist, plus many more hybrids. Many are shrubby, but a few form large trees.

Bay Willow
Salix pentandra 18m
A broadly domed, open-crowned tree when growing in its typical open stream-side habitat, but more slender and upright when growing in woodlands. Both leaves and shoots are glossy green, the shoots being olive-green and the leaves showing a bluish tint beneath.

Reproductive parts In contrast to other willows, the bright-yellow upright male catkins appear at the the same time as the new growth of leaves, rather than just before them. Female catkins are dull yellowish-green, longer and more pendulous.

Habitat and distribution A fairly common native of moorlands, stream-sides and boggy areas, and also in damp, upland woods, through much of northern Europe. Only very occasionally planted as an ornamental tree for its fine foliage.

Crack Willow
Salix fragilis 25m
A large tree when mature, with a broadly domed crown and a thick bole with large branches arising from low down near the base. The dull grey-brown bark is covered with thick interlocking criss-crossed ridges. The shoots are dull reddish-brown, becoming brighter in early spring as the leaves emerge. The leaves are long and glossy, with toothed margins, and are widely spaced on the shoots. The lower surface is less glossy and slightly paler than the upper surface, and the leaves have short green petioles.

Reproductive parts Male flowers are yellow, pendulous catkins, opening at about the same time as the leaves in early spring. Female catkins are green and pendulous, growing on a separate tree.

Habitat and distribution A very widespread European native, found in damp lowland woodlands and along river and canal banks. Hybridizes freely and is not always true to the type species.

Comments The twigs snap easily and cleanly (hence *fragilis*) and root very readily if stuck in the ground. Even pieces which snap off accidentally and are carried along in a river will root themselves if they lodge in a riverbank. Often, lines of trees of the same sex will be found along riverbanks, all derived from pieces of the same individual tree.

Bay Willow

Crack Willow

Crack Willow

Crack Willow

White Willow
Salix alba 25m

A large, broadly columnar tree with a dense crown when growing in an open site, but more slender when crowded by other trees. Distinguished from the similar Crack Willow by its smaller greyish-blue leaves.

Reproductive parts Male catkins are small, elongated-ovoid and pendulous. Female catkins are longer, slender and green.

Habitat and distribution A widespread European native tree, often growing in damp, lowland habitats.

Comments Easily raised from cuttings and grows well in damp soil, especially near ponds and rivers. Becomes more scarce in northern regions.

Similar species
Violet Willow *S. daphnoides* 12m Best recognized by its attractive violet-blue bloomed twigs and shiny leaves. The catkins are also distinctive with their attractive black flecks.

Violet Willow

S. acutifolia Sometimes also known as 'Violet Willow'; this has more drooping twigs with a waxy feel, turning violet in winter, and longer, narrower leaves which are shiny green on both sides. A native of Russia, but sometimes planted by streamsides and in large gardens.

Corkscrew Willow
Salix matsudana 'Tortuosa' 18m

A distinctive willow, easily recognized by its contorted stems and pointed, twisted leaves. The leaves open early in spring and are a pleasing bright green, becoming darker green in summer and lasting on the tree well into the autumn. Older shoots are less twisted, but the bark still shows the signs of earlier curves and even the boles of older trees show some torsion.

Reproductive parts Male flowers are small, without petals, and are borne in yellow catkins up to 2cm long. Female flowers are borne in smaller, greenish catkins on separate plants, opening in spring at about the same time as the leaves.

Habitat and distribution A fast-growing tree, becoming more common in large gardens and growing rapidly, even in dry soils, although it is often planted near water. The species originated in N China but is now found only in cultivation, occurring in parks and gardens over much of Europe.

Comments This is a form of the Peking Willow, which is usually a more upright tree.

Chinese Weeping Willow
Salix babylonica 20m

An attractive tree with graceful 'weeping' branches and foliage reaching down to the ground. The leaves are up to 16cm long and 1.5cm wide, and finely toothed with a pointed tip, growing on a petiole about 5mm long. Mature leaves are dark green and slightly glossy on the upper surface. Twigs are brownish and slender at first, becoming more gnarled and thicker with age.

Reproductive parts Catkins are up to 2cm long and 0.4cm wide, and produced in May.

Habitat and distribution A native of China but widely cultivated in Europe and often naturalized in wet habitats, although not as popular a tree as the more golden-looking Weeping Willow *S. × chrysocoma*. Not tolerant of hard winters so less common in the north and in upland regions.

Similar species
Weeping Willow *S. × chrysocoma* 20m A familiar and popular tree, probably a hybrid between the Chinese Weeping Willow and the White Willow. Its pendulous branches and elegant foliage make it a well-loved tree in its usual waterside settings.

White Willow

Corkscrew Willow

Weeping Willow

White Willow 'Argentia'

Corkscrew Willow

Boreal Willow
Salix borealis

A small shrubby tree with a dense mass of multi-forked branches arising thickly from a short bole. The leathery leaves are linear and toothed, up to 7cm long, with prominent venation and whitish hairs on the underside.

Reproductive parts The catkins emerge at the same time as the leaves on short pedicels. Male catkins are yellow and slightly curved, up to 2.5cm long. Female catkins are greenish, approximately 3cm long at first and lengthening to about 7cm when mature.

Habitat and distribution A widespread tree in N Scandinavia and Russia in wet habitats.

Similar species

Dark-leaved Willow *S. nigricans* Very similar, but has more glaucous leaves (which turn black when dried) and smoother twigs and branches. Common on riverbanks and lake margins in N and central Europe.

S. pedicellata A shrub or small tree, sometimes reaching 10m, with ridges on the wood evident only after the bark has been peeled. Young shoots are downy, becoming smoother with age. The ovoid to oblong leaves have a slightly wavy margin, a smooth upper surface and a slightly downy lower surface. At the base of the petiole are small irregular stipules.

Reproductive parts Male and female flowers are borne on separate trees in short, compact catkins up to 4cm long.

Habitat and distribution A variable species found in wet habitats in the Mediterranean area.

Common Osier
Salix viminalis 6m (10m)

A spreading shrub or small tree, rarely allowed to grow to its full potential, being regularly cropped to provide a crown of long flexible twigs ('withies') for weaving baskets. The natural crown is narrow with slightly pendulous branches. The long, straight twigs are flexible and covered with greyish hairs when young, but becoming smoother and a shiny olive-brown with age. The narrow leaves taper to a point, and are up to 15cm long; the margin is usually waved and rolled under, the underside being covered with grey hairs.

Common Osier

Reproductive parts Male and female catkins appear before the leaves on separate trees, are erect or slightly curved and are crowded near the ends of the twigs. Males are yellow and females are browner, both growing to about 3cm long.

Habitat and distribution A common native tree of lowland Europe, particularly in wet habitats such as fens and riversides. Often planted for withies. Sometimes occurs on remote islands, where it was once planted by fishermen to provide the materials for weaving lobster pots.

Dark-leaved Willow

Grey Willow

Grey Willow
Grey Willow, flowers and down

Grey Willow
Salix cinerea 6m

A large shrub or sometimes a small tree with characteristic thick, downy, grey twigs. If the bark is peeled off 2-year-old twigs the wood shows a series of fine longitudinal ridges. The leaves are oblong and pointed, and usually about 4 times as long as broad, on 2 short petioles with irregular stipules at the base. Leaves often have an inrolled margin.

Reproductive parts Catkins are produced in early spring on separate trees, before the leaves: male catkins are ovoid and yellow, female catkins are similar but greener, eventually releasing many finely plumed seeds. This species and the Goat Willow *S. caprea*, are often called 'Pussy Willow' when their silky-grey buds, resembling cats' paws, followed by bright-yellow catkins, appear in the spring.

Habitat and distribution A very common tree over much of Europe, apart from the drier and hotter south, usually growing in wet habitats such as fenlands, streamsides and damp woodlands.

Almond Willow
Salix triandra 10m

A small tree, although more often an untidy shrub, with smooth bark which flakes off in small patches. The shoots are greenish or reddish-brown, tend to snap easily, and terminate in brown, ovoid, smooth buds. Leaves are ovate, up to 10cm long, with a serrated margin and pointed tip, usually smooth and a dark glossy green. The petiole is up to 1.5cm long and smooth.

Reproductive parts The catkins usually appear at the same time as the leaves on short leafy shoots and are erect and cylindrical. Male catkins are up to 5cm long and greenish-yellow, remaining on the tree for some time. Female catkins are shorter and more compact.

Habitat and distribution A widespread native of much of Europe, including the cooler, wetter areas of the Mediterranean region, but absent from the far north. Usually occurs on wetter soils.

Goat Willow or Sallow
Salix caprea 12m (18m)

Depending on its situation this may be a multi-branched, dense, shrubby tree, or a taller tree with a straight, ridged stem and sparsely domed crown. The thick, stiff twigs are hairy at first, but become smoother and yellowish-brown with age. If the twigs have the bark peeled off they are smooth. (Compare with Grey Willow.) Leaves are large, up to 12cm long and oval, with a short twisted point at the tip. The upper surface is dull green and slightly hairy, the lower surface is noticeably grey and woolly; in windy weather this can suddenly change the appearance of the tree from green to grey as all the leaves are blown around. The leaf margins have small, irregular teeth, and the short petiole sometimes has 2 ear-like sinuous stipules at its base.

Reproductive parts Male and female catkins, on separate trees, appear before the leaves, often very early in the spring in sheltered places. Measuring up to 2.5cm long, they are ovoid and covered with greyish silky hairs before opening, when they become bright yellow. Female catkins are greener and produce numerous silky-haired seeds.

Habitat and distribution A widespread and common native of Britain and Europe, in woods, hedgerows and scrub, and often in drier places than other similar species.

Comments An important food plant for numerous species of Lepidoptera, most notably the Purple Emperor butterfly.

Similar species

Common Sallow *S. atrocinerea* 10m Leaves are narrower than those of Goat Willow, and lack the twisted point at the tip. The upper surface is often reddish-green or slightly buff-coloured.

Almond Willow

Goat Willow

Goat Willow

Goat Willow, male catkins

Goat Willow

Grey Willow

Common Osier

Common Osier

Hoary Willow
Salix elaeagnos 6m (16m)
A slender tree best recognized by its very narrow, hairy leaves; unlike many other willows the leaves have a matt white undersurface which is neither shiny nor silky. The leaves may be up to 15cm long, but are usually less than 1cm wide and have smooth, untoothed margins. Mature leaves are a dark shiny green above with dense white hairs below. Young twigs are also covered with dense grey or white hairs, but these are soon lost and older twigs are brownish or yellow-brown and smooth.
Reproductive parts Male and female catkins appear, on separate trees, just before the leaves. They are slightly red-tinged and mostly crowded towards the tips of the twigs. Male catkins may be up to 3cm long, appearing dense and spreading; female catkins are smaller and more erect on the twigs.
Habitat and distribution A native of central and S Europe, but sometimes planted elsewhere for ornament.

POPLARS *Populus* About 30 species exist, most of which grow rapidly to form large trees. Numerous hybrids occur.

Western Balsam Poplar
Populus trichocarpa 35m (60m)
A large and fast-growing tree, often increasing in height by 2m a year. Mature trees are columnar with a tapering crown. The tall, tapering trunk has dark-grey bark with shallow grooves and fissures. The stout shoots bear pointed, tapering leaves with a glossy-green upper surface and a white underside. The leaves turn yellow in autumn.
Reproductive parts Catkins, produced in April, are slender and pendulous: male catkins are reddish-brown and female catkins greenish. The seeds are hairy (hence *trichocarpa*) and produced abundantly.
Habitat and distribution A native of the Pacific coasts of the USA and Canada, mostly occurring in damp habitats.
Comments This tree is often planted in sites which do not allow for its rapid growth and large size when mature. It is probably the largest broadleaved tree to be found in its native Canada. It roots easily from cuttings, and small trees regenerate well when pruned back to the base. A useful species for shelter-belts if there is enough room for it.

White Poplar
Populus alba 20m (40m)
An easily identified tree in windy weather in summer, when the pure white undersides of the leaves are turned up and the whole tree looks white. The simple, deeply lobed leaves are covered with a dense white felt underneath, but are grey-ish-green above. The shoots are also covered in white felt, but this usually wears off by the end of the growing season. The leaves are shed early in the autumn, and sometimes turn a pleasing bright yellow for a few days before falling. The bark on the trunk is also white and in mature specimens is broken by diamond-shaped scars.
Reproductive parts Male catkins are long and oval, white and fluffy, and female catkins are more slender and greenish-yellow.
Habitat and distribution A native of S Europe, but one of the first trees to be introduced into Britain, perhaps because of its rapid rate of growth and ability to flourish even in the poorest of soils and on the most exposed sites. Common near the coast, where it grows in thickets as a result of suckering, but less frequent inland.

Western Balsam Poplar

Western Balsam Poplar

Western Balsam Poplar

White Poplar

White Poplar

White Poplar

Grey Poplar
Populus canescens 37m

When fully mature, this grows into an impressively large tree with a good solid bole and whitish bark with diamond-shaped fissures. The leaves are borne on long petioles and are rounded to oval and toothed with regular blunt, forward-pointing teeth. The upper surface of the

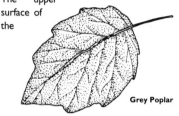

Grey Poplar

leaves is glossy grey-green and the lower surface is covered with a greyish-white felt. In spring the tree has a whitish appearance when the wind displaces the leaves, but it is

Grey Poplar

not as brilliantly white as the White Poplar. By mid- to late summer the leaves lose some of the white felt and the tree looks greyer. This tree suckers freely and so sometimes appears to be growing in thickets of the same species.

Reproductive parts Male and female catkins are borne on separate trees. Female trees with green, pendulous catkins are rare. Male catkins are elongated and pendulous, giving the whole tree a purplish colour when they start to swell before opening in spring.

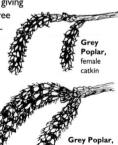

Grey Poplar, female catkin

Grey Poplar, male catkin

Habitat and distribution A native of Europe and introduced into Britain very early, probably at the same time as the White Poplar. The best specimens in Britain are found in chalky areas of the south and in the limestone valleys of Ireland, but this tree is tolerant of a wide range of climates and soil types and so is found in N Scotland as well as in many coastal places.

Aspen
Populus tremulus 18m

A slender to slightly conical tree with a rounded crown supported on a tall, tapering trunk. It is best known for its delicately fluttering leaves, which quiver and rustle in the slightest breeze. Leaves are alternate, rounded to slightly oval, and have shallow teeth all round the margin. They are green on both surfaces, but paler below, and are borne on long, flattened petioles. The bark of young trees is smooth and greyish-green at first, but with age becomes browner and ridged, with some deeper crevices. In autumn the leaves may turn golden-yellow, especially in the north, but further south they normally fall quickly without a colour change. Leaves newly produced in late summer are often a deep-red colour.

Reproductive parts Catkins may be up to 8cm long and are borne in clusters at the ends of twigs, males and females occurring on different trees. Male catkins are reddish-purple, and females are green with a pinkish tinge. Seeds are produced prolifically often germinating after 24 hours.

Habitat and distribution Aspen suckers readily and is often found growing in small groves all of the same sex. Rooted suckers do not transplant well however. A native tree in Britain and Europe, common in many places, especially on poor damp soils, but in the warmer south of Europe it is confined to the mountains.

Comments This is one of the few trees that can easily be recognized by just sound. The characteristic dry rustling of the leaves, especially on almost still days when no other leaves are moving, is quite distinctive

Grey Poplar

Grey Poplar

Grey Poplar

Aspen

Aspen

Aspen, catkins

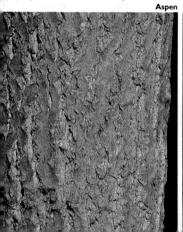

Black Poplar
Populus nigra var. *betulifolia* 32m

A large, spreading tree when fully mature, with a domed crown and a thick, blackish, gnarled bole covered with distinctive burrs and tuberous growths. Large specimens are not often seen in natural habitats however, as it often grows among other trees in woods and copses, when it becomes taller and more straggling. The leaves are triangular and long-stalked with a finely toothed margin and are a fresh shiny green on both surfaces. Shoots and buds are smooth and golden-brown when young.

Black Poplar

Reproductive parts Male catkins are pendulous and reddish, female catkins are greenish. Both appear in April in Britain.
Habitat and distribution A native of Britain and Europe, preferring heavier soils and damp conditions, but, because of its resistance to industrial air pollution, it has been a popular tree for planting in cities, where it can sometimes be found growing in parks and even along road-sides. It grows, but does not thrive in these conditions. It is known in the north of England as 'Manchester Poplar'.

Lombardy Poplar
Populus nigra 'Italica' 36m

One of the most distinctive of all broadleaved trees, recognized by its narrowly columnar habit. The stout, gnarled bole supports numerous short ascending branches which taper towards the nar-row pointed crown. In other respects this tree is similar to the Black Poplar with slightly more triangular leaves.
Reproductive parts All of the typical slender Lombardy poplars are males, bearing reddish catkins. Female trees known as var. 'Gigantea', are far less common, and have thicker branches which spread out more and give the tree a broader crown.
Habitat and distribution A native of Italy, from where it was introduced into Britain in the mid-eighteenth century. It was popular at once and cuttings were sent all over the country. It grows well in a wide range of soils and climates. Lombardy poplars are widely planted, often in long lines which look less than satisfactory when one or two trees die and leave gaps. In some collections they are planted in close-packed groups which look more pleasing.
Similar species
Berlin Poplar *P.* × *berolinensis* 27m A hybrid between the Lombardy Poplar and an Asiatic species of balsam poplar which arose in Berlin. It has a narrow crown rather like the Lombardy, but is more

Berlin Poplar

spreading and trees may be female. The leaves are oval and pointed with a finely toothed margin and are a shiny yellowish-green above with a whitish underside. Young shoots are downy at first and slightly winged. This species is tolerant of harsher conditions than the Lombardy Poplar, so is often planted in more extreme climates than that of Britain

Black Poplar

Lombardy Poplar

Black Poplar, young trees

Lombardy Poplar

Black Poplar

Hybrid Black Poplar
Populus × canadensis 30m

Very similar to Black Poplar, one of the parent species, and in many areas far more common. The other parent is the N American tree, Cottonwood. An upright or sometimes more spreading tree depending on situation, with a narrow, or occasionally columnar crown. The trunk lacks the burrs seen in Black Poplar, but has deep grooves and fissures in the greyish bark. Young twigs may be greenish or slightly reddened. Leaves are alternate, oval to triangular and sharply toothed with fringes of small hairs.

Many forms of the Hybrid Black Poplar occur, and they are best separated by the appearance of the leaves and the overall form of the tree. Black Italian Poplar is one of the commonest forms and is sometimes planted in parks and beside lakes. Its heavy branches often break off alarmingly in storms as the tree passes maturity.

Reproductive parts The catkins are similar to those of Black Poplar.

Habitat and distribution A commonly planted tree, sometimes for ornament, but usually for its strong timber which is mainly used for making packing crates and boxes. Does not thrive in very wet or cold areas.

Similar species
Balm of Gilead *P. candicans (gileadensis)* The most distinctive feature is the abundance of sticky buds, borne on downy shoots, which give off a strong scent of balsam. The leaves are also aromatic when newly opened, heart-shaped and downy on the underside and borne on a downy petiole. The mature tree is open-crowned and suckers freely; large thickets are sometimes produced and the tree can become troublesome if introduced into the wrong place. Not to be confused with the closely related Balsam Poplar.

Balsam Poplar
Populus balsamifera 30m

A conical to slightly spreading tree with numerous ascending branches arising from a tapering bole. The bark is thinner than other poplars and narrowly grooved. Th base of the bole is often surrounded many suckers. Young shoots and th 2.5cm-long, pointed buds are covered wi a shiny resin, making them look as if the have just been varnished. Leaves are up 10cm (the larger ones on the most vigo ous suckers), oval and pointed at the t with finely toothed margins. The upper le surface is a dark shiny green and the lowe surface is paler and more downy.

Reproductive parts Greenish catkin are produced in late spring or early sum mer. Male catkins are up to 7.5cm lor and female catkins are up to 12.5cm lon and they occur on separate trees.

Habitat and distribution A native N America, and common along rive banks, on lake shores and in wet woo lands. Cultivated in Europe mainly fo timber, although the fragrant resin sometimes extracted. Cultivated tree appear to be all males.

Cottonwood or
American Black Poplar
Populus deltoides 30m

A large tree with distinctive large, tria gular to oval leaves which may b 10–18cm long; the margins are ciliate and the heart-shaped leaf bases hav glands on them. The twigs are frequentl sharply angled. Mature trees have broad, flattish crown and large, spreadin or slightly ascending branches. The bark greyish-brown and ridged.

Reproductive parts Pendulous catkir are produced in spring. Male catkins ar yellowish, tipped with red on the sta mens. The female catkins elongate in fru and may be up to 20cm long.

Habitat and distribution A native c eastern N America where it grows lowland woods and wetter grassy area Introduced into Europe where it ha become naturalized in some places an is sometimes planted along roadsides o in plantations.

Hybrid Black Poplar

Hybrid Black Poplar

Hybrid Black Poplar
Balm of Gilead

Hybrid Black Poplar 'Eugeni'
Balm of Gilead

BOG MYRTLE FAMILY, Myricaceae

Evergreen shrubs or small trees, sometimes with aromatic leaves.

Myrtle
Myrica faya 8m

A small evergreen tree or large shrub with distinctive reddish, hairy twigs. The alternate leaves may be 4–11cm long, narrowly oval, with a down-rolled margin and a smooth shiny-green upper surface.
Reproductive parts Flowers are produced in the form of branched catkins on young shoots. Female flowers have 2 or more bracteoles, but male flowers, produced on the same tree, have none. Fleshy, reddish fruits are produced in late summer.
Habitat and distribution A native of some of the Atlantic islands where it occurs in the drier zones of broadleaved evergreen forests. Possibly native in central and S Portugal.
Similar species
Bog Myrtle *M. gale* Usually little more than a shrub, with leathery aromatic leaves. Confined to lowland acid bogs.

WALNUT FAMILY Juglandaceae

A family of 7 genera and about 60 species spread across the Americas, SE Europe, SE Asia and Japan. Leaves are usually alternate and pinnate, flowers are without petals, small and grouped in catkins, with males and females on the same plant. The fruit is usually a nut, sometimes large and edible, or sometimes small and winged

HICKORIES *Carya* Nineteen species occur in N America, with a further single species in SW China. The male catkins are in parts, and the internal pith is solid.

Shagbark Hickory
Carya alba (*ovata*) 20m (40m)

A large, upright to slightly spreading tree with a broad, flattened crown. Best known for its grey bark which soon split into long flaking scales. Winter tree reveal the rather sparse branches which support reddish twigs tipped with scaly buds. Compound leaves consist of 5 (sometimes 3 or 7) leaflets up to 20cm long, longer near the tip of the leaf. Each leaflet is oval to oblong, toothed, with tufts of short white hairs between the teeth. The terminal leaflet is short stalked. Leaves feel tough and leathery, or sometimes oily.
Reproductive parts Male catkins are green, up to 15cm long, and produced in spreading clusters. Female flowers are small and yellowish-green, produced in small terminal clusters. Fruits are rounded, up to 6cm long and on short stalks, and contain small white seeds
Habitat and distribution A native of eastern N America, but planted for timber in Europe. A useful timber tree, providing high-quality durable wood used for building and smaller items such as axe handles.

Shagbark Hickory, autumn

Bog Myrtle

Shagbark Hickory

Shagbark Hickory

Bitternut
Carya cordiformis 30m

A large tree with a high conical crown. The bark is greyish and smooth at first but becomes more wrinkled and scaly with maturity, and flakes away revealing orange patches beneath. The branches are mostly straight and ascending and terminate in greenish twigs tipped with elongated yellowish buds covered with large scales. Compound leaves are composed of 9 leaflets (rarely there may be 5–8), and the terminal leaflet is stalkless. Individual leaflets are elongated, pointed at the tip with markedly toothed margins.

Reproductive parts Male catkins are up to 7cm long, yellowish-green and pendulous. Fruits are up to 3.5cm long and rounded to pear-shaped with 4 wings, concealing grey, smooth seeds.

Habitat and distribution A native of eastern N America from Texas and Florida to as far north as SE Canada. Introduced into Britain and Europe as an ornamental tree, for which it makes a fine specimen with good coloration in autumn. Also planted occasionally for timber.

Similar species
Pignut *C. glabra* 20m Makes a fine specimen tree, but is rarely planted. It has the smoothest bark of all the hickories, which may be purplish in old trees, and leaves resembling the Common Ash, but with much finer autumn colour.

WINGNUTS *Pterocarya* Attractive, strong trees, often surrounded by suckers. Winter buds are protected by 2 closely adpressed hairy leaves. The pith in the centre of the twigs is divided into chambers which can be clearly seen if a twig is cut diagonally. Winged seeds are borne in long pendulous catkins.

Caucasian Wingnut
Pterocarya fraxinifolia 35m

A large, spreading, deciduous tree with a domed crown and a short but stout bole from which large numbers of branches arise close to the same point. The tree suckers freely and some long-established specimens have clusters of smaller trees crowded around the main trunk, especially where the ground beneath the tree is not subject to grazing or mowing. The bark is grey and deeply fissured and gnarled. The compound leaves are composed of 11–20 pairs of leaflets, each up to 18cm long, ovate to lanceolate with a pointed tip and sharply toothed margins. The midribs bear long brownish or white stellate hairs on the underside. There is usually a fine display of bright-yellow leaves in autumn.

Reproductive parts Male catkins are solitary, female catkins are pendent with many flowers and give rise to the characteristic seeds which are broad-winged nutlets.

Habitat and distribution A native of SW Asia but often planted in gardens in Europe as an ornamental tree; some very fine specimens can be found in long-established botanical gardens and arboreta.

Similar species
Chinese Wingnut *P. stenoptera* 25m Usually a smaller and more slender tree than the Caucasian Wingnut, best recognized when in leaf by the toothed wings on the central blade of the compound leaf which has fewer leaflets. The winged fruits are pink and contrast attractively with the leaves. Does not sucker as freely as the previous species.

Hybrid Wingnut *P.* × *rehderana* 27m A hybrid between the Caucasian and Chinese Wingnuts which arose in a botanical garden in Boston, Massachusetts, and is intermediate in characteristics between the two parents, although it is apparently far more vigorous in its growth. It produces suckers copiously, and roots well from cuttings. The central blade of the compound leaf is slightly winged.

Caucasian Wingnut

Caucasian Wingnut

Bitternut

Caucasian Wingnut

WALNUTS *Juglans* Fifteen species exist, from N and S America and Asia. They produce large edible nuts and also excellent-quality timber. The central pith in the twigs is chambered, and this can be checked by slicing through a twig. They can be propagated from seed and, in the case of good fruiting varieties, by grafting on to a healthy stock.

Common Walnut
Juglans regia 30m

A fine, spreading, deciduous tree with a domed crown on a straight bole when grown in ideal conditions, but sometimes more twisted when found in woodlands or orchards. The bark is smooth and brownish at first but becomes grey and fissured with maturity. The lowest branches are spreading to ascending and often very large near the base, but divide rapidly into numerous twisted twigs with dark purple-brown buds. The compound leaves are composed of 7–9 elliptical leaflets, up to 15cm long, thick and leathery to touch, with pointed tips and untoothed margins. Crushed leaves are slightly aromatic. The leaves are late to open in the spring and look reddish at first, becoming green later in the summer.
Reproductive parts Male catkins are yellow and up to 15cm long, female flowers are small and greenish with a yellow, protruding, branched stigma. The fruits are about 5cm long and rounded with a smooth green skin dotted with slightly raised glands. This encases the familiar edible walnut seed.
Habitat and distribution A native of SE Europe and Asia, but spread by cultivation from an early age and may have reached Britain with the Romans. It is naturalized in some areas but is common in established gardens and collections.
Similar species
Japanese Walnut *J. ailantifolia*. Similar to *J. regia*, but leaves are much larger with 11–15 pointed, toothed leaflets, hairy on

both surfaces and borne on hairy shoots. Fruits borne in clusters of up to 20.
Black Walnut *J. nigra* 32m (50m) An even more attractive tree than Common Walnut with a tall, straight bole and a high, domed crown of brighter green leaves. Individual leaflets are smaller (6–12cm) but there are more of them (15–23) in the compound leaf;

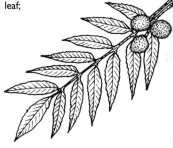

Black Walnut

they have a similar leathery texture. The blackish-brown bark is broken up into a diamond pattern of deep cracks. The fruits are similar to those of Common Walnut but not as edible, although the green husk yields a similarly persistent dark dye. A native of eastern N America.

Butternut
Juglans cinerea 26m

Differs from Black Walnut in having grey bark; where the 2 species occur together naturally in eastern N America the grey bark is quite noticeable. Leaflets are larger and more widely spaced than in Black Walnut; the central leaf stalk is densely hairy, and those leaflets near the leaf base are smallest.
Reproductive parts Edible fruits are borne in clusters of up to 12.
Habitat and distribution A native of woods and thickets in eastern N America. A fine ornamental tree and also sometimes planted for its good-quality timber.

Common Walnut

Japanese Walnut

Common Walnut
Common Walnut

Japanese Walnut

BIRCH FAMILY, Betulaceae

A large family of 6 genera and about 150 species of medium-sized trees and shrubs. Flowers are in the form of catkins, with the separate sexes growing on the same tree; the male catkins are the more conspicuous. Seeds are borne in smaller cone-like catkins, or in the form of nuts with hard shells or sometimes wings.

BIRCHES Betula About 40 species occur across the whole of the northern hemisphere, some surviving further north than any other tree species. Most grow into medium-sized trees with good hard timber used for making plywood, and sometimes for paper pulp. Few birches grow large enough to provide sizeable beams or planks for building. Flowers are in the form of catkins and the seeds are very small winged nutlets which are dispersed by the wind over great distances and in large numbers. They are rapid colonizers of disturbed ground, and some birches are very invasive. The seeds are of great importance as a winter food for small birds, and the leaves are food for innumerable insect larvae.

Silver Birch
Betula pendula 26m (30m)

A slender, fast-growing deciduous tree with a narrow, tapering crown when young and growing vigorously, but with a weeping habit in older trees, especially if growing in an open, uncrowded situation. Branches are ascending in young trees but twigs and shoots are pendulous, slender and smooth, mostly brown and pitted with many white resin glands. Old trees have a thick bark, deeply fissured at the base of the bole and breaking up into rectangular plates; higher up the bole the bark is a smooth silvery-white, often flaking away and revealing greyer patches below. A pattern of black diamond shapes is often seen on the trunk of older trees.

Silver Birch

Leaves are up to 7cm long, triangular and pointed with large teeth separated by many smaller teeth. They are thin and smooth when mature and borne on hairless petioles.

Reproductive parts Male catkins are produced in groups of 2–4 at the tips of young twigs and appear very early in the winter when they are brownish in colour; in spring, when the leaves are opening, they are yellow and pendulous. Female catkins are shorter, more erect and greenish, produced in the

Silver Birch, seed

axils of leaves. After pollination they become browner and thicker, eventually reaching a length of 3.5cm The seeds are winged and papery and usually produced copiously.

Habitat and distribution A native of a wide area of Europe, including Britain, but not the extreme south, or far north. Often planted as an ornamental tree in gardens and parks. A fast-growing tree and an early colonizer, although it does not thrive in shade or compete with even more vigorous species. Prone to attacks by fungi.

Silver Birch, winter

Silver Birch, autumn

Silver Birch

Silver Birch, female catkins

Silver Birch, catkins

Downy Birch
Betula pubescens 25m

The bark is mostly smooth and brown or greyish, but does not break up into rectangular plates at the base like that of the Silver Birch. The branches are more irregular and densely crowded, and mostly erect, never pendulous. The twigs lack the whitish resin glands, but do have a covering of downy white hairs. The leaves are more rounded at the base than those of the Silver Birch and are more evenly toothed; there are white hairs in the axils of the veins on the underside, and the petiole is hairy. The crown in winter looks untidy compared with Silver Birch. A very variable species but usually easy to recognize by the soft, downy feel of the tips of the twigs in spring, and by the reddish bark on young wood.

Reproductive parts The catkins are very similar to those of the Silver Birch but the winged seeds have smaller wings that are about the same size as the seed. Female flowers are produced in April–May.

Downy Birch, seed

Habitat and distribution A native of most of Europe, and common in some areas where soils are poor or peaty; common in mountainous areas in the south and widespread in the north.

Similar species

Paper-bark Birch or **Canoe-bark Birch** *B. papyrifera* 23m A native of northern N America from the east to the west coast. Best recognized by its leaves which are large, but have only 5 pairs of veins and are borne on hairy stalks arising from a warty twig. The bark is mostly white and smooth, flecked with grey or sometimes orange or brown. The freely peeling bark was once used by Native Americans to make canoes.

Erman's Birch *B. ermanii* 24m Easily recognized by its pinkish bark which hangs in tatters down the bole of mature trees; younger trees have a smoother white bark. The tree is more spreading and has a stouter bole than the Silver Birch, with which it frequently hybridizes. A native of E Asia, and introduced into Britain from Japan. The best specimens are seen in established gardens where the peeling bark is a fine winter feature.

Downy Birch

Downy Birch, catkins

Downy Birch, mature woodland

White Birch

White Birch, autumn

Erman's Birch

ALDERS *Alnus* A family of about 30 species, mostly found in wet habitats and especially characteristic of riverbanks. The roots have numerous bacteria-containing nodules to fix nitrogen, like members of the Pea family, so they can cope well on infertile soils. The clusters of bright-orange nodules are often exposed when the roots of riverside trees are seen at low water-levels. Alders are useful in the protection of riverbanks from erosion and provide valuable cover for riverside wildlife. Seeds are borne in small, woody, cone-like catkins. The durable wood can withstand alternate wetting and drying.

Common Alder
Alnus glutinosa 25m
A small, spreading and sometimes multi-stemmed tree with a broad domed or conical crown. The bark is brownish and fissured into square or oblong plates. Branches are ascending in young trees, but spreading later. The twigs are smooth, except when young when they have a sticky feel (hence *glutinosa*), and have raised orange lenticels. The buds are about 7mm long, and borne on 3mm-long stalks.

Common Alder

The stalked leaves are noticeably rounded, up to 10cm long, with a slightly notched apex and a wavy or bluntly toothed margin. The 5–8 pairs of veins have long hairs in the axils on the underside of the leaf. **Reproductive parts** In winter the purplish male catkins, in bunches of 2–3, are an attractive feature, even though they are only around 3cm long; by the end of winter they open up, revealing yellow anthers, and are more colourful. Female catkins are smaller (1.5cm) and cone-like, reddish-purple at first and then turning green, usually in bunches of 3–8. They form hard green 'cones' which grow through the summer and persist until the following spring. Their small winged seeds are an important source of winter food for finches like redpolls and siskins. **Habitat and distribution** A native of Britain and Europe, absent only from the very far north and south. Common by water, and found at altitudes up to 500m. **Comments** A useful timber for wet situations, so is used for pier pilings, lock gates and making clogs. Also useful for making charcoal and was an ingredient for gunpowder. The wood has an attractive bright-orange colour when freshly cut. Growing trees help stabilise river banks and prevent erosion with their tough roots.

Common Alder, young cones

Common Alder, catkins

Common Alder, mature bark

Common Alder, mature cones

Green Alder
Alnus viridis 5m

Rarely more than a large shrub or small tree, with pointed, sessile, shiny-red buds and mostly smooth, greenish twigs. The leaves are more pointed than those of Common Alder and sharply toothed, hairy on the midrib and in the joins of the veins on the underside. When first open they are sticky to the touch.

Green Alder

Reproductive parts Male catkins, appearing with the leaves, are up to 12cm, yellow and pendulous; female catkins are 1cm long, erect and greenish at first, becoming reddish later, and usually found in stalked clusters of 3–5. The cone-like ripe catkins are rounded, green and tough at first, becoming blackened later and persisting until the following spring.

Habitat and distribution A native of the mountains of central and E Europe, found mostly in alpine woods and along streamsides.

Grey Alder
Alnus incana 25m

A fast-growing alder more at home on dry soils than most other alders. The bark is smooth and grey and the shoots and new leaves are covered with a dense layer of soft greyish hairs (hence *incana*). The hairs persist on the underside of the leaf as it matures. The leaves are triangular and toothed, terminating in a point, and the margins do not roll inwards.

Reproductive parts The catkins and fruits are very similar to those of other alders, although the green fruits are more globose before ripening to the typical dark, woody alder cone.

Habitat and distribution A native of Europe, introduced into Britain but not often planted. A good species for waste land and reclamation schemes.

Similar species

Red Alder *A. rubra* 25m Resembles Grey Alder, but the toothed margin of the leaf is inrolled (check with a hand-lens). Leaves may be up to 20cm long. Catkins and cones are very similar to those of Common Alder. A native of the western USA and Canada from Alaska to California, where it occurs in hilly country. Not often planted in Europe, but where it does occur, such as in Scotland, it grows rapidly at first, then slows down.

Smooth Alder *A. rugosa* is a N American species which has red hairs in the axils of the leaf veins on the singly toothed leaves. Often planted in central Europe, and naturalized in many places.

Italian Alder
Alnus cordata 29m

An attractive tree with a bold, conical shape, fine glossy leaves and the best show of catkins and cones. The best feature for identification is the glossy heart-shaped leaves (hence *cordata*) which have short tufts of orange hairs along the midrib on the underside. The bark is pale grey and fairly smooth and the twigs are slightly downy.

Reproductive parts The male catkins are yellow and produced prolifically; the female catkins are borne in small clusters, ripening in early summer. The woody 'cones' are larger than those of any other Alder species.

Habitat and distribution A native of Corsica and S Italy, and planted widely elsewhere in parks and gardens, and often along roadsides.

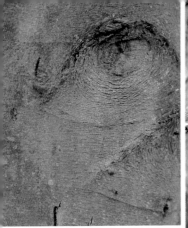

Grey Alder

Grey Alder

Green Alder, catkins and cones

Italian Alder, cones

HORNBEAM FAMILY, Carpinaceae

About 45 species occur in the northern hemisphere; they are related to Birches and Alders. The male catkins are protected inside winter buds. Leaves are sharply toothed and have conspicuous parallel veins. They produce winged seeds which are a favourite food of birds like the Hawfinch.

Hornbeam
Carpinus betulus 30m

A fine tree with a bold outline in winter. The bole is often gnarled and twisted and the bark is silvery-grey with deep fissures lower down and occasional dark bands. The densely packed branches are ascending and twisted, bearing greyish-brown, partly hairy twigs. The leaves are oval and pointed with a rounded base and short petiole, and have a double-toothed margin; the 15 pairs of veins are hairy on the underside. The leaves produce a colourful display of yellow, through orange to russet-brown in autumn, and trees which are planted in hedgerows keep their leaves long into the winter.

Reproductive parts Male catkins are up to 5cm long and yellowish-green with red outer scales. The fruits are produced in clusters of winged nutlets up to 14cm long, usually consisting of about 8 pairs of small hard-cased nuts with a 3-pointed papery wing.

Habitat and distribution A native of a large area of Britain and Europe, occurring in pure stands in some woodlands, in hedgerows and as a specimen tree in parks and gardens. Tolerant of heavy clay soils.

Comments Hornbeam was regularly coppiced in the past to provide a timber crop. The tough wood was prized in the past for its durable qualities: it was useful for wheel hubs, mill-wheels, piano hammers and chopping blocks. The tough seeds are a favourite food of the Hawfinch, which is one of the few birds able to crack them open, so this bird's range is closely linked to the distribution of the Hornbeam.

Similar species

Oriental Hornbeam *C. orientalis* 11m The leaves resemble those of Hornbeam but are smaller, always looking slightly folded, and the tree is normally much smaller and neater. The shoots are thinner and covered with long silky hairs. A native of SE Europe and Asia Minor, occasionally seen in Britain as a specimen tree in large gardens.

European Hop-Hornbeam *Ostrya carpinifolia* 19m A spreading tree with a domed crown and leaves resembling those of the Hornbeam. As a specimen tree grown in the open it has a fine bole

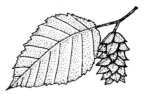

European Hop-Hornbeam

and almost level branches, but in a woodland it may have more than one bole and many ascending, crowded branches. The fruits are borne in clusters with a superficial resemblance to bunches of hops. It is a native of Europe from France eastwards to the Caucasus. In Britain it occurs mainly in well-established gardens.

Hornbeam, catkins

Hornbeam, Witches Broom, galls

Hornbeam, seeds

Hornbeam

HAZEL FAMILY, Corylaceae

About 15 species, of which only 4 reach tree status, all confined to the northern hemisphere. The prominent male catkins open early in the winter, and the female flowers are little more than tiny buds. The fruits are edible hard-shelled nuts.

Hazel
Corylus avellana 6m (12m)

Often no more than a spreading, multi-stemmed shrub, but sometimes grows into a taller tree with a shrubby crown and a short but thick and gnarled bole. The bark is smooth and often shiny, peeling horizontally into thin papery strips. Twigs are covered with stiff hairs and the oval buds are smooth. The leaves may be up to 10cm long, rounded, with a heart-shaped base and a pointed tip. The margins are double-toothed and the upper surface is hairy. On the underside of the leaf the veins have white hairs. The short petiole is also hairy and the whole leaf has a bristly, rough feel.

Reproductive parts Male catkins first appear in the autumn and are short and green, but when they open early in the spring they are up to 8cm long, pendulous and yellow. Female flowers are red and very small, and produce hard-shelled nuts in bunches of 1–4, the nuts being partly concealed in a leafy, deeply toothed involucre. The nut is up to 2cm long, brown and woody when ripe.

Habitat and distribution A widespread native tree across most of Europe, occurring in hedgerows and woodlands where it is an important component of the understorey. Frequently coppiced to provide poles for a variety of uses and of immense importance to woodland wildlife for its edible leaves and fruits.

Comments Some hazels, which have been coppiced and re-coppiced many times, are now extremely old trees, having greatly exceeded their normal life span through the constant regeneration caused by cutting them back and allowing them to re-grow.

Similar species

Turkish Hazel *C. colurna* 22m A larger tree with a stout bole and a conical crown. The best feature for identification

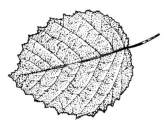

Turkish Hazel

is the involucre, which completely encloses the nut and is finely toothed and often recurved. Leaves are similar to those of Hazel, but are more likely to look lobed. A native of SE Europe and Asia Minor, and also found as an introduction further north and west.

Filbert *C. maxima* 6m Very similar to Hazel except for the nuts, which are mostly solitary or in bunches of 2–3 and entirely enclosed in an undivided involucre which is constricted over the nut and toothed at the tip. A native of the Balkans but widely planted elsewhere for the superior quality of its nuts, and sometimes naturalized.

Hazel

Hazel, coppice

Hazel, catkins

Hazel, nuts

Hazel, spring with catkins

Filbert, nuts

Hazel 'Contorta'

BEECH FAMILY, Fagaceae

A large family containing many well-known trees. Eight genera and more than 1,000 species occur, mostly in the northern hemisphere, but many occur far to the south. The flowers are small, sexes are usually separate and on the same tree. Fruits are in the form of nuts, protected by a cupule.

BEECHES *Fagus* Large, imposing trees with smooth bark, male flowers in rounded clusters, and 1–2 nuts borne in woody and sometimes spiny husks.

Common Beech
Fagus sylvatica 40m
A large and imposing deciduous tree with a broad, rounded crown. The bark is usually smooth and grey, but may occasionally become rougher. The buds are up to 2cm long, smooth and pointed, and reddish-brown. The branches are often crowded and ascending, but sometimes arch outwards. The leaves are up to 10cm long, oval and pointed, with a wavy margin and a fringe of silky hairs when freshly open. The petiole is up to 1.5cm long.

Common Beech, flowers

Reproductive parts Male flowers are pendent and borne in clusters at the tips of twigs. The female flowers are paired, borne on short stalks, and surrounded by a brownish, 4-lobed involucre. The nuts are up to 1.8cm long, 3-sided, shiny and brown, and enclosed in a prickly case in pairs.

Habitat and distribution A widespread native of W and central Europe, preferring drier soils such as chalk, but found on a wide variety of dry and free-draining soils. Frequently planted as an ornamental tree, in shelter belts and for timber. The timber is mostly used for making furniture; it does not last well out of doors.

Comments Beech trees cast such a dense shade and produce such copious leaf litter that little grows beneath them, apart from fungi, and no other tree species can compete.

Similar species

Copper Beech *F. sylvatica* 'Purpurea' A densely purple tree, often looking rather overbearing and casting a very dense shade. The leaves have the same shape as those of Common Beech, but the new leaves are red and the older leaves are a deep opaque purple.

Dawyck Beech *F. sylvatica* 'Dawyck' A columnar form of Common Beech discovered in Dawyck, Scotland, in the mid-nineteenth century. It resembles Lombardy Poplar from a distance, but is more densely branched with otherwise normal beech leaves, flowers and fruits. Still rare, but sometimes seen in parks and gardens and on roadsides.

Eastern Beech or **Oriental Beech** *F. orientalis* 23m Leaves are larger than those of Common Beech and widely separated, with 7 or more pairs of veins. A native of the Balkans, Asia Minor and the Caucasus, rare elsewhere. Grows vigorously and forms a fine tree in good conditions.

Common Beech

Common Beech, mast

Common Beech

Common Beech, spring

Common Beech, winter

Copper Beech

Dawyck Beech

SOUTHERN BEECHES *Nothofagus* About 40 species occur in S America and Australasia. A few are deciduous, but most are evergreen with fine, glossy foliage.

Rauli or Southern Beech
Nothofagus procera 28m

An attractive tree with a fine conical shape on a stout bole and with striking foliage, particularly in autumn. The leaves are alternate, up to 8cm long and more or less pointed at the tip. The margin is wavy, but minutely toothed and, on the underside, the 15–22 pairs of veins are covered with fine silky hairs. The buds are about 1cm long, pointed and reddish-brown, borne on thick green twigs which darken with age. The lower branches are usually level, and the upper branches are more ascending.

Reproductive parts Male and female flowers occur on the same tree. Male flowers are solitary and grow in the leaf axils, female flowers are also usually solitary and give rise to a 4-lobed hairy capsule which contains 3 shiny brown nuts.

Habitat and distribution A native of Chile, introduced early this century and found in parks, gardens and commercial plantations. Grows very rapidly at first, often as much as 2m a year, and soon makes an attractive specimen tree.

Similar species

Roble Beech *N. obliqua* 30m Altogether more delicate in appearance than the Rauli, with leaves which have a wavy margin, and finer twigs which branch in a fairly regular alternate pattern, slender ascending branches, and pendent shoots on the upper crown. Leaves have only 7–11 pairs of veins (compare with Rauli's 15–22). Grows very fast, but comes into leaf later than Rauli, and gives a good autumn colour display. A native of Chile and W Argentina, and found in Britain and Europe as a specimen tree and occasionally as a commercial timber species.

Dombey's Southern Beech *N. dombeyi* 28m Evergreen, but rather tender until well established. Bark of young trees is smooth and black, but becomes wrinkled and browner with age, with scales peeling away to leave red patches.

Antarctic Beech *N. antarctica* 16m First discovered in its native Chile and Tierra del Fuego in the 1830s. It has been grown in Britain since then. Hardy, but prefers some shelter. Forms an attractive small tree with delicate, shiny foliage and reddish, shiny bark in young trees. The leaves have only 4 pairs of veins and remain curled for most of the season, turning a pleasing yellow and then brown in autumn.

Rauli, winter buds

Rauli

Roble Beech

Roble Beech

Dombey's Southern Beech

Dombey's Southern Beech
Antarctic Beech

Antarctic Beech

SWEET CHESTNUTS *Castanea* Ten species occur in the northern hemisphere, most being found in more southerly areas with a temperate climate. Most are large trees with long leaves and edible nuts.

Sweet Chestnut
Castanea sativa 35m

A handsome, large-leafed deciduous tree with a fine bole and attractive autumn colours. The bark in young trees is silvery and smooth with fine vertical fissures, but in older trees the bark becomes more deeply fissured and the grooves become markedly spiralled up the trunk. In old trees the lowest branches are often very large and spreading, the upper branches being more ascending and twisted. The glossy leaves are up to 25cm long, lanceolate, the margins serrated with spine-tipped teeth, pointed at the tip, and sometimes with a slightly heart-shaped base.

Reproductive parts Male catkins are creamy-white, long and pendulous, producing a sickly-sweet smell. The female flowers are borne in groups of 2 and 3 at the base of the male catkins, are greenish and erect, and give rise to the familiar spine-covered green capsules which split open to reveal 3 shiny, brown-skinned nuts. Flowers are produced in June–July, and the fruits are ripe in October– November.

Habitat and distribution A widespread native of most of Europe and N Africa, and frequently planted elsewhere. Occurs on a range of soils, but does especially well in well-drained, slightly acidic soils, and on hillsides.

OAKS *Quercus* About 500 species exist in the northern hemisphere, many of them occurring in warmer climates, with Mexico having about 125 species. Some species hybridize freely, and a number of long-established, named hybrids exist. Around half are evergreens. Some of the deciduous oaks produce brilliant autumn colours. All propagate by means of acorns. Many are fine and imposing trees producing high-quality, long-lasting timber and are of considerable commercial importance. Oaks are often slow-growing but long-lived, and some are of immense importance to wildlife for food and shelter, dominating the landscape in many areas.

English Oak or Common Oak
Quercus robur 36m (45m)

A large, spreading, deciduous tree with a dense crown of heavy branches. The bark of mature trees is thick and deeply fissured. Shoots and buds are hairless. The leaves have very short stalks (5mm or less) and are deeply lobed with 2 auricles at the base. The first flush of leaves is often eaten rapidly by insects, and is replaced by a second crop in midsummer. Very old trees (700–800 years) may have dead branches emerging from the upper canopy (giving rise to the description 'stag-headed') and a hollow trunk.

English Oak

Reproductive parts Male and female catkins are produced just as the first flush of leaves appears. The male catkins die off after pollination when the leaves are fully open. Acorns are borne on long stalks in roughly scaled cups, in groups of 1–3.

Habitat and distribution A widespread native tree of Britain and Europe, preferring heavier clay soils. Often the dominant tree in old woodlands, especially in lowland areas, but occurs in more hilly country up to 1,500m.

Sweet Chestnut

Sweet Chestnut, seeds and cases

Sweet Chestnut, autumn

Sweet Chestnut, seedcases
English Oak, flowers

English Oak, acorns
English Oak

English Oak

Sessile Oak or Durmast Oak
Quercus petraea 40m (43m)

A sturdy deciduous tree with a domed shape and relatively straight branches radiating around a longer and more upright bole than that of the English Oak. The grey-brown bark has deep vertical fissures. Buds are orange-brown with long white hairs. Leaves are borne on yellow stalks 1–2.5cm long and lack auricles at the base, distinguishing them from those of the English Oak. The leaf is flattened, dark green and hairless above, paler below with hairs along the veins.

Reproductive parts The drooping green male catkins are borne in May and fall off as the leaves open fully. Acorns are long and egg-shaped, stalkless, and sit directly on the twig in small clusters.

Habitat and distribution A common and widespread tree in western parts of Britain in hilly areas on poor soils, often forming woods rich in epiphytes. Once heavily coppiced for fuel and bark for tanning, but now valued more for its importance to the landscape and the wildlife it supports.

Downy Oak
Quercus pubescens 24m (27m)

A deciduous oak, forming a large, sturdy tree under good growing conditions. Resembles English Oak, but leaves are smaller, up to 13cm long and 6cm wide, with shallower, forward-pointing lobes and very hairy on the petiole. Young leaves are densely downy at first but become smoother and grey-green above when mature. The deep-grey bark is grooved with numerous deep fissures which break up to form small plates or rough scales. Twigs and buds are both covered with greyish downy hairs, buds looking more orange-brown beneath the down.

Reproductive parts Catkins are produced in late May; acorns form in early autumn. Acorns are sessile, borne in stalkless shallow cups about 1.5cm deep, and covered in closely packed downy scales.

Habitat and distribution Native in central, S and W Europe, and occasionally planted elsewhere as a specimen tree. Known as the 'Green Oak' in parts of S Europe where it occurs widely in dry hilly countryside.

Hungarian Oak
Quercus frainetto 30m (33m)

A deciduous oak which grows rapidly into a fine, broadly domed tree. The large leaves are deeply lobed and may be up to 25cm long and 14cm wide. Their size and shape makes them visible against the sky at the edge of the crown, unlike any other oak. The bark is pale grey and finely fissured, breaking up into numerous fine ridges. The largest branches are long and straight, emerging from a sturdy bole, and terminate in finely downy greyish-green or brownish twigs.

Hungarian Oak,
acorn

Reproductive parts The pendulous yellow catkins are produced in May and early June and are followed by acorns borne in cups about 1.2cm deep covered in downy, blunt, overlapping scales.

Habitat and distribution Native to the Balkans, central Europe and S Italy. Widely planted elsewhere in parks and large gardens because of its splendid appearance when mature.

Comments May be seen away from its native range as a very old tree grafted on to the stock of English Oak, which sometimes produces its own shoots from the base and shows a set of quite different leaves and twigs.

Sessile Oak, acorns

Downy Oak

Sessile Oak, woodland

Hungarian Oak

Hungarian Oak

Cork Oak
Quercus suber 17m (20m)

A medium-sized evergreen oak forming a rounded tree with numerous large twisted branches arising low down on the bole. In very old trees some branches may trail on the ground. The thick, pale greyish-brown bark forms deep fissures and ridges if left to mature, and has a soft corky texture. Leaves are up to 7cm long, borne on 1cm petioles, and resemble holly leaves, with spiny tips to the shallow lobes. Mature leaves are dark green and smooth above, but paler, almost grey and downy below.

Reproductive parts Acorns are 2–3cm long, egg-shaped, and borne in cups covered with long projecting scales.

Habitat and distribution A native of the hills and lower mountain slopes of the Mediterranean region, where its bark is regularly stripped for the cork, especially in Spain and Portugal, to supply corks for wine bottles. After stripping, the tree has a red trunk, but the cambium and inner tissues are unharmed by this and the bark regrows and can be harvested again after a few years. It has been introduced to Britain and N Europe, growing well as far north as Scotland, but is more successful in warmer regions.

Turkey Oak
Quercus cerris 38m (40m)

A deciduous oak with a broadly conica shape, becoming more spreading an domed with age. Branches appear swolle near the base and spread upwards. Th thick grey-brown bark becomes fissure and forms regular, almost square plates i older trees. Buds are covered with lon hairs. Leaves are 10–12cm long, borne o 1–2cm-long, slightly downy petioles, deepl lobed with up to 10 lobes or larg teeth. The upper leaf surface feels rough and is deep green, the lower surface i downy when new and greyish. Trees tha have been pruned produce more variabl leaves.

Reproductive parts Catkins produce in May–June. Acorns ripen in late summe and are partly encased in a deep cup cov ered in long outward-pointing scales

Habitat and distribution A native of Europe, introduced into Britain by Lucombe of Exeter in 1735, and now widely planted in parks and gardens an sometimes occurring in woodlands. A fas growing tree, forming a fine sturdy specie men when mature, it makes a useful specie for ornamental plantings, although the tim ber is not highly prized as it cracks easily. seems to be very tolerant of different so types and of atmospheric pollution.

Turkey Oak, acorn

Cork Oak, bark harvested

Cork Oak

Turkey Oak

Cork Oak

Turkey Oak

Lucombe Oak

Quercus × hispanica 'Lucombeana'
35m

A tall evergreen oak, resulting from a cross between the Cork Oak and the Turkey Oak, which originated in Exeter, Devon, in the eighteenth century. Named after Lucombe's nursery, and still most common in parks and gardens around Exeter. The long, glossy leaves are toothed and remain on the tree throughout all but the hardest winters. Some of the earliest trees, dating from the original hybridization, have a very thin crown in the winter, losing a large proportion of their leaves, but later crosses have a more dense crown. The bark is variable, with some specimens showing more features of the cork oak, and others having a smoother, darker bark.

Reproductive parts Male catkins are produced in early summer, and acorns are borne in the autumn in small scaly cups.

Habitat and distribution Most common in SW of England, especially near the sea, but may be found in mature parks and gardens in sheltered regions elsewhere.

Holm Oak

Quercus ilex 28m (30m)

An evergreen oak which grows into a fine, broadly domed tree, branching from low down on the bole. The crown is often very dense and twiggy. The bark is very dark with shallow fissures, eventually cracking to form squarish scales. Young shoots are covered with a white down, as are leaf stalks and the lower surfaces of the leaves. Leaves are variable: usually ovate to oblong with a pointed tip and a rounded base on mature trees, but more like holly leaves on a young tree. Leaves have a dark glossy upper surface, but are paler below with raised veins and are supported on a 1–2cm hairy petiole.

Holm Oak, acorn

Reproductive parts Male catkins are produced in spring and their golden colour contrasts attractively with the silvery new leaves and the darker twigs and branches. Acorns are up to 2cm long and sit deeply in a cup covered with rows of small hairy scales.

Habitat and distribution A native of hillsides and valleys in S Europe, Holm Oak has been widely planted further north, but does not do well in very cold climates. It is much valued as a shelterbelt tree in coastal areas where its rather oppressive form is used to protect more tender species from winds and salt spray. It has become naturalized in many areas near the coast.

Lucombe Oak

Lucombe Oak

Holm Oak, mature leaves

Holm Oak, new leaves

Holm Oak

Pyrenean Oak
Quercus pyrenaica 15m (18m)

A relatively slender oak with a more open crown than most other species. It is best recognized by its rough, scaly bark and deeply lobed leaves. The long leaves, up to 20cm long, with petioles about 2cm long, are often borne on pendulous shoots, and are covered with soft grey, downy hairs at first, but become smooth above with maturity.

Reproductive parts Male catkins are produced in June and July, often after other oaks have finished flowering, and are conspicuously long and yellow. In good years they can be abundant and make a brief but colourful display. The acorns are about twice the length of the cup, which is covered in blunt overlapping scales.

Habitat and distribution A native tree in Iberia, N Italy and Morocco, occasionally planted elsewhere in N Europe, mainly in parks and large gardens.

Comments Can be cultivated by grafting shoots on to 2m stocks of English Oak. May also sucker freely in its native regions.

Kermes Oak or Holly Oak
Quercus coccifera 5m

A small evergreen oak, often remaining as a dense shrub or rather straggly large bush, branching repeatedly from near the base. Bark is greyish and smooth at first, becoming finely patterned in older trees. Young twigs are yellowish with a covering of branched hairs, but become hairless with maturity. Leaves are tough and holly-like, dark green above and a little paler below, up to 4cm long with pronounced spines. The petiole is short or almost absent.

Reproductive parts The small acorns are up to 1.5cm long and sit in a shallow cup protected by strong spiny scales. They take 2 years to mature so trees always have some acorns on them.

Habitat and distribution A widespread species in the warmer regions of S and central Europe, especially along the shores of the Mediterranean, where it occasionally forms a dense scrub on stony hillsides, but is unable to survive in Britain or N Europe.

Comments Was once highly prized as the host plant for the coccid insects used to extract the red dye 'cochineal', used as a food colouring.

Pyrenean Oak, flowers

Kermes Oak

Pyrenean Oak, typical woodland

Kermes Oak, acorns

Red Oak
Quercus rubra 35m

A large deciduous oak which matures into a broadly conical tree. The bark is pale silvery-grey, sometimes more brownish, and mostly smooth, although it can become more fissured with age. The large leaves are 10–20cm long, and can be up to 30cm long in younger trees and on vigorous shoots. They are deeply lobed, with smaller teeth terminating in fine hairs at the tips of the lobes. The leaves are green above and a paler matt green below during the growing season, but develop rich red and brown hues in autumn. Young trees produce the finest red colourings, and older trees may be yellower or brownish.

Red Oak, acorn

Reproductive parts Pendulous male catkins are produced in spring as the leaves are just beginning to open, giving the whole tree a golden-yellow appearance. In the first season acorns are minute and do not develop, but in their second season they mature to form rounded acorns set in a neat scaly cup.

Habitat and distribution A native of N America, but widely planted in Britain and Europe for its fine autumn colouring and vigorous growth. Often seen on roadsides and in municipal parks, and is becoming naturalized in some areas where soil conditions are suitable.

Pin Oak
Quercus palustris 26m (30m)

A broadly conical deciduous tree with a short bole and smooth greyish-brown bark. The branches are numerous and mostly ascending. The leaves are a distinctive feature; they are up to 15cm long and deeply lobed with bristles at the tips of the pointed lobes. In summer the leaves are glossy green on both surfaces, but a little paler on the underside with tufts of brownish hairs in the vein axils.

Reproductive parts The male catkins are pendulous and yellowish-green, opening in early summer. The acorns are up to 1.5cm long and only partially enclosed in a shallow scaly cup.

Habitat and distribution A native of woodlands on swampy ground in SE Canada and NE United States. Introduced into Britain and Europe as an ornamental tree and occasionally planted on roadsides and in parks, especially on wetter soils.

Similar species

Scarlet Oak *Q. coccinea* 28m The 15cm-long leaves are even more deeply lobed but are less strongly bristle-tipped. In summer the leaves are glossy green above and paler below with small hair-tufts in the vein axils below. In autumn they turn a brilliant red, especially in the cultivar *Q. coccinea* 'Splendens'. The dark greyish-brown bark is smooth in young trees but becomes slightly ridged with maturity. The acorns are up to 2.5cm long and rounded, half-enclosed in a slightly glossy cup. A native of drier woods and sandy ground in eastern N America. Planted in Europe as an ornamental tree for its brilliant autumn colours.

Red Oak, male catkins

Red Oak, autumn

Red Oak 'Aurea'

Pin Oak

Scarlet Oak

Scarlet Oak

Golden Oak of Cyprus
Quercus alnifolia 8m

A small, rather shrubby evergreen oak with numerous branches, a short bole and dark-grey bark pitted with orange-brown lenticels. The 5cm-long leaves are leathery, with a toothed margin, a smooth, dark glossy-green upper surface and a distinctive golden-felted underside.

Reproductive parts The male catkins are yellowish-green and pendulous, and the female catkins are smaller and inconspicuous, growing on the same tree in spring. The acorns are up to 3cm long, sitting in a small scaly cup.

Habitat and distribution A native of the mountains of Cyprus, usually forming an understorey in dense coniferous woodlands. Only rarely seen elsewhere in specialist collections.

Comments The leaves of this tree are an important source of food for the rare Cyprus Mouflon, a species of wild sheep still found in the Troodos Mountains.

Algerian Oak or Mirbeck's Oak
Quercus canariensis 25m

A large, broadly columnar, deciduous or semi-evergreen tree with a domed crown, a stout bole and thick, dark-grey, furrowed bark. The leaves are ovate to elliptic, up to 15cm long and 7.5cm wide with up to 12 lobes. Young leaves are hairy and reddish at first, but they become darker green and smooth above

Algerian Oak, acorn

and paler green below when mature in late summer. Some of the leaves fall in the autumn after a brief display of yellow colours, but about half remain on the tree through the winter.

Reproductive parts The male catkins are yellowish-green and pendulous, and the separate female catkins, growing on the same tree in spring, are small and difficult to see. The acorns are up to 2.5cm long and ovate, one-third hidden in a densely scaly cup.

Habitat and distribution A native of the woods of N Africa and SW Europe but is hardy in much colder climates so is sometimes planted further north in Europe. Despite its scientific name, this tree is not thought to be a native of the Canary Islands.

Japanese Evergreen Oak
Quercus acuta 15m

A small evergreen oak whose glossy dark-green leaves have entire or sometimes sparsely toothed margins and pointed tips. The bole is short and the branches are numerous, giving the tree a bushy appearance and making it look more like a laurel or rhododendron than an oak. Young shoots are covered with an orange down which is gradually lost during the summer. The dark-grey bark is dotted with pale-grey raised spots and is slightly wrinkled.

Reproductive parts The male catkins are greenish and pendulous, the female catkins are small and borne on erect spikes. Some develop into large orange acorns in scaly cups, still growing on the flower spikes.

Habitat and distribution A native of the hills and mountains of Japan, occasionally planted as an ornamental tree in Europe.

Golden Oak of Cyprus

Algerian Oak, winter leaves

Algerian Oak

ELM FAMILY, Ulmaceae

This family includes about 150 species of both deciduous and evergreen trees and shrubs occurring in tropical and northern areas. The leaves are normally alternate, the small flowers lack petals and the fruits may be winged, in the form of a nut, or fleshy with a single stone.

ELMS *Ulmus* A family of mostly large deciduous trees with small flowers which open before the leaves, except for a few which flower in autumn. Leaves are asymmetric at the base. Many species propagate freely from root suckers.

Wych Elm
Ulmus glabra 40m

A large, often spreading tree, frequently with several prominent trunks arising from a stout bole. The bark is smooth and greyish in younger trees, but becomes browner when older and forms many deep, mostly vertical cracks and ridges. The main branches are spreading, sometimes becoming almost horizontal; the youngest twigs are thick, reddish-brown and covered with short stiff hairs, but older twigs are smoother and greyer. In winter the buds are reddish-brown and hairy, and oval with blunt-pointed tips. The leaves are up to 18cm long, rounded or oval with a long tapering point at the tip. The base of the leaf is unequal: a good pointer to all the elms. The long side of the leaf base extends beyond the 2–5mm-long petiole to the twig. The leaves have a

Wych Elm

rough feel to them; the upper surface is hairy, and the lower surface has softer sparser hairs. Rarely produces suckers like other elms, so reproduces only by seed.

Reproductive parts The flowers, open before the leaves in February and March, are sessile and have purple anthers, but being high up on the tree are not conspicuous. The fruits are about 2cm long, on a short stalk, and papery.

Habitat and distribution A widespread native of a large area of Europe, including Britain, occurring in woods and especially hedgerows, often near flowing water. An attractive feature of many riversides in the north of England.

Comments Susceptible to Dutch elm disease, so much reduced in numbers. It will be slow to recover as it does not sucker like other elms.

European White Elm
Ulmus laevis 20m (35m)

A broadly spreading tree with an open crown. Young trees have a grey, smooth bark, but it becomes deeply furrowed with age. Twigs are reddish-brown and softly downy, but become smooth with age. The leaves are up to 13cm long, with a markedly unequal base and toothed margin. The leaf veins are paired, and the longer side has 2–3 more veins than the other. The upper leaf surface is usually

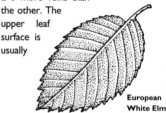

European White Elm

smooth but the underside is normally covered with a soft greyish down.

Reproductive parts Flowers are produced in long-stalked clusters. Fruits are winged and papery, with a fringe of hairs, and are borne in pendulous clusters.

Habitat and distribution A native of Europe, but probably extinct in Britain.

Wych Elm, seeds

Wych Elm, flowers

Wych Elm

English Elm
Ulmus procera 36m

Probably incorrectly named, as it is likely to have been brought to Britain by early European colonizers, and is sadly no longer a prominent feature of the English countryside as a result of a devastating attack by Dutch elm disease. Its high domed crown and lofty form give it a distinctive outline. The bark is dark brown and deeply grooved, breaking up into small squarish plates, and the main branches are large and ascending. The twigs are thick, reddish and always densely hairy. Winter buds are 3mm long, ovoid, pointed and hairy (check with a hand-lens). The leaves are rounded or slightly oval with a short tapering tip, and the base is unequal, but the longest side does not reach beyond the petiole to the twig. The leaf feels rough to the touch and the 1–5mm-long petiole and the midrib are finely downy. **Reproductive parts** The flowers have dark-red anthers and open before the leaves in February and March. Ripe fruits are rarely produced, but if present are shed in midsummer. The fruit is up to 1.5cm long, papery, and grows on a very short stalk. **Habitat and distribution** A native of S and E Europe, found in hedgerows and woodland edges. Introduced in places and formerly much prized for its leaves, which were fed to cattle, and its durable timber, used for making furniture, floorboards and coffins.

Similar species
Smooth-leaved Elm *U. carpinifolia* 32m The specific name refers to the fact that the leaves resemble Hornbeam, having similar venation and a smooth surface although feeling leathery to touch. In other respects it resembles English Elm, but has more pendulous masses of contorted shoots and small leaves. Once widespread in SE England, but badly affected by Dutch elm disease.

Coritanian Elm *U. coritana* A spreading tree with stout twigs and rather broad leaves which show a distinct curve towards the side of the leaf where the margin is shortest. The base is markedly unequal, with the long side sometimes forming a lobe. Restricted to SE Britain.

Cornish Elm *U. angustifolia* 36m A narrow conical crown, short stiff twigs and narrower leaves separate this species from English Elm which it replaces in the extreme SW of Britain and parts of Ireland, and possibly in W France. The leaf is narrower at the base, sometimes concave and with a straight midrib and an almost equal base.

Plot's Elm *U. plotii* The narrow, upright crown with an arching leading shoot, long pendulous twigs and narrow leaves distinguish this species from English Elm. The leaf is widest in the middle with a straight midrib and pointed tip, and an almost equal base. Confined to Britain.

English Elm

English Elm

English Elms, decaying from
Dutch Elm Disease (above)

Smooth-leaved Elm
Cornish Elm

Smooth-leaved Elm
Cornish Elm

Zelkova Five species, closely related to the Elms, which occur in the E Mediterranean, the Caucasus, China and Japan. Only one grows to be a large tree. Susceptible to elm disease.

Caucasian Elm
Zelkova carpinifolia 31m

A fine tree with a very dense, multi-stemmed crown composed of numerous almost upright branches. The bole is normally short, up to 3m, and heavily ridged, and it has a greyish, flaking bark which falls away in rounded scales leaving orange patches exposed. The youngest twigs have a covering of whitish down over a greenish background colour. The leaves are up to 10cm long, oval and pointed with numerous large rounded teeth on the margins and 6–12 pairs of veins. The upper surface is dark green and slightly hairy, and the lower surface is slightly paler with hairs on either side of the veins. The petiole is very short, often no more than 2mm long.

Reproductive parts Male flowers, produced in April, are sessile and composed of clusters of yellow-green stamens arising from the older part of the twig where there are no leaves. Female flowers are solitary and carried in the axils of the last few leaves on the shoot. The fruits are spherical, around 5mm in diameter and slightly 4-winged.

Habitat and distribution A native of the Caucasus, and found as an ornamental or specimen tree in parks and gardens in the rest of Europe. Noted for its fine display of autumn colours. Mature trees produce suckers readily and the tree can spread like a hedgerow elm.

Similar species

Keaki *Z. serrata* Young twigs are hairy at first, becoming smoother with age. Leaves are more markedly toothed and smooth below. Fruits are smooth and rounded.

NETTLE TREES *Celtis* A family of about 70 species, related to the Elms, occurring in the tropics and cooler areas to the north. The fruits are fleshy berries and the leaves have 3 prominent veins at the base.

Southern Nettle Tree
Celtis australis 12m (25m)

A straight, silver-grey, smooth-barked bole is the most striking feature of this deciduous tree which is often seen in town squares. The crown is sparse and fairly open and the twigs are reddish-brown. The nettle-like leaves, feeling rough to the touch, are up to 15cm long and spear-shaped; they terminate in a twisted tip. The base may be heart-shaped or rounded, and the margin is wavy with sharply pointed teeth. The upper surface of the leaf has short hairs which give the leaf its rough texture, while the lower surface has a softer white down.

Reproductive parts Flowers are produced in the axils of leaves on young twigs, opening in May. Male flowers grow where new growth is starting, whilst hermaphrodite flowers grow towards the tip of a shoot. The flowers are brownish on the outside with yellow anthers protruding. The fruit is small and fleshy, with a single hard-cased seed inside it, reddish at first, becoming blackened when ripe.

Habitat and distribution A native of S Europe and SW Asia, popular in Italy and France as a shade tree along streets.

Similar species

Hackberry *C. occidentalis* 15m Resembles Southern Nettle Tree in leaves and fruits, but has a strange bark with many protuberances and winged projections. A native of the eastern USA from Texas north to Canada, brought to Europe in the early seventeenth century, but never widely planted.

Southern Nettle Tree, fruit and leaf

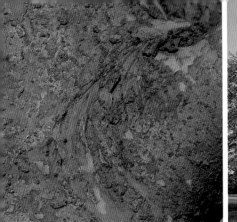

Caucasian Elm

Keaki

Southern Nettle Tree

Keaki

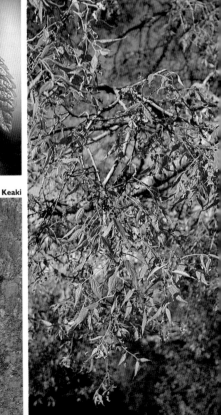

Keaki

MULBERRY FAMILY, Moraceae

A large family from the tropics with around 1,000 species, 12 of which are known as Mulberries. Two of these are hardy in Britain and NW Europe; their male and female flowers are in the form of separate catkins, but growing on the same tree, and the fruits are edible berries.

Common Mulberry or Black Mulberry *Morus nigra* 13m (15m)

A gnarled and twisted bole, and densely packed twisting branches and twigs make a mature mulberry look like an ancient tree but it is fast-growing and soon acquires the aged look. The crown may be broader than the tree is tall. The dark orange-brown bark is deeply fissured and shreds of the outer layers are always peeling off. The downy shoots release a milky juice if snapped. The leaves are up to 20cm long and oval with a markedly heart-shaped base and a toothed margin terminating in a pointed tip. The petiole is up to 2.5cm long and hairy.

Reproductive parts Flower spikes are produced on short downy stalks in May; male flowers are about 2.5cm long and pale yellowish-green, the females are about 1–1.25cm long and give rise to a hard raspberry-like fruit which has an acidic taste until it is fully ripened, when it turns a deep wine-red or purple colour. Fruits are usually ripe in late summer to early autumn.

Habitat and distribution A native of Asia, but long cultivated and naturalized in Europe, especially the warmer south. Prized for its fruit. In Britain it is found mainly in the south, where it thrives in sheltered gardens.

White Mulberry *Morus alba* 15m

A deciduous tree which forms a narrow rounded crown on a broad bole which may quickly reach up to 2m in girth. The bark is heavily ridged and grey, sometimes with a pinkish tinge. The shoots are thin, covered with fine hairs at first, and bear minute, pointed brown buds. The leaves are up to 18cm long, oval to rounded with a heart-shaped base and a hairy, grooved petiole up to 2.5cm long. They feel thin and smooth to the touch, and have a toothed margin, with downy hairs on the veins on the underside.

Reproductive parts Female flowers are produced on stalks and are spike-like and yellowish. Male flowers are slightly longer spikes than the females and look whiter with prominent anthers. The fruit is in fact a cluster of drupes which may change from white or pink to purple when fully ripe. The fruits are edible but not especially tasty or useful.

Habitat and distribution A native of China and neighbouring regions of Asia, but long known as a cultivated tree in S Europe where it occurs in gardens and churchyards and along roadsides. The leaves are used as food for silkworms, so trees are frequently propagated by taking large (1m-long) woody cuttings in winter and allowing them to root. They soon produce a copious supply of fresh leaves for the caterpillars, and will also grow on to become mature trees.

Common Mulberry

White Mulberry, autumn

Common Mulberry, fruit

White Mulberry, autumn

Osage Orange
Maclura pomifera 16m

A small deciduous tree with a flattish or domed crown and numerous spines on the shoots and branches, especially in young specimens. The bark is markedly cracked, covered with interlocking ridges, and sometimes has an orange tinge. In winter, the zigzag shoots with their spines at the angles are distinctive. The leaves are up to 12cm long, oval to lanceolate with a pointed tip, shiny green on the upper surface and paler and downy below, particularly on the midrib and prominent veins.
Reproductive parts Male flowers are produced in June in thick clusters or short spikes on a very short stalk, and are greenish and inconspicuous. Female flowers are similar and give rise to green globular compound fruits, ripening in October, with a superficial resemblance to a green orange.
Habitat and distribution A native of the south and central USA from Texas to Arkansas, but has become naturalized in the warmer parts of Europe. As its seedlings are susceptible to frost it does not propagate well in Britain and is not often seen, although some sheltered gardens in the south have good specimens.

Fig
Ficus carica 5m (8m)

A deciduous tree with distinctive fruits and leaves, and long familiar as a cultivated tree in gardens. The bark is smooth and pale grey, or almost white in the Mediterranean sun, and sometimes marked with finer lines. The branches are thick and form a spreading domed crown in a tree, when given room to spread out. The alternate leaves are up to 20cm long, on a 5–10cm petiole, and are deeply lobed, usually in 3 segments, sometimes 5. They feel rough and leathery with prominent veins on the underside.
Reproductive parts Flowers are hidden from view, being produced on the inside of a pear-like fleshy receptacle which is almost closed at the apex. This ripens in the second year into the familiar fleshy sweet-tasting fig.
Habitat and distribution Possibly native in the Balkans and the Iberian peninsula, and also in SW Asia, but long cultivated in much of Europe, including Britain. It is occasionally found naturalized, sometimes forming dense thickets, but is most likely to be seen in cultivation, thriving in walled gardens in the north of its range, but sometimes seen as an isolated tree providing welcome shade in the Mediterranean countries.
Comments Cultivars have been developed and these are more likely to be seen in gardens. The fruits are eaten either fresh or dried.

PROTEA FAMILY, Proteaceae

A large family of over 1,000 evergreen trees and shrubs, mostly native to the southern hemisphere, but introduced widely around the world. Leaves are alternate and sometimes pinnate. The flowers can be very showy, although petals are very small, the main display being provided by a large divided calyx.

Chilean Firebush
Embothrium coccineum 12m

A small, slightly spreading and untidy-looking evergreen tree with slightly pendulous shoots, 22cm-long lanceolate leaves and purple-grey flaking bark.
Reproductive parts The species is best known for its clusters of striking red flowers produced in May. These are up to 10cm long, and swollen at the tip which, when open, divides into 4 segments. Fruits are grooved capsules which retain the 3cm-long style at the tip.
Habitat and distribution A native of Chile and Argentina, but planted in Britain and W Europe for its colourful flowers.

Osage Orange **Fig**

Fig

Fig, fruit **Chilean Firebush**

KATSURA FAMILY,
Cercidiphyllaceae

A very small family with probably only a single species, once thought to be closer to the Magnolias, but now considered to be more primitive and perhaps nearer to the Planes.

Katsura Tree
Cercidiphyllum japonicum 25m

A tall, conical-crowned deciduous tree, sometimes with a single bole, but more often with several main stems, and vertically fissured peeling bark. The leaves are in opposite pairs, up to 8cm long, rounded, with pointed tips and heart-shaped bases. When they first open they are an attractive pink colour, but they turn green in summer, then red in the autumn. **Reproductive parts** Flowers are produced in the leaf nodes in April. Male flowers are small clusters of reddish stamens, female flowers are darker-red clusters of styles. Fruits are claw-like bunches of 5cm-long pods which change from grey, through green, to brown. **Habitat and distribution** A native of the mountain forests of Japan, but becoming very popular as an ornamental garden tree in Britain and W Europe. If given similar conditions to its native habitat, such as damp soils, and some protection from frosts in late spring, it produces a very fine display of spring foliage, and grows on into a pleasing tree.

MAGNOLIA FAMILY,
Magnoliaceae

A family of 12 genera and up to 200 species, most occurring in Asia, particularly the Himalayas, China and Japan; a few also occur in the south of the USA and further south into S America. They can be either trees or shrubs, deciduous or evergreen with alternate, untoothed and occasionally lobed leaves. The flowers are often showy and sometimes scented.

TULIP TREES *Liriodendron* Only 2 species occur, and they are relics of the pre-Ice-Age flora, surviving in N America and China.

Tulip Tree
Liriodendron tulipifera 45m

An impressive deciduous tree which, despite the promise of its name, produces more attractive foliage than flowers. The strikingly shaped leaves, which are a clean fresh green through the summer, turn a bright gold in the autumn and the whole tree glows with colour on a sunny day. The leaves are up to 20cm long and 4-lobed with a terminal notch, looking rather as if they have been cut out with scissors. They are completely smooth and hairless and grow on a slender 5–10cm-long petiole. **Reproductive parts** The flowers, which give the tree its name, are superficially tulip-like. When first open they are cup-shaped and not very conspicuous as the perianth segments are greenish and blend in with the leaves. Later the flowers open more fully, revealing the rings of yellowish stamens surrounding the paler ovaries. The flowers are often produced high up on the tree in the middle of dense foliage, and not until the tree is at least 25 years old and quite sizeable, so they are sometimes overlooked. The conical fruits reach a length of 8.5cm and are composed of numerous scale-like overlapping carpels. **Habitat and distribution** A native of the eastern USA and quite common in many areas in open countryside where some fine specimens can be seen. Introduced into Europe in the seventeenth century and commonly planted in gardens and parks in Britain and W Europe as an ornamental tree, and also in plantations for its easily worked timber, sometimes called 'whitewood'.

Katsura Tree, autumn

Tulip Tree

Katsura Tree

Tulip Tree, flower

Katsura Tree

Tulip Tree

MAGNOLIAS *Magnolia* A genus of about 35 species, many with beautiful showy but primitive flowers. Numerous cultivars exist and these are popular garden trees.

Evergreen Magnolia or Bull Bay
Magnolia grandiflora 30m

A large, spreading evergreen tree with a broadly conical crown. The branches are large and the bark is a smooth, dull grey. The youngest shoots are covered with a thick down and terminate in red-tipped buds. The elliptical leaves are up to 16cm long and 9cm wide with a smooth or sometimes wavy margin. The upper surface is a shiny, dark green, and the underside is rust-coloured and downy, as is the 2.5cm-long petiole.

Reproductive parts The conspicuous flowers, composed of 6 white petal-like segments, are borne at the tips of the shoots and are conical in bud, later opening out to a spreading cup-shape, reaching a diameter of 25cm. The fruit is conical and up to 6cm long, composed of scale-like carpels on a single orange stalk. Flowers from midsummer to late autumn.

Habitat and distribution A native of the south-eastern USA, introduced into Europe in the eighteenth century. Very popular as a garden specimen and does especially well if grown against a wall and given some frost protection, although in more sheltered areas it will form a splendid free-standing tree.

Comments There are at least 35 other species of Magnolia, found over a wide range of the USA and Asia. Many of them are in cultivation, being among the most popular garden trees.

LAUREL FAMILY, Lauraceae

Mostly evergreen trees and shrubs. The family numbers about 1,000 species, mainly found in the tropics, but with a few hardy species occurring in more northern areas. Many are aromatic.

Sweet Bay or Poet's Laurel
Laurus nobilis 17m (20m)

A moderate-sized evergreen tree with a conical crown and smooth dark-grey or almost black bark. The branches are mostly ascending and also dark grey, terminating in reddish twigs and conical dark-red buds. The leaves are up to 10cm long, narrowly oval or lanceolate with wavy margins. They feel tough and leathery and have a pleasing aroma when crushed. The upper surface is glossy dark green and the underside is paler; the glands that release the scent can be seen through a hand-lens.

Reproductive parts Flowers are borne below the petioles against the shoot and open in creamy-yellow clusters. Fruits are small, shiny-black berries up to 1.5cm long.

Habitat and distribution A native of the Mediterranean area, but widely planted and naturalized as far north in Europe as Britain. Not always seen in a natural shape, as it lends itself well to pruning and clipping and can be trained into neat symmetrical shapes and grown in tubs. Popular in walled kitchen gardens, where the aromatic leaves are collected for use as a flavouring.

Comments Long favoured as a culinary herb, bay leaves can be used to flavour stews, sauces, soups and fish recipes. Once used by the Romans to make laurel wreaths or garlands to adorn poets and heroes.

Similar species

Californian Laurel *Umbellularia californica* 20m Similar foliage, but leaves are paler green or yellowish-green. Flowers grow in small, dense, rounded clusters and the fruits are rounded and greenish, ripening to purple. The crushed leaves give off a stronger scent than those of Sweet Bay which can induce painful headaches and nausea in some people. A native of the evergreen forests of the west coast of N America from California to Oregon, but cultivated in milder parts of Europe where some fine trees exist.

Evergreen Magnolia

Evergreen Magnolia

Sweet Bay

Californian Laurel

Avocado
Persea americana 9m (18m)

A rather untidy-looking evergreen tree which is covered with aromatic oil-releasing glands. The alternate leaves are up to 20cm long and elliptical to oval with pointed tips and smooth margins. They feel leathery to touch and are glossy green above and bluish-green below.

Avocado, flower

Reproductive parts Flowers are borne early in the spring at the tips of shoots beyond the leaves in short spikes; each flower is up to 2cm across, white and composed of 6 perianth segments. The fruit is the familiar green-skinned, pear-shaped berry on a short stalk. It has a tough warty outer skin and sometimes changes from green through yellow to brown or even purple. It contains a single large, woody seed.

Habitat and distribution Probably a native of Central America, and grown commercially for its edible fruits in many warm countries, especially in the Mediterranean area. In plantations it is grown as a small, neat bush for ease of harvesting, but trees that have become naturalized are much more untidy and larger.

Sassafras
Sassafras albidum 20m

A medium-sized, columnar, deciduous tree with thick, reddish-brown, furrowed and aromatic bark. The leaves are mostly elliptic and untoothed, measuring up to 15cm long and 10cm across, but may sometimes develop large lobes on either side. The upper surface is bright green and the lower surface is bluish-green, and the leaves turn through yellow and orange to purple in the autumn. Trees that have spread through suckers can form large clumps which produce a brilliant autumn display. Crushed leaves have a pleasing smell and to some they taste of orange and vanilla. After leaf-fall the thin green shoots are an attractive feature.

Sassafras, fruits and flower

Reproductive parts The male and female flowers are very small, greenish-yellow and without petals, growing in small clusters on separate plants and opening in the spring. The fruit is an ovoid berry, about 1cm long, ripening to a dark blue.

Habitat and distribution A common native tree of eastern N America, growing in woods and thickets, and used as a raw ingredient for root beer and tea. Seen in Europe in arboreta and well-established gardens.

vocado, fruit

Sassafras

Sassafras

WITCH HAZEL FAMILY, Hamamelidaceae

About 25 genera and 100 species occur in temperate and sub-tropical regions. They range from trees to shrubs and may be evergreen or deciduous. Many are very popular ornamental garden plants.

Sweet Gum
Liquidamber styraciflua 28m

A large tree with attractive foliage and sharply lobed leaves with a toothed

Sweet Gum, flowers and fruit

margin. They are alternate and give off a resinous scent when crushed, unlike maple leaves which they resemble.

Reproductive parts The flowers are globuse; fruits spiny and pendulous, 2.5–4cm across, resembling those of Plane.

Habitat and distribution Familiar as a colourful autumn tree in many parks and gardens. Imported as timber called satinwood. A widespread and common native tree of the south-eastern USA as far south as Central America.

Persian Ironwood
Parrotia persica 12m

A small, spreading deciduous tree with a short bole and mostly level branches. The bark is smooth and peels away in flakes, leaving attractive coloured patches; older trees have a pattern of pink, brown and yellow. Young twigs are hairy, and terminate in blackish hairy buds. The leaves are up to 7.5cm long, oval with a slightly tapering tip and a rounded base. The margins are wavy or sometimes slightly toothed.

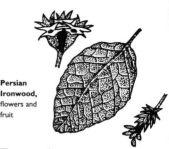

Persian Ironwood, flowers and fruit

They are glossy green above and appear slightly crushed or crinkled, and the underside is slightly hairy.

Reproductive parts The flowers appear before the leaves in early spring; they are short-stalked clusters, reddish and inconspicuous. The fruits are dry capsules which split open to release small pointed, shiny-brown seeds.

Habitat and distribution A native of the Caucasus and N Iran, introduced into Europe as an ornamental tree.

Witch Hazel
Hamamelis mollis 4m

Rarely more than a small sprawling shrub, but sometimes grows into a small domed tree with dense, mostly ascending branches. The leaves, resembling hazel leaves, are alternate and mostly oval with pointed tips, a toothed margin and an unequal base.

Reproductive parts Best known for its winter flowers, produced long before the leaves open and providing a welcome sign of early spring in a winter landscape. They are composed of long yellow, ribbon-like petals and red stamens, and are noticeably sweet-scented. They are often produced prolifically on bare twigs, making the shrub stand out conspicuously.

Habitat and distribution A native of China, introduced into Britain late in the nineteenth century and now found in parks and gardens and sometimes naturalized in open woodlands.

Similar species

Japanese Witch Hazel *H. japonica* Showy, spring-flowering with a spreading habit and colourful autumn leaves.

Sweet Gum

Sweet Gum

Persian Ironwood

Persian Ironwood

Witch Hazel, flowers

Japanese Witch Hazel, flowers

PITTOSPORUM FAMILY, Pittosporaceae

A large family of 9 genera and over 200 species, mostly originating in Australasia. The leaves are alternate and usually untoothed and the 5-lobed flowers develop into either dry or succulent fruits. Some are cultivated and numerous attractive varieties occur in gardens.

Pittosporum
Pittosporum tenuifolium 10m

A small tree with densely packed branches and usually a very stout bole with smooth, dark-grey bark. The leaves are oblong, sometimes elliptical, up to 6cm long and 2cm across with a markedly wavy margin. The upper surface is a glossy, sometimes pale green; the underside is less shiny. The shoots are normally a dark purple-black.

Reproductive parts The heavily scented tubular flowers are about 1cm long with 5 deep-purplish lobes and yellow anthers. They may be in clusters or solitary, growing in the leaf axils and opening in spring. The fruit is a rounded capsule, about 1cm long, ripening from green to black.

Habitat and distribution A native of forests from sea-level to high altitudes in New Zealand. Introduced as a garden shrub into Europe, where it is popular as a specimen plant and for hedging. Numerous cultivars exist with varying degrees of variegation in the foliage, from purple to golden-yellow. Young trees especially need protection from hard frosts and icy winds.

White Holly or Mock Orange
Pittosporum undulatum 20m

A medium-sized evergreen tree with a spreading habit and a dense pyramidal crown. The bark is generally smooth and grey. The leaves are about 13cm long and up to 6cm wide, mostly ovate with a wedge-shaped base, a tapering tip and a slightly wavy margin; the upper surface is shiny and green.

Reproductive parts The fragrant white flowers are borne in lax, flat-topped clusters; the 5 petals are narrow and pointed. The main flowering period is late spring or early summer. The fruits are smooth, rounded orange capsules about 1.2cm long.

Habitat and distribution A native of SE Australia, introduced into Europe as an ornamental tree and widely cultivated in parks and gardens. Mainly confined to S and W Europe where it is becoming naturalized, especially on some of the Atlantic islands.

Pittosporum crassifolium 10m

A small, upright evergreen tree or large shrub with black bark and a rather untidy, congested crown. The leathery leaves are up to 8cm long and 3cm wide, ovate to lanceolate with a blunt tip. They have a dark-green upper surface, a paler, slightly woolly underside and a slightly inrolled margin.

Reproductive parts The flowers grow in scattered and rather lax clusters; the 5 petals are wine-red or even darker, contrasting with the yellow anthers. The fruit is an ovoid, blunt capsule up to 3cm long with a matt, light-green outer skin at first, divided internally into 3–4 fibrous woody valves containing shiny seeds.

Habitat and distribution A native of New Zealand introduced into Europe as an ornamental species. It is tolerant of exposure to salt spray so is extensively used by the coast for shelter and has become naturalized in parts of SW England and W France. Very hard winters damage the foliage and the trees die back, but if the dead wood is cut out they sprout back vigorously.

Pittosporum

Pittosporum, flowers

Pittosporum crassifolium, fruit

Pittosporum crassifolium

White Holly, flowers

PLANE FAMILY, Platanaceae

A family of 8 species of large deciduous trees, mostly native to the USA and Mexico apart from one which occurs in the Balkans and one in SE Asia. Leaves are large and normally palmate. Male and female flowers are in separate pendulous clusters on the same tree.

Oriental Plane
Platanus orientalis 30m

A large deciduous tree, often with spreading branches and a broad, domed crown. In older specimens the branches droop down to the ground. The main trunk is frequently covered with large tuberous burrs, but the bark is mostly smooth and pale brown, flaking away to reveal rounded yellow patches. Young shoots are yellow-brown and hairy, older twigs are greyer. The leaves are large, usually reaching 18cm in length and width. They are deeply divided into 5–7 lobes which are themselves notched; the central lobe is the longest, and the leaf is supported on a 5cm-long petiole which has a swollen base enclosing a bud.

Reproductive parts Male flowers are up to 6cm long and composed of 2–7 rounded, yellowish flower heads. The female flowers are up to 8cm long and are composed of up to 6 rounded, dark-red flower heads; flowers are open in May–June. As they ripen into fruits the catkins reach a length of 15cm and the heads grow to 3cm in diameter; they contain many 1-seeded carpels with long hairs attached to their bases.

Habitat and distribution A native of the Balkan peninsula and areas further to the east into W Asia. Commonly planted in parks and gardens, and alongside roads elsewhere in Europe. It is not suitable for narrow roads as its spreading habit makes it too large.

London Plane
Platanus × *acerifolia* (× *hispanica*) 44m

A large deciduous tree resulting from a cross between the American and Oriental Planes, and known since the mid-seventeenth century. The main trunk is usually very tall and the crown of an old tree is often spreading with tangled branches. The greyish-brown bark is thin and flakes away in rounded patches leaving paler, yellowish areas beneath. The leaves are up to 24cm long and mostly 5-lobed and palmate, but not as deeply divided as those of Oriental Plane; they are very variable, however, and the degree of lobing may differ greatly.

London Plane

Reproductive parts Flowers are very similar to those of Oriental Plane. Some flower spikes may bear only one or 2 flower heads.

Habitat and distribution A widespread tree in towns, where the peeling bark is a useful way of ridding the tree of soot and dust deposits. Very sturdy and resistant to gales and storms, and also quite disease-resistant. Very much a feature of London streets and squares, but also popular in other cities.

American Sycamore or **Western Plane** *P. occidentalis* 35m A native of E north America, with glossy green, palmately lobed leaves and flaking, greyish bark. Flowers are small, in separate clusters.

Oriental Plane, ripening fruits

London Plane

London Plane

American Sycamore

ROSE FAMILY, Rosaceae

A very large and important family of over 100 genera and about 3,000 species of trees, shrubs and herbaceous plants. The trees can be deciduous or evergreen, and have alternate, simple leaves or a range of leaf types including complex pinnate leaves. Flowers are usually 5-petalled, with the ovary beneath the petals, but the fruits are very varied and the family is divided mainly on the basis of the types of fruits produced.

Quince
Cydonia oblonga 7.5m
A small, irregularly spreading, deciduous tree with a flattened crown and dense branches. The shoots are noticeably woolly at first, but lose this as they become older. Leaves are up to 10cm long with entire margins; the upper surface is green and mostly smooth, and the lower surface is greyer and markedly downy.
Reproductive parts The attractive pink-tinged white flowers, which are at their best in April–May, are up to 5cm in diameter and bowl-shaped, containing yellowish anthers and stigmas. The fruit is up to 3.5cm long, resembling a small pear, greenish at first and becoming golden-yellow when mature with a pleasing fragrance.
Habitat and distribution A native of SW Asia, but long cultivated in Europe for its fruits. Many of the cultivated varieties have much larger fruits which may be 12cm long. Mostly found in orchards and gardens, but naturalized in hedges and open woodlands in the south.

PEARS *Pyrus* About 20 species occur in temperate regions of Europe and Asia. Some produce edible fruits and many produce good-quality durable timber which is used for inlay work and turnery. Many ar found in cultivated forms and are impor tant commercial species.

Willow-leaved Pear
Pyrus salicifolia 10m
A small deciduous tree with a rounde crown and mostly level branches wit pendulous, very downy twigs. The bark i rough and scaly and usually dark brown The narrow leaves are up to 9cm long an resemble willow leaves, being silvery-gre on both surfaces at first, but greener o the upper surface later in the season
Reproductive parts The white flower are about 2cm in diameter and usuall open at the same time as the leaves. Th fruit is about 3cm long, pear-shaped o sometimes more pointed, and brow when ripe, growing a downy pedicel.
Habitat and distribution A native of wide area from Siberia through the Cau casus to Iran. Cultivated in Europe main as an ornamental tree for its silver foliage and slightly weeping habit.

Plymouth Pear
Pyrus cordata 8m
A small, slender or slightly spreadin deciduous tree with spiny branches an purplish twigs. The alternate leaves ar oval and up to 5cm long, although they ar usually much smaller. The margin is fine toothed and the leaf is downy whe young, becoming a dull green when olde
Reproductive parts The flowers ope at the same time as the leaves in May an the tree is often covered with white blos som. The fruit is up to 1.8cm long, resem bling a tiny pear on a long stalk, and i golden-brown at first, ripening later to re and marked by numerous brown lenticels
Habitat and distribution A scarc native of SW Britain, W France and th Iberian peninsula, usually found i hedgerows and copses.

Quince

Willow-leaved Pear, fruit

Plymouth Pear, fruit

Plymouth Pear

Plymouth Pear

Wild Pear
Pyrus pyraster 20m

A medium-sized deciduous tree, sometimes becoming fairly large and spreading, but often rounded in outline and no more than 8-10m tall. The branches may be spreading, or sometimes ascending, and are normally spiny; the twigs are smooth and greyish-brown. Leaves are up to 7cm long, elliptic or rounded, or sometimes heart-shaped near the base, but nearly always with a toothed margin near the apex. The leaves are hairless when fully grown and are borne on a petiole up to 7cm long.

Reproductive parts The long-stalked flowers open at the same time as the leaves in April–May and are white. The petals, sometimes looking slightly crushed, are borne in clusters of about 5. The tree is often densely covered with blossom and can be a most attractive sight in a woodland in spring. The small, hard fruits are rounded, about 3.5cm in diameter and yellowish-brown, sometimes blackened, and pitted with numerous tiny lenticels. They grow on a thin stalk.

Habitat and distribution A native of a wide area of Europe, found in open woodlands and copses, usually solitary, but easy to spot for a short time in spring when the white blossom is open. Difficult to identify with any certainty as so many hybrids and varieties exist, especially in areas where other *Pyrus* species occur.

Common Pear or Cultivated Pear
Pyrus communis 20m

A normally upright and slender deciduous tree with a stout bole covered in dark-brown bark which breaks up into small square plates. The branches are ascending in young trees, but become more spreading in older specimens, and may bear some spines. Young twigs are reddish-brown and sparsely hairy, and become smoother with age. The leaves are up to 8cm long, and usually oval to elliptic in shape, but there is always some variation; the margins have numerous small teeth and the leaves are smooth and almost glossy when mature.

Reproductive parts The flowers are pure white and open before the leaves have fully expanded. Blossom is often produced prolifically: a flowering pear orchard is a spectacular sight on a sunny spring day. The pear-shaped fruits may be up to 12cm long, with a soft, but slightly gritty, sweet-tasting flesh.

Habitat and distribution A native of W Asia originally, but now widespread across Europe, apart from the very cold north and the very hot and dry south, and cultivated for its highly edible fruits. Many hundreds of cultivars exist and there are numerous hybrids. Single trees may be seen naturalized in hedgerows and woodlands, sometimes indicating where an old dwelling once existed.

Similar species
P. bourgaeana 10m A rare species, confined to Spain and Portugal, with ovate or heart-shaped leaves up to 4cm long, white flowers and spiny lower branches. The fruits are small, up to 2.5cm in diameter and rounded on a thick stalk, and are usually yellow, ripening to matt brown. Most often found along riverbanks and hill streamsides.

P. elaeagrifolia 10m A small, often slender tree with spreading, spiny branches and twigs covered with grey hairs. The alternate leaves are up to 8cm long, lanceolate, sometimes toothed at the tip, and covered with a thick white down, even at the end of the growing season. White, almost sessile flowers open with the leaves. Thick-stalked fruits are about 1.3cm long, and pear-shaped, sometimes globular, remaining green when ripe. A native of the Balkans, Turkey and W Russia, and usually found in dry habitats.

Wild Pear

Common Pear

Common Pear

Common Pear

Common Pear
Pyrus elaeagrifolia

Pyrus elaeagrifolia

Sage-leaved Pear or Aurelian Pear
Pyrus salvifolia 10m

A small tree with spreading spiny branches and blackish, almost hairless old twigs. Leaves are up to 5cm long, elliptic, smooth above and grey and woolly below.

Reproductive parts White flowers open with the leaves and are followed by a pear-shaped fruit up to 8cm long. The pedicel and the young fruit are woolly; later the fruit becomes yellow and has an unpleasant bitter taste, but it can be used by the brewing industry to make perry.

Habitat and distribution Occurs in cultivation, and as a wild tree in W and central Europe from France to Russia. Prefers dry habitats and open conditions. Very variable and possibly a hybrid between the Common Pear and *P. nivalis*.

Almond-leaved Pear
Pyrus amygdaliformis 6m

A small tree, often with dense, sparsely spiny branches and greyish, woolly young twigs. The leaves are up to 8cm long and usually lanceolate with a sparsely toothed margin. Young leaves are downy, but full-grown leaves are shiny above and slightly downy below.

Reproductive parts The white flower clusters open at about the same time as the leaves. The thick-stalked fruits are rounded and about 3cm in diameter ripening to a dark yellow.

Habitat and distribution A native of southern Europe, the Balkans and some of the larger Mediterranean islands, usually found in dry habitats and nearly always solitary.

Similar species

Snow Pear *P. nivalis* 20m A medium-sized tree with ascending branches and normally lacking spines. Leaves are up to 9cm long and smooth, with the blade running decurrently down the petiole. The white flowers open just after the leaves. Fruits are up to 5cm long and are rounded, greenish-yellow when ripe and covered with tiny purple dots. Occurs in dry, sunny habitats and woodland clearings, from France to Russia.

APPLES *Malus* About 25 species occur in northern temperate regions, although there are countless varieties and cultivars used for their highly important edible fruit and sometimes for their attractive blossom. They are hardy trees, growing in a variety of soils and climates, and some produce good-quality timber suitable for turnery. Most important fruiting varieties are propagated by grafting on to healthy stocks.

Crab Apple
Malus sylvestris 10m

A small tree, sometimes tall and slender if growing in woodland, or more spreading if found in a hedgerow. May be spiny on twigs and branches; smooth brown shoots often sport long thorns. The bark is deep brown, and cracks into small oblong plates. The leaves are up to 11cm long, toothed and smooth above and below when fully open.

Reproductive parts The flowers are up to 4cm across and usually white, although they may show a pinkish tinge. Cultivated varieties of apple which have become naturalized always show the pink tinge. The fruits are up to 4cm in diameter and rounded, yellowish-green when ripe and very tough and sour to taste. They often lie on the ground beneath the tree uneaten until they start to rot before deer or rabbits will try them.

Habitat and distribution A native tree of a wide area of Europe from Britain eastwards to Russia, but not found in the far north. Occurs widely in woodlands and hedgerows and is most easily spotted when in blossom or when the green fruits start to fall. One of the parent species of the hybrid Cultivated Apple, but of little importance itself as a food species.

Sage-leaved Pear, fruit

Snow Pear, fruit

Crab Apple

Crab Apple

Crab Apple, fruit

Japanese Crab or
Japanese Hybrid Apple
Malus floribunda 8m

A compact, densely crowned small tree on a thick bole with dark brown, fissured bark. The twigs are slightly pendulous and reddish when young, remaining densely hairy. The alternate leaves are up to 8cm long, oval with a pointed tip and a toothed margin. The underside is downy when the leaves first open, but becomes smooth later.

Reproductive parts The fragrant flowers appear soon after the leaves and are usually so dense that they hide the leaves. At first the buds are a rich pink, then they become paler as they open and the blossom gradually fades to white. The fruits are rounded and up to 2.5cm across, but sometimes smaller. They ripen to a bright yellow, and are often present in the same abundance as the flowers.

Habitat and distribution Probably a hybrid between two Japanese garden species, as this tree has not been found growing in the wild. Frequently planted in gardens and parks all over Europe for its attractive blossom and convenient small size.

Similar species
Siberian Crab *M. baccata* Slender leaves and compact flower heads of white blossom make this a popular garden tree. The fruit is green at first but ripens to bright red and remains on the tree long after the leaves have fallen, providing a late feed for winter migrant birds. A native of China. *M. florentina* An attractive small tree with good blossom, small fruits and colourful autumn foliage. Possibly a hybrid between a *Malus* species and *Sorbus torminalis* which it resembles. Mostly seen in gardens. *M.* × *zumi* A hybrid crab apple popular for its small red fruits.

Cultivated Apple
Malus domestica 15m

A familiar orchard tree producing copious edible fruits. The bark is usually brown and fissured and the twigs are downy. Leaves are up to 13cm long, elliptic and rounded at the base with a slightly pointed tip and toothed margin. They are slightly downy on the upper surface and normally very downy on the lower surface.

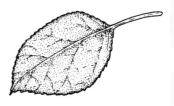

Cultivated Apple

Reproductive parts The flowers are white or tinged with pink and, in some varieties, produced abundantly in short-stalked clusters. The fruits are normally larger than 5cm in diameter and indented at the pedicel. A great variety of shapes, sizes, tastes and colours exist.

Habitat and distribution Almost always found in cultivation in orchards and gardens across a wide range of Europe and N America, but not in the coldest northern regions, or the hotter and dryer southern regions. Occasionally naturalized, or found in isolated places where human habitation once occurred. A hybrid species, probably between the wild Crab Apple *M. sylvestris* and *M. dasyphylla*, and possibly *M. praecox*.

Comments The wood of the Apple tree is excellent for wood-turning, making mallet heads and for imparting a rich fragrance to wood-smoke on log fires. Apple trees in old orchards are often parasitized by mistletoe, which becomes very obvious in winter when the leaves have fallen.

Japanese Crab Apple

Siberian Crab Apple

Cultivated Apple, fruit

Cultivated Apple

Malus florentina

Cultivated Apple, Cox's Orange Pippin

Malus florentina

Malus × zumi

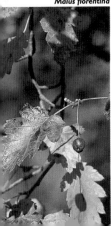

WHITEBEAMS AND ROWANS *Sorbus*

About 80 species of medium to small trees and shrubs, mostly with showy umbels of white flowers and clusters of colourful berries. Rowans generally have pinnate leaves and whitebeams have simple, usually toothed leaves. They hybridize at times and confusing leaf forms occur. There are some very rare and local species restricted to isolated localities.

Rowan or Mountain Ash
Sorbus aucuparia 20m

A small to medium-sized deciduous tree with a fairly open, domed crown. The silvery-grey bark is usually smooth but sometimes feels slightly ridged. The branches are ascending and quite widely spaced with purple-tinged twigs which are hairy when young but become smooth later. The buds are oval with curved tips and mostly purple and covered with greyish hairs. The compound leaves are pinnate, composed of 5–8 pairs of toothed leaflets, each one up to 6cm long, ovoid and markedly toothed. The central rachis is rounded near the base, and grooved between the leaflets.

Reproductive parts The flowers are produced in dense heads in May; each flower is up to 1cm in diameter with 5 creamy-white petals. The fruits are rounded, under 1cm long and bright scarlet, hanging in colourful clusters and persisting after the leaves have fallen.

Habitat and distribution A native of a wide area of Europe, occurring in woodlands and open land on a variety of soils, apart from very wet ones, and growing at a higher altitude on mountains than many other species. Often planted as a town tree in squares and along roadsides.

Comments The bright scarlet fruits of the Rowan are a favourite food of birds in winter and often attract migrants like Waxwings into busy town centres.

True Service Tree
Sorbus domestica 20m

Resembles Rowan, but the rich brown bark is fissured and ridged and often peels in vertical shreds. The buds are smooth, rounded and green, unlike the purple, pointed buds of the Rowan. The alternate leaves are pinnate, composed of up to 8 pairs of oblong, toothed leaflets about 5cm long, and softly hairy on the underside.

Reproductive parts Flowers are produced in May in rounded, branched clusters; each flower is about 1.5cm in diameter and composed of 5 creamy-white petals. The small pear- or sometimes apple-shaped fruits are up to 2cm long and green or brown like a russet apple. They have a very sharp taste when ripe, but after a frost they become more palatable.

Habitat and distribution A native of the Mediterranean region and other warm parts of southern Europe, but long cultivated elsewhere and sometimes naturalized. Uncommon outside its native area.

Similar species
Sargent's Rowan *S. sargentiana* 10m A small and sometimes densely branched deciduous tree, with dark brown twigs and ovoid, glossy-red, slightly resiniferous buds. The large compound leaves are pinnate, with 4–5 pairs of 5cm-long, sharply toothed leaflets which are hairy on the underside and usually late to open. The white flowers are about 6mm across, in dense, stalked clusters, and these give rise to bunches of as many as 200 bright-red fruits. It is a well-known garden tree now, since its discovery in W China by Charles Sargent. Its brilliant fiery-red autumn foliage colour is making it increasingly popular.

Rowan

True Service Tree

Rowan
Rowan, regenerating

Sargent's Rowan

Wild Service Tree
Sorbus torminalis 25m

A medium-sized deciduous tree with a spreading or sometimes domed habit, depending on its situation. Its bark is finely fissured into squarish brown plates, thought to be the origin of one of its vernacular English names: 'Chequers'. The twigs are shiny and usually dark brown, terminating in rounded shiny-green buds about 5mm long. The leaves are up to 10cm long with 3–5 pairs of pointed lobes and a sharply toothed margin; the basal lobes project at right-angles, whilst the other lobes are pointed forwards. The leaves are amongst the first to change colour in the autumn, producing a rich display of reds and russets, and making the tree easy to find at this season.

Reproductive parts The white flowers, produced in May, are up to 1.5cm in diameter and produced in loose clusters on woolly pedicels. The fruit is up to 1.8cm in diameter, rounded and brownish, with numerous lenticels in the skin, and is normally ripe in September.

Habitat and distribution A native of much of Europe, including Britain, and normally found in copses and woodlands, especially ancient woodlands on heavier soils. This tree is often used as an indicator of ancient woodland.

Comments A further clue to the tree's other name is that a drink used to be made from the fruits and called 'checkers'.

Whitebeam
Sorbus aria 25m

A medium-sized deciduous tree, or sometimes little more than a shrub, with a spreading or, more often, domed crown. The smooth grey bark is sometimes ridged. The branches are spreading; the twigs are brown on the upper surface and usually green below and are hairy when young, becoming smooth later. The buds are up to 2cm long, ovoid and green and tipped with white hairs. The simple oval leaves are up to 12cm long, toothed or shallowly lobed at the margins and very hairy, especially on the underside which is white. When the leaves first open the white undersides are exposed and from a distance the whole tree looks white, but gradually it becomes greener as the upper leaf surfaces turn down and the leaves lose their white covering of hairs.

A number of cultivars are commonly planted in gardens and streets; 'Lutescens' has purple twigs, smaller leaves and a very neat, compact habit. 'Decaisneana' has larger leaves and the fruits are white-spotted on yellow stalks. 'Majestica' has larger, thicker leaves, sometimes up to 15cm long, and stronger, more upright branches.

Reproductive parts The white flowers are produced in stalked clusters, opening in May, and the fruits are ovoid, about 1.5cm long, bright red by September and covered with many small lenticels.

Distribution and habitat A widespread native tree in Britain and Europe, found in hedgerows and woodland edges, mainly on limestone and other calcareous soils, but often planted in towns and along roadsides.

Similar species
A large number of very similar and closely related species of *Sorbus* occur throughout Britain and Europe, many of them very rare and restricted to a small, local area. There are also numerous hybrids.

Greek Whitebeam *S. graeca* A small tree, but often little more than a large shrub with 9cm-long, leathery, double-toothed leaves, green above and woolly-white below. The fruits are rounded, 1.2cm long and red with conspicuous lenticels. A native of the Balkans and eastern Europe, but very similar to a number of other species occurring in the same area.

Wild Service Tree, autumn

Whitebeam, leaf underside

Whitebeam

Wild Service Tree, fruit

Wild Service Tree, buds

Species similar to Whitebeam

Rock Whitebeam S. rupicola A small tree, and often little more than a shrub, with simple, ovate leaves which are toothed with irregularly sized sharp, rather coarse teeth which curve on the outer edge and are all directed towards the apex. The leaves are densely woolly on the underside. The fruits are up to 1.5cm in diameter and rounded, becoming bright red when ripe and covered with many lenticels. A native of parts of Britain, Ireland, Scandinavia and Russia, usually in limestone areas.

S. umbellata A small tree or large shrub with simple, 7cm-long, roughly triangular leaves with shallow lobes bearing coarse teeth. The leaves are densely woolly and white on the underside. The white flowers are about 1.5cm across and the yellowish fruits are about 1.5cm in diameter and rounded. A native of the Balkans and Russia.

Austrian Whitebeam S. austriaca A small tree with leaves up to 8cm long, oval or elliptical with toothed lobes sometimes slightly overlapping, green above and white and hairy below. The typical Sorbus fruits are red, rounded, up to 1.3cm in diameter and pitted with large lenticels. A native of Austria, the northern Balkans and eastern Europe. Most common in hills and on lower mountain slopes.

S. lancastriensis A shrubby species mainly confined to limestone rocks in NW England. Leaves are ovate and toothed, downy beneath. Flowers and fruits are borne on slightly downy stalks. Fruits up to 1.5cm long and red with prominent lenticels when ripe.

S. anglica A shrubby species found mainly on rocky hillsides in SW England, Wales and Ireland, usually confined to limestone areas. Leaves are ovate, lobed and toothed, with a shiny upper surface and whitish, downy underside. Several similar species occur in other parts of Britain, Scandinavia, the Alps and the Pyrenees, including S. subsimilis.

Hupeh Rowan S. hupehensis A native of mountainous regions of China, noted for its unusual pink-tinged white berries. A popular garden tree in Europe.

Swedish Whitebeam
Sorbus intermedia 15m

A medium-sized tree with a stout bole, a broad crown and smooth grey bark with the occasional wide fissure. Young twigs are very hairy, but become smoother with age. The green buds are covered with grey hairs and become dark reddish-brown. The leaves, up to 12cm long, are oval and deeply lobed, looking like an intermediate stage between the entire leaf of Whitebeam and the compound leaf of Rowan. They are a glossy green above, but yellowish and downy below.

Reproductive parts The white flowers grow in flattish clusters; each flower is up to 2cm in diameter and 5-petalled. The oval fruits are about 1.5cm long, scarlet and speckled with lenticels.

Habitat and distribution A native of Scandinavia and the Baltic area, but because of its resistance to air pollution it is a popular urban tree, surviving in city centres and busy suburbs. The berries make a colourful display until found by birds.

Similar species
S. mougeottii 20m Very similar to Swedish Whitebeam, but the leaves are lobed only a quarter of the way to the midrib and the fruits have just a few small lenticels. A native of the western Alps and the Pyrenees and possibly a hybrid between Rowan and Greek Whitebeam.

Rock Whitebeam, berries

Swedish Whitebeam

Sorbus anglica, berries

Sorbus subsimilis, berries

Sorbus lancastriensis, berries

Hupeh Rowan, berries

Service Tree of Fontainebleau or Broad-leaved Whitebeam
Sorbus × latifolia 18m

A spreading tree with a rounded crown, and twigs which are downy at first but become shiny red-brown later. The leaves are alternate and rather leathery, up to 10cm long, and broadly oval with indistinct triangular lobes and double-toothed margins. The upper surface is shiny green, but the lower surface remains downy with greyish hair along the 7 to 9 pairs of veins. The trunk is often divided, with several stems arising from near the base.

Reproductive parts The white 5-petalled flowers can be up to 2cm in diameter, and grow on downy stalks in branched clusters. The rounded fruits are up to 1.5cm long, ripening to yellowish-brown, and the skin is pitted with large lenticels.

Habitat and distribution Probably a hybrid between Whitebeam and Wild Service Tree. This species was first recorded in the forests surrounding Fontainebleau, France, and is now to be found in suitable wooded habitats in W and central Europe. Many other similar hybrids are known from Britain and Europe, each one limited to a certain area. Most are capable of setting seed and growing true to type, thereby qualifying as distinct species.

Similar species
Devonshire Whitebeam or **French Hales** *S. devoniensis* 7m A medium-sized tree, or sometimes a large hedgerow shrub, with simple, toothed, leathery leaves, dark glossy green above and white below. Endemic to SW England.

Bastard Service Tree
Sorbus hybrida 14m

A medium-sized deciduous tree with a dense, rounded to conical crown. The greyish bark is usually slightly fissured. The twigs have a pink tinge and grow darker near to the tips. The buds are about 8mm long and covered with reddish-brown scales. The slightly leathery leaves are up to 10cm long, with the basal portion almost pinnate and the apex more shallowly lobed. The margins of the lobes are toothed near the tips and the leaf is grey-green on the upper surface and woolly-white below.

Bastard Service Tree

Reproductive parts The white flowers are produced in May and are up to 1cm in diameter; the fruit is about 1.2cm in diameter, rounded, bright red and pitted with small lenticels.

Habitat and distribution Native to woodlands in SW Scandinavia and planted elsewhere as a town or garden tree.

Similar species
S. meinchii A similar small tree to the Bastard Service Tree, with leaves that have a lower portion with free leaflets and the upper portion lobed. Flowers and fruits are very similar. Confined to Norway.

Service Tree of Fontainebleau

Devonshire Whitebeam

Service Tree of Fontainebleau

Devonshire Whitebeam

Devonshire Whitebeam, fruit

Loquat
Eriobotrya japonica 10m

A small evergreen tree or large shrub with hairy twigs and thick shoots and branches. The leaves are up to 25cm long, and mostly elliptic with toothed margins and prominent veins. They have a leathery texture, with a glossy-green upper surface and reddish-brown or sometimes grey down beneath.

Reproductive parts The flowers are borne in a densely packed branching terminal spike covered with down at first, opening to reveal white flowers 1cm across. The almost rounded white petals are sometimes hidden by the dense brown hairs. The fruit is rounded, yellow and fleshy, and about 6cm long, containing one or more seeds. It is sweet-tasting and edible. The fruits are borne in open clusters at the tips of the twigs.

Habitat and distribution A native of China, introduced to S Europe and cultivated as an orchard species, and sometimes for its ornamental glossy foliage. Will survive further north in Europe in sheltered places such as walled gardens.

SNOWY MESPILS *Amelanchier* Generally small trees or large shrubs with spineless branches and alternate leaves. Flowers are sometimes solitary or, more usually, in lax terminal spikes, and normally white. The rounded fruits, which are usually juicy, sweet and edible, retain the dried calyx at the tip.

Snowy Mespil
Amelanchier ovalis 5m

A small deciduous tree or shrub whose twigs are woolly when young. The leaves are up to 5cm long with coarsely toothed margins and downy undersides when first open.

Reproductive parts The flowers are produced in upright spikes of up to 8 white-petalled flowers with separate styles and these give rise to blue-black fruits.

Habitat and distribution A native of a wide area of Europe from France eastwards to Russia, and usually found on stony ground, especially limestone hills, and in open woodlands.

Similar species

American Snowy Mespil or **Allegheny Serviceberry** *A. laevis* 20m A small, smooth-barked tree with similar leaves to the Snowy Mespil's which produce a brilliant display of bright-red

American Snowy Mespil, flowers and fruits

autumn foliage. Flowers are borne in drooping spikes and the 6mm-long fruit is purple when fully ripe, retaining the sepals at the apex. Naturalized in parts of S England, but usually seen in gardens where its autumn colours make it a popular tree. *A. spicata* Very similar to Snowy Mespil, with finely toothed leaves, and flowers with fused styles and a hairy ovary. A N American species grown as an ornamental tree in N Europe and sometimes naturalized.

Canadian Snowy Mespil *A. canadensis* The leaves are mostly oblong and the apex of the ovary is smooth, otherwise similar to *A. spicata*. A native of NE America, grown as an ornamental garden tree.

Loquat, with fruit

Loquat

Snowy Mespil, unripened fruit

Snowy Mespil

Canadian Snowy Mespil

June Berry
Amelanchier grandiflora (lamarckii) 9m

A small deciduous tree with hairy young twigs, a short bole and a slightly spreading habit. The leaves are up to 7cm long, elliptic and finely toothed. When first open they have a purple tinge and a woolly texture, but they become smoother and green when older.

Reproductive parts Flowers are borne in drooping, slightly hairy spikes; the petals are white and up to 1.8cm long, but narrow. Each flower is supported on a 2.2cm-long pedicel. The fruits are deep purple when fully ripe and retain the dried sepals at the tip; they also often have a bloom like black grapes.

Habitat and distribution Probably a hybrid between two similar wild species, first arising in N America and subsequently introduced as a garden tree into Europe, where it is now sometimes naturalized.

COTONEASTERS *Cotoneaster* A family of about 70 shrubs of various sizes and habits and a single tree. Leaves are normally entire and the twigs are thornless. Flowers are usually white and the fruit is a berry.

Himalayan Tree Cotoneaster
Cotoneaster frigidus 20m

Sometimes grows as a medium-sized tree on a single upright bole, or may be a spreading shrub with many stems; there are no thorns or spines on the twigs. Sometimes the bole is blown over and many stems grow up vertically from the old one. The crown is usually domed. Young trees have a smooth, pale-grey bark. The leaves are simple and elliptical with entire margins and a dark-green upper surface; the lower surface is densely hairy and white. Leaves persist for a long time and are semi-evergreen.

Reproductive parts The flowers are small, but grouped into dense white clusters about 5cm across, and held upright at the tips of shoots. The fruits are about 5mm long and round and red all the way through. They are popular with birds, but often not taken until late in the winter.

Habitat and distribution A popular garden tree in NW Europe. Grows well in western areas, where the climate is similar to its native Himalayas; that is, with high rainfall and cool summers.

Medlar
Mespilus germanica 9m

Sometimes a small, rounded tree, or often a spreading and rather untidy shrub. The bark is greyish-brown, and in old trees breaks up into oblong plates with deep fissures between them. Young shoots are densely hairy. The leaves are up to 15cm long, and lanceolate to ovate with entire or sometimes very finely toothed margins and deep veins. They are often a yellowish-green colour and almost shiny above, with dense white hairs on the underside.

Reproductive parts The solitary white flowers are up to 6cm in diameter, with sepals longer than the petals and about 40 red anthers. The curious fruit is about 3cm long, divided into 5 carpels, with a brown russet-like skin and a sunken apex. It is edible, but not until it has started to rot, when it can be used in preserves.

Habitat and distribution A native species of the woodlands of SE Europe and Asia Minor, but has been in cultivation elsewhere for a long time. Usually found in old gardens, but is also naturalized in some woodlands.

June Berry

Himalayan Tree Cotoneaster

Himalayan Tree Cotoneaster

Medlar, fruit

Medlar

THORNS *Crataegus* A large and rather confusing group with many very similar species and numerous local forms. They are characterized by thorny twigs, and many also have attractive flowers and fruits, and good autumn colours. They are usually tough and resilient and survive in harsh conditions, including in city centres. Most are large shrubs or small trees, and can be pruned and trained into good stock-proof hedges.

Cockspur Thorn
Crataegus crus-galli 10m

A small, usually spreading deciduous tree with a flattish crown and a short bole. The bark of young trees is smooth and greyish-brown; in older trees it is fissured. The purple-brown twigs carry many 7–10cm-long sharp spines. The leaves are up to 8cm long and about 3cm wide, increasing in width above the middle, with a toothed margin. Both surfaces are smooth and shiny, dark green in summer and turning a rich orange in autumn, often before other species have started to show colour changes.

Reproductive parts The white flowers are about 1.5cm in diameter and grow in loose clusters, opening in May. The red globular fruits are ripe in October and persist after the leaves have fallen.

Habitat and distribution A native tree in NE America, and often planted in Europe as a garden or roadside tree, mostly for its striking orange autumn colours. Not as common as the 2 hybrids that follow.

Similar species

Hybrid Cockspur Thorn *C.* × *lavallei* A common tree in town gardens and on roadsides, recognized in winter by its level branches with twigs growing thickly on the upper side, and pale-grey, scaly bark. The leaves are narrow and glossy green, turning dark red late in the autumn.

Broadleaf Cockspur Thorn *C.* × *prunifolia* 8m A small, spreading tree with a short bole and a rounded crown. The leaves are oval and toothed, smooth and shiny and turn from glossy green, through yellow, orange and copper to a deep red by the end of autumn before they finally fall. The twigs and 2cm-long stiff thorns are a deep, glossy purple-brown. The fruits are rounded and red, up to 1.5cm long. A popular tree on roadsides and in gardens, and makes a good stockproof hedge.

Several other related *Crataegus* species occur in parks and gardens, chosen mostly for their spring blossom and colourful fruits in autumn. They may be grown as specimen trees, or sometimes incorporated into hedgerows. *C. latifolia* and the **Scarlet Hawthorn** *C. pedicellata* both have showy flowers and attractive summer foliage.

Cockspur Thorn

Hybrid Cockspur Thorn

Scarlet Hawthorn

Common Hawthorn
Crataegus monogyna 15m (18m)

A small, spreading deciduous tree or hedgerow shrub. It may grow on a single stout bole, or be multi-stemmed with a spreading crown. The bark is usually heavily fissured into a fairly regular pattern of vertical grooves; the outer layers are greyish-brown, and the lower layers are more orange. The branches and twigs are usually densely packed and there are numerous sharp spines. The leaves are up to 4.5cm long, roughly ovate and deeply lobed, usually with 3 segments. The lobes are pointed with just a few teeth near the apex. The leaves have a tough feel to them and are dark green above, paler below, with a few tufts of hair at the axils of the veins. The petiole is about 2cm long and pink-tinged.

Reproductive parts Flowers are produced in late spring in flat-topped clusters of about 10–18 white or sometimes pink-tinged flowers. Hawthorns growing in the open, and receiving plenty of sunlight, often flower prolifically and produce a heavy scent. Each flower is about 1.5cm in diameter with a single style in the centre. The fruits are rounded, sometimes more ovate, bright red or sometimes darkening to maroon. They are an important winter food for birds and small mammals.

Habitat and distribution A very common native across most of Europe, found in woods and hedgerows, and rapidly colonizing waste ground, roadsides and other disturbed habitats. Particularly abundant in drier limestone habitats. A useful species for training into stockproof hedgerows.

Comments Common Hawthorn hybridizes readily with other *Crataegus* species and identification can be very difficult in regions where they occur together.

Azarole
Crataegus azarolus 8m

A small tree with a spreading habit and flattish crown. The branches and twigs bear strong axillary spines up to 1cm long and young shoots are downy, becoming smooth later. Leaves are up to 5cm long, deeply lobed with up to 5 narrow, toothed, forward-pointing lobes, and the leaf base is often decurrent on a very short petiole.

Reproductive parts The flowers are borne on hairy stalks in a very compact cluster of up to 18 white flowers about 1.5cm in diameter. The anthers are reddish and there are 2–3 styles. The fruits are rounded with a slightly flattened base and resemble tiny greenish or orange-red apples, each one containing up to 3 seeds.

Habitat and distribution Naturalized in much of the Mediterranean, but probably native only to Crete and W Asia. Found mainly in scrub areas on limestone soils, and as a component of the maquis on hillsides. Long cultivated for its edible fruits, used in making preserves.

Oriental Hawthorn
Crataegus laciniata 10m

Young twigs, flower stalks and leaves are covered with long white hairs. Eventually young twigs become smooth and blackish. Leaves are deeply lobed, about 4cm long.

Reproductive parts Flowers grow in dense clusters of up to 16, fruits hairy at first, ripening to orange or red, containing 3–5 seeds.

Habitat and distribution Native to SE Europe, Spain and Sicily, found mainly on dry slopes and woodland edges and in scrub.

Common Hawthorn

Oriental Hawthorn

Common Hawthorn, spring

Azarole

Common Hawthorn, berries

Midland Hawthorn
Crataegus laevigata 10m

Often no more than a large shrub, but does sometimes grow into a dense but shapely, small, flat-topped tree. The grey bark cracks into regular-shaped plates which reveal browner patches beneath. There are some spines in the twig axils, but these are rarely more than 1cm long. The leaves are up to 6cm long, but not as

Midland Hawthorn

deeply or conspicuously lobed as those of Common Hawthorn. The lobes are more rounded and toothed to the base.

Reproductive parts Flowers, open in May–June, are borne in rather lax clusters of up to 9 normally white flowers which are up to 2.4cm in diameter and have 2–3 styles. Fruits are about 1cm long, rounded, and a deep-red colour. They are ripe between August and October.

Habitat and distribution A widespread native tree of W and central Europe, including Britain, but not as frequent as Common Hawthorn. Prefers shadier woodlands on heavier soils, and is often found in the understorey of oak-woods, although it does occur on more open limestone slopes. Hybridizes freely with other *Crataegus* species where they occur together.

Similar species

C. calycina 11m A small tree, or more often a shrub, with infrequent spines up to 11cm long. Leaves are up to 6.5cm long and broad, with 3–7 lobes, the basal lobe more deeply cut and finely toothed to the base. The underside of the leaf is slightly downy on the veins and the petiole. Flowers are borne in a lax raceme of up to 9 white flowers about 2cm in diameter. The 20 or so anthers are conspicuously red and there is a single style. The oval fruits are dark red and about 1.5cm long. A native of most of Europe, but not Britain or the warmer south. Prefers cooler, more shady habitats such as dense woodland, and replaces Common Hawthorn in the north and east.

Five-seeded Hawthorn *C. pentagyna* 8m A small Hawthorn with pendulous upper branches, pale-brown bark which splits to reveal yellow patches underneath, and spines about 1cm long. The slightly leathery olive-green leaves are about 5cm long, ovate and divided into 3–7 lobes; the lower 2 lobes often diverge widely. Flowers are borne in a lax cluster of typical white blossom; each flower has about 20 dark anthers and 3–5 styles. The fruit is rounded, sometimes ovate, and ripens to a dark blackened red or almost completely black. A native of the Balkans and E Europe, found mainly in open habitats and scrub.

CHERRIES, PLUMS AND PEACHES *Prunus*
A large group of trees and large shrubs with attractive flowers and mostly with edible fruits. The single style in each flower leads to the production of only one seed, or stone, inside each fleshy fruit, unlike the number of seeds in apples or pears, for example. Many are cultivated for their attractive spring flowers, and still more have been domesticated for their edible fruits. Wild species occur in a range of habitats and many are grown in gardens and commercial orchards.

Peach
Prunus persica 6m
A small deciduous tree, often rather bushy and rounded with smooth, reddish twigs, which are angular when cut across, and straight branches. Its true shape can be difficult to see, as this species is often trained against a wall for shelter. The leaves are alternate, lanceolate and finely toothed, and often creased into a V-shape.

Peach

Reproductive parts The attractive pink flowers are usually solitary, opening at the same time as the leaf buds. There are 5 petals, about 20mm long, and a cluster of yellow-tipped anthers. The fruit is the familiar peach which can be up to 8cm long and is rounded with a downy skin, flushed pink, and sweet, juicy flesh when ripe. The seed is contained inside a woody, thickly ridged 'stone'.

Habitat and distribution Probably a native of China, but long cultivated in gardens and orchards in Europe. It thrives in the warmer parts of Europe and is occasionally naturalized in the south. Further north it requires the protection of a walled garden. The Nectarine is a smooth-skinned cultivar of the Peach.

Almond
Prunus dulcis 8m
A small, open-crowned deciduous tree which is one of the first to burst into blossom in the spring. The blackish bark breaks up into small oblong plates. The ascending branches are rather spiny with numerous thin twigs if the tree is growing in the wild, but many of the numerous cultivated forms are more regularly branched and lack spines. The alternate leaves are up to 13cm long, finely toothed and folded lengthways.

Reproductive parts The pink or white flowers are paired and almost sessile, opening before the leaves early in the spring. The 5 petals are up to 2.5cm long and form a cup-shaped flower. The fruit is about 6cm long, a flattened ovoid shape and covered with velvety green down. Below this is a tough fleshy layer, and inside this is the ridged and pitted 'stone' which has to be cracked open to reveal the edible almond seed inside.

Habitat and distribution Probably a native to central and SW Asia and N Africa, but long cultivated around the Mediterranean for its edible seeds, and also for its attractive spring flowers. Grows well in most of Europe, but needs protection from frosty winds in the north of its range.

Peach

Almond

Almond, fruit

Almond, spring blossom

Almond

Apricot
Prunus armeniaca 10m

A small, rounded deciduous tree with a mass of twisted branches and smooth reddish twigs. The bark is greyish-brown with fine fissures. The heart-shaped leaves are reddish when first open, later becoming green above and more yellowish beneath, on a red petiole with 2 glands near the leaf base.

Apricot, flower

Reproductive parts The white or pale-pink short-stalked flowers are normally solitary, or sometimes paired, and open before the leaves early in the spring. The fruit is up to 8cm long and rounded, with a downy red-tinged skin surrounding a rather acid-tasting juicy flesh which becomes sweet only when fully ripe. The stone is a flattened elliptical shape and smooth, with 3 raised lines along one edge.
Habitat and distribution A native of central Asia and China, and commonly grown for its edible fruits in southern Europe, but also found further to the north in sheltered areas.

Myrobalan or Cherry Plum
Prunus cerasifera 8m

A small deciduous, rather bushy tree with many fine and sometimes spiny branches and glossy-green twigs. The bark is dark brown and pitted with rows of white

lenticels, and in older trees is fissured. The leaves are borne on 1cm pinkish, grooved petioles, are up to 7cm long and ovate, and taper at the base and the tip. The margins have numerous rounded teeth and the underside has downy veins.
Reproductive parts The white,

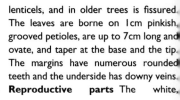

Myrobalan

stalked flowers are mostly solitary and open at about the same time as the leaves. The fruits are up to 3.5cm long, rounded, with a smooth red or yellow skin. The flesh becomes sweet and the smooth stone inside is rounded but has a thickened margin.
Habitat and distribution A native of scrub and copses in the Balkans, but widely planted elsewhere for its edible fruits used for pies and preserves, and also frequently naturalized.

Similar species
P. cerasifera var. *pissardii* has dark reddish-green leaves and pale-pink or rose-tinted flowers. It is often planted in town streets and parks for ornament.

Briançon Apricot *P. brigantina* Smaller and more spreading than Myrobalan, and has more sharply toothed leaf margins. Its flowers grow in small clusters and the fruits are rounded and yellow. An alpine species found on dry, open hillsides up to about 1,800m in France and Italy.

Myrobalan 'Atropurpurea'

Myrobalan

Myrobalan 'Atropurpurea'

Briançon Apricot

Blackthorn or Sloe
Prunus spinosa 6m

A rather untidy-looking, densely branched and spiny deciduous tree often surrounded by numerous suckers. The bark is dark blackish-brown and the spreading branches terminate in spiny twigs. The leaves grow on a 1cm-long petiole, are up to 4.5cm long, oval and pointed at the tip with toothed margins. The upper surface is smooth and a dull green, the lower surface is downy along the prominent veins.

Reproductive parts The mostly solitary white flowers open before the leaves; they are almost sessile or short-stalked and have 5 petals about 8mm long. They are often produced so prolifically that whole hedgerows can turn white for a brief period in early spring. The fruits are up to 1.5cm long, rounded to slightly ovoid, black or blue-black with a whitish bloom on the thin skin. The flesh inside is very acidic, and the stone is mostly smooth. The fruit is sometimes collected for use in making preserves or country wines.

Habitat and distribution A widespread and common native of much of Europe apart from the far north. Often forms dense, impenetrable thickets, and grows in hedgerows, copses and open woodlands.

Plum
Prunus domestica 10m

A small deciduous tree with straight branches and spiny twigs when growing as a wild plant; domesticated varieties usually have no spines. The bark is a dull brown and the twigs are also brown and smooth. The leaves are alternate, up to 8cm long, with toothed margins, a smooth green upper surface and a downy lower surface.

Reproductive parts The flowers are mostly white or sometimes green-tinged and hang in small clusters of 2–3 on a 1–2cm-long pedicel, opening at about the same time as the leaves in early spring. The fruits are up to 7.5cm long, rounded or more often oval, with a smooth skin. Depending on variety, in the domesticated forms, it may be yellow, red, purple or even green when ripe. The flesh is acidic at first, though never as sharply astringent as that of a sloe, but nearly always becomes sweet when ripe. The flattened oval stone is usually rough and slightly pitted.

Habitat and distribution Probably a hybrid between Blackthorn and Myrobalan, widely planted and naturalized throughout Europe, often found in copses and hedgerows and nearly always near human habitation. Numerous cultivars exist, each with a particular quality of fruit favoured for its flavour, colour or texture of flesh and suitability for cooking.

Similar species

Bullace *P. domestica* ssp *instita* The branches are usually spiny and the young twigs and flower stalks are downy. The rounded fruits are about 5cm long. The cultivated Greengage and Damson are the same sub-species.

P. cocomilia A smaller tree than the Plum with leaves no more than 4cm long and 2.5cm wide, smaller white flowers with petals up to 6mm long, and oval fruits, yellow, tinged with red. A scarce native of the mountains of S Italy, Sicily and the Balkans.

Blackthorn

Plum, fruit

Plum

Blackthorn, fruit

Blackthorn

Sour Cherry
Prunus cerasus 8m

A small deciduous tree with a very short, branching bole and a rounded shrubby outline, often surrounded by suckers. The bark is reddish-brown and the twigs are smooth. The leaves are up to 8cm long and borne on a 1–3cm-long petiole, oval to elliptic and sharply pointed at the tip, with a tapering base and toothed margin. Young leaves are slightly downy on the underside, and the upper surface is always smooth and shiny.

Sour Cherry, flower

Reproductive parts The long-stalked white flowers are usually open just before the leaves in April–May, and grow in clusters of 2–6. The fruits are up to 1.8cm long and rounded with a slightly depressed apex, and are usually bright red or blackish-red. The flesh is soft and tastes acidic, and the stone is rounded and smooth.

Habitat and distribution A species native to SW Asia, but widely cultivated elsewhere for its fruit which is used mainly in preserves when it loses much of its acidity. Also naturalized over most of Europe, occurring in hedgerows and copses and on waste ground.

Wild Cherry or Gean
Prunus avium 30m

A large deciduous tree with a good tapering bole and a high, domed crown. The bark is reddish-brown and shiny, with circular lines of lenticels, peeling horizontally into tough papery strips, and occasionally becoming fissured. The branches spread widely and terminate in smooth reddish twigs. The leaves are up to 15cm long, ovate with a long pointed apex and forward-pointing irregular teeth on the margins. The upper surface is smooth and dull, and the lower surface is downy on the veins. The 2–5cm-long petiole has 2 glands near the leaf.

Reproductive parts The white flowers grow in long-stalked clusters of 2–6, opening just before the leaves. The 5 petals are up to 1.5cm long. The fruits are up to 2cm long, rounded with a depressed apex and a dark-purple or red-black, or more rarely yellow, shiny skin. The flesh may be sweet-tasting or rather bitter. The stone is rounded and smooth.

Habitat and distribution A widespread native of much of Europe except the far north and east; less common in the drier Mediterranean regions. Grows in woods and copses, often in hilly areas, and is also cultivated for its fruit or its fine timber, used in turnery.

Comments This tree is often used as a stock for grafting other varieties of Cherry and is usually cultivated by cuttings. Birds are particularly fond of the fruits.

Wild Cherry

Wild Cherry

Wild Cherry

Wild Cherry, fruit

Sargent's Cherry
Prunus sargentii 13m (25m)

A deciduous tree which grows to a greater height in its natural habitat in the high hills of Japan than in the parks and gardens of Europe. The purple-brown, rather glossy bark is ringed with horizontal bands of lenticels. The branches are ascending or spreading and the dark-red twigs are thin and smooth. The leaves are up to 15cm long, ovate with a long-pointed tip, sharply toothed margins and a 2–4cm-long petiole. They are smooth on both surfaces.

Reproductive parts The flowers are pale pink and borne on 1–2cm stalks in clusters of 2–4, opening just before the leaves, usually in April. The petals are up to 2cm long. The fruits are up to 1.1cm long, ovoid and dark crimson, although they are rarely seen in cultivated trees.

Habitat and distribution A native of Japan where it normally grows above 750m, and the Sakhalin Islands where it may be found at lower altitudes.

Comments Usually grafted on to a stock of Wild Cherry, which grows faster than the graft and looks disproportionately large beneath the crown of fanned-out branches. Very popular as a garden and street tree, favoured for its early spring blossom and rich autumn colours, although rather a drab tree at other times.

Japanese Cherry
Prunus serrulata 15m

A small to medium-sized deciduous tree with purple-brown bark ringed by horizontal lines of prominent lenticels. The ascending branches usually fan out from the bole and terminate in smooth twigs. The leaves are up to 20cm long, ovate and drawn out to a long tapering tip, the margin is sharply toothed and the smooth petiole is up to 4cm long with up to 4 red glands near the base.

Reproductive parts The white or pink flowers grow in clusters of 2–4, opening just before the leaves; there are a number of cultivars so the flowers may be long-

stalked on a petiole up to 8cm, have notched petals, and vary in shade from pure white to deep pink. The round fruit are up to 7mm long and a deep purple-crimson, but they are unlikely to develop in cultivated trees.

Habitat and distribution Probably a native of central China, then introduced into Japan at a very early date, and subsequently brought to Europe where it is a very popular garden tree. Centuries of breeding and selection have made the modern trees different from their wild ancestors, which are rarely seen.

Similar species
Yoshino Cherry *P.* × *yedoensis* Similar to the Japanese Cherry, but the young twigs are downy, the flowers occur in clusters of 5–6 on 2cm pedicels and the pale-pink petals are deeply notched. A hybrid first seen in Japan, now popular as a street tree.

Saint Lucie Cherry
Prunus mahaleb 12m

Sometimes little more than a spreading shrub, but occasionally a small tree with greyish-brown bark ringed with lenticels and young twigs covered with short greyish hairs. The alternate leaves are up to 7cm long and almost rounded, with a short point at the tip and a rounded or nearly heart-shaped base. The margin is finely toothed, the upper surface is glossy and the lower surface finely downy.

Reproductive parts The white, scented flowers, which open in April–May, grow in clusters of 3–10 in groups of racemes at the end of leafy shoots. The 5 petals are about 8mm long and surround the yellowish anthers. The fruit is a 0.6–1cm-long ovate or rounded black berry with bitter-tasting flesh surrounding a smooth rounded stone.

Habitat and distribution A native of central and S Europe, growing in woodland glades and thickets, and naturalized elsewhere in N Europe. Several cultivated varieties exist and are grown for ornament in N Europe.

Sargent's Cherry

Japanese Cherry

Japanese Cherry, autumn

Japanese Cherry

Yoshino Cherry

Saint Lucie Cherry, fruit

Spring Cherry
Prunus subhirtella 20m

A densely crowned deciduous tree with greyish-brown bark, slender branches and numerous downy, crimson twigs. The leaves are up to 6cm long on a 1cm-long crimson, downy petiole, ovate to lanceolate with a long-pointed tip and an irregularly toothed margin. The veins are downy on the underside.

Reproductive parts The pinkish-white short-stalked flowers open just before the leaves in March or April; the petals are about 1cm long and notched. The purplish-black fruits are rounded but not produced freely in street trees. The Autumn Cherry *P. subhirtella* 'Autumnalis' is a common cultivar which is unusual in that it produces flowers throughout the winter from October to April.

Habitat and distribution A native of Japan, commonly planted as a street and garden tree. Various cultivars have been developed, some with a weeping habit, and some with double flowers. These are usually grafted on to stocks of Wild Cherry.

Similar species

Tibetan Cherry *P. serrula* Closely resembles Spring Cherry, but the deep-purple bark peels to reveal a rich and glossy mahogany-coloured inner layer. The branches spread widely on top of the fine bole; they are often pruned away to reveal more of the bark, the principal decorative feature of this tree. The bark is often very smooth in places where passers-by have been tempted to rub their hands on it. The leaves are up to 12cm long, lanceolate and pointed, and the white flowers open at the same time as the leaves in April–May. Bright-red fruits about 1cm long sometimes form.

Bird Cherry
Prunus padus 17m

A deciduous tree with smooth dark, grey-brown bark which releases a strong, unpleasant smell if rubbed. The thin branches are mostly ascending and terminate in twigs which are smooth, but finely downy when young. The alternate leaves are tough, with a dark-green upper surface and slightly blue-green underside, elliptical to elongate and up to 10cm long, finely toothed on the margins and tapering at the tip.

Reproductive parts The white flowers open after the leaves and grow in 15cm-long spikes which may be pendulous or ascending, composed of up to 35 5-petalled flowers smelling of almonds. The fruits are up to 8mm long, shiny black and sour-tasting, rather like sloes.

Habitat and distribution A widespread native across Europe, including Britain, but not the warmer Mediterranean regions. In the far north it takes the place of Wild Cherry. Usually found in limestone areas, on streamsides and in damp woods and hedgerows. Sometimes planted for ornament elsewhere as it is hardy, its blossom makes a good show for a short time in spring and its leaves are colourful in early autumn.

Similar species

Rum Cherry or **Black Cherry** *P. serotina* 22m (35m) A spreading deciduous tree with a stout trunk and greyish bark which peels away in strips and is fissured in older trees; a strange, bitter smell is released if the bark is damaged. The leaves are larger than those of the Bird Cherry at up to 14cm long, shiny above and with fine forward-pointing teeth on the margin; the midrib on the underside has patches of hairs along it, which help separate this species from other similar cherries. The flowers are very similar, but the spike may contain fewer than 30 flowers, the pedicels are shorter and the white petals are toothed at the margins. The black fruits contain a bitter-tasting flesh and a rounded smooth stone. A native of N America, planted for timber and ornament in much of Europe, and naturalized in many places, including S England.

Bird Cherry

Spring Cherry 'Rosea'

Bird Cherry 'Plena'

Bird Cherry 'Plena'

Tibetan Cherry

Portugal Laurel
Prunus lusitanica 8m
A small, spreading evergreen tree, or usually a shrub, with smooth or occasionally flaking black bark. The twigs are reddish and smooth and bear dark-green, glossy and slightly leathery leaves up to 13cm long. The leaves are lanceolate to elliptic and tapering at the tip, with a rounded base and a toothed margin. The reddish petiole is about 2cm long.
Reproductive parts The white flowers are borne in long tapering spikes, up to 26cm long and composed of about 100 strongly scented flowers. They grow out of the leaf axils and exceed the length of the leaves, and are usually pendent. The fruits are up to 1.3cm long, ovoid or rounded with a tapering tip, purplish-black when ripe and containing a smooth, rounded stone with a ridged margin.
Habitat and distribution A native of Portugal, Spain and SW France, but frequently planted elsewhere in the milder parts of W Europe for ornament and as a hedgerow shrub; it can survive regular clipping. May occasionally grow to a height of about 20m.

Cherry Laurel
Prunus laurocerasus 8m
An evergreen shrub or small, spreading tree with dark greyish-brown bark, pitted with numerous lenticels, and smooth pale-green twigs. The leathery leaves are up to 20cm long and 6cm wide, oblong with a short-pointed tip and rounded or tapering base, and a smooth margin with just a few very small teeth at intervals.
Reproductive parts The fragrant white flowers are borne in an erect spike about 13cm long, which is about the same length as the leaf plus the petiole (Portugal Laurel has a flower spike which greatly exceeds the leaf in length). The fruits are rounded and green at first, turning red and then finally blackish-purple. They contain a smooth rounded stone with a slightly ridged margin.

Habitat and distribution A native of the E Balkans and commonly planted as an ornamental species since the sixteenth century in the S and W of Europe; it is often found naturalized and also exists in a number of cultivars. Produces suckers freely, so often spreads out from the original planting to produce dense thickets.

PEA FAMILY, Leguminosae
A very large family of trees, shrubs and herbaceous plants which bear their seeds in pods. Their roots have colonies of nitrogen-fixing bacteria living on them in tiny nodules. All of the tree species have tough, durable wood and many of them are thorny. Most have compound leaves and very attractive flowers.

Plume Albizia
Albizia lophantha 7m
A small, spreading tree with striking fern-like foliage composed of pinnate leaves on downy petioles. Each leaf is divided into 16–20 pinnae, with each pinna supporting 40–60 6mm-long, curved leaflets which are smooth above and silky below.
Reproductive parts The yellow plume-like flowers are supported on very hairy peduncles; these are followed by flattened pods about 7.5cm long and 1cm across, containing oval or rounded seeds.
Distribution and habitat Introduced to the Mediterranean from SW Australia and used as an ornamental garden species.
Similar species
Pink Siris *A. julibrissin* 13m A small tree with smooth, spreading branches and pinnate leaves up to 40cm long; each leaf supports up to 25 pinnae and each pinna bears about 35–50 curved, ovate leaflets up to 1.5cm long, green above and white below. The pinkish-orange plume-like flowers are borne on branched hairy stalks and give rise to brown pods up to 15cm long, markedly constricted between the 10–15 seeds. A native of Asia, growing in lowland woods and marshy areas.

Portugal Laurel

Portugal Laurel

Cherry Laurel

Cherry Laurel

Plume Albizia, flowers

Pink Siris, flowers

Judas Tree
Cercis siliquastrum 10m

A small, spreading and rather flat-crowned deciduous tree with ascending branches, spreading near the tips, terminating in red-brown buds and twigs, and often with more than one bole. Old trees have more drooping branches. The simple, alternate leaves are rounded, sometimes notched at the tip and heart-shaped at the base. They are smooth on the upper surface and bluish-green when young, becoming more yellow when older, but paler and bluer on the underside.

Reproductive parts The 5-petalled, pink, pea-like flowers are borne in small short-stalked clusters, opening before the leaves and bursting out of the bole, large branches and smaller twigs. These are followed by a pod up to 10cm long, which is slightly constricted around the seeds, reddish at first, and then brown when mature and becoming dehiscent.

Habitat and distribution A native tree of the E Mediterranean region, occurring mainly in dry, stony country, but widely planted elsewhere as an ornamental tree and naturalized in many places. Survives in sheltered places in N Europe on dry calcareous soils.

Comments Once used as a sweetener by adding the petals to food.

Carob or Locust Tree
Ceratonia siliqua 10m

A small evergreen tree with a compact, domed crown and a dense mass of branches. The bole is short, often gnarled and fluted, and covered with greyish bark. The alternate leaves are pinnate, composed of 2–5 pairs of tough, leathery oval or rounded leaflets about 4cm long with a notched tip, a wavy margin and a shiny-green upper surface.

Reproductive parts The greenish flowers are small and borne in spikes of a single sex; male and female flowers may occur on the same or separate trees. There are no petals, and the 5 sepals drop early, leaving a tiny green disc supporting the stamens or a single style. The flattened pods are up to 20cm long, dark violet-brown and pendent, containing shiny-brown flattened oval seeds embedded in a white pith.

Habitat and distribution A native of the Mediterranean area, common in dry stony areas and often cultivated for fodder.

Honey Locust
Gleditsia triacanthos 45m

A tall deciduous tree with a high, domed crown. The branches and even the bole have numerous strong spines, some in clusters on the bole, and others branched. The alternate leaves are either pinnate, being composed of up to 18 pairs of 2–3cm-long leaflets, or bipinnate, consisting of up to 14 leaflets no more than 2cm long. The leaf axes end in spines, not a smaller leaflet as in many other pinnate leaves.

Reproductive parts The tiny flowers, which usually open in June, are no more than 3mm long, may be male, female or both, and grow in compact clusters in the leaf axils; the greenish-white oval petals number from 3 to 5. The striking flattened pods with their thickened edges can be up to 45cm long, but they are markedly twisted or curved and become dark brown when ripe.

Habitat and distribution A native of the Mississippi basin of N America, introduced to Europe as an ornamental tree, and occasionally for hedging on account of its powerful spines. Commonly planted in city centres in the USA. Cultivars lacking the spines are occasionally seen as specimen trees in parks and gardens in Europe.

Judas Tree, in flower

Judas Tree, flower

Carob

Carob, pods

Honey Locust

Mount Etna Broom
Genista aetnensis 10m

A small, upright tree with pendulous branches and twigs. The opposite leaves are very small and short-lived; they fall rapidly and photosynthesis is carried out by the green shoots which make the tree look as green in winter as it is in summer.

Reproductive parts The flowers are produced abundantly in midsummer and cover the whole tree in bright-yellow blossom. Each flower is about 12mm long and formed like a typical pea-flower with a keel and wings. The pods are ovoid and compressed laterally, containing only a few seeds.

Habitat and distribution A native of Sardinia and Sicily, occurring in dry hilly country, but commonly planted elsewhere in Europe as an ornamental tree.

Golden Wreath or Willow Wattle
Acacia cyanophylla 10m

A dense, shrubby small tree with one or more main stems, often suckering at the base. The bark is smooth and grey in young trees, becoming browner and fissured in older trees. The twigs are usually pendulous and pliant and finely ridged. The leaves are rather variable, between 10–20cm long and up to 3cm wide, mostly lanceolate, but sometimes curved and sickle-shaped, and may be green or blue-green with a smooth, shiny surface.

Reproductive parts The yellow flowers are minute but grouped together in globular heads which themselves hang in racemes of 2–8. The pods are up to 12cm long, markedly constricted between the seeds, and brown when ripe.

Habitat and distribution A native of W Australia and commonly planted in S Europe where it is used to stabilize sand-dunes, occasionally appearing as an ornamental tree elsewhere.

Comments The Wattles were given that name by early English settlers in Australia who used the branches for weaving hedges and as the basis for walls; in England they would have used hazel for this and called the woven panels 'wattle', so the most readily available material in Australia was given the same name.

Mimosa or Silver Wattle
Acacia dealbata 30m

An imposing, medium-sized tree with smooth, greenish-grey bark and silvery-white young shoots and foliage. A dense covering of fine hairs causes the silvery colour. Older trees have an almost black, fluted bark. The foliage is fern-like and composed of tripinnate leaves; the leaflets are only 5mm long, and there are numerous glands where the leaflets touch the rachis of the leaf.

Reproductive parts The bright-yellow flowers are minute, but 30–40 are grouped together in small globular heads which are themselves borne on long racemes of 20–30 heads. The tree flowers prolifically and can be a spectacular sight in spring. The pods are up to 10cm long and flattened, but not constricted between the seeds.

Habitat and distribution A native of SE Australia and Tasmania which grows well in the warmer regions of Europe. It can be used as a timber tree, for soil stabilization and for ornament. Hardy in the S and W of Britain, but cut down by severe winters.

Similar species

Sydney Golden Wattle A. *longifolia* 10m A small tree or shrub with a dense crown and bright green foliage. The leaves are about 15cm long and 3cm wide and striped with pronounced veins. The strong-smelling flowers are borne in single yellow spikes about 5cm long, and the pods are about 15cm long, mostly straight, and pinched between the seeds which have white stalks. A native of the coastline of New South Wales, Australia and introduced into Europe for sand-dune stabilization and for ornament.

Mimosa, in flower

Mimosa

Sydney Golden Wattle

Blackwood
Acacia melanoxylon 40m

A large tree with an erect trunk and dark greyish-brown, roughly grooved bark. The branches arise from low down on the trunk and are usually horizontal, but may be pendulous in older trees. The alternate leaves are up to 13cm long, lanceolate, blunt-tipped and sometimes slightly curved with 3–5 prominent veins. There may be some fern-like pinnate leaves as well, especially on younger trees.

Reproductive parts The creamy-white flowers are minute and grouped together in small globular heads in clusters in the leaf axils. The pods reach a length of 12cm and are flattened and twisted, containing seeds on bright-red stalks.

Habitat and distribution A native of SE Australia and Tasmania, brought to Europe as a timber tree and now naturalized in SW Europe. The timber is used as a veneer.

Similar species
Golden Wattle *A. pycnantha* 12m The leaves are bright green, lanceolate and have a single vein, and the flowers are bright duster-yellow, strongly scented and composed of racemes of 20–30 globular flower heads. It is the state flower of Australia, and found in the cooler areas of Victoria and S Australia. Naturalized in SW Europe, and planted elsewhere for tanning and occasionally for ornament.

Swamp Wattle *A. retinodes* 10m A small tree with a short bole, upward-curving branches and very narrow leaves less than 2cm wide but up to 15cm long. The pale-yellow, minute flowers are grouped into small globular heads, about 6mm in diameter, arranged in groups of 5–10 on a short, branched raceme. The pod is straight with slight constrictions between the seeds which are on scarlet stalks. A native of S Australia, introduced into Europe for ornament and now naturalized in the S and W.

Green Wattle *A. mearnsii* 15m The pinnate foliage is fern-like and dark green and the rachis has small glands between the pinnae. The flowers are yellow, minute and grouped into globular heads on a long trailing spike the same length as the leaf. The narrow pod is about 7mm wide and markedly pinched between the seeds. From SE Australia and Tasmania and naturalized in Spain and Portugal. Planted for ornament elsewhere in S Europe.

Pagoda Tree
Sophora japonica 24m

A medium-sized deciduous tree. It has furrowed bark, and an open, spreading crown with numerous twisted branches, and grows best in open, sunny sites. The young twigs are hairy and blue-green, becoming smoother and greener with age. The alternate leaves are pinnate, up to 25cm long and composed of 3–8 pairs of dark, shiny-green leaflets which are often hairy on the underside.

Reproductive parts The white or pale-pink flowers are pea-like and borne in clusters about 20cm across at the tips of twigs, usually late in the season (August–September). The pods are up to 8cm long, greenish and constricted between the seeds. Only large, mature trees produce flowers.

Habitat and distribution A native of E Asia, discovered in gardens in Japan and brought to Europe in the eighteenth century. Now planted in many parts of Europe and occasionally naturalized.

Blackwood, flowers

Pagoda Tree

Blackwood

Swamp Wattle

Common Laburnum
Laburnum anagyroides 7m

A deciduous tree with a narrow, sparse crown and a slender bole whose smooth greenish-brown bark is marked with occasional blemishes. The branches may be slightly pendulous and the shoots are grey-green and covered with long, silky, clinging hairs. The leaves are alternate and divided into three, each leaflet being up to 8cm long, elliptic and blunt-pointed at the tip, on a 2–6cm-long petiole, and hairy on the underside when young.

Reproductive parts The attractive yellow pea-like flowers are fragrant and copiously produced in 10–30cm-long pendulous racemes in early summer. The pods are up to 6cm long, with a smooth blackish-brown, dry outer skin. They remain on the tree until late in the year, twisting open to reveal the pale inner skin and the dark seeds.

Habitat and distribution A native of S and central Europe, but widely planted elsewhere in parks and gardens; one of the most popular and widespread of ornamental trees. An upland species in its native range, it thrives in towns and open countryside and is often naturalized.

Comments The seeds are very poisonous.

Similar species
Alpine Laburnum or **Scotch Laburnum** *L. alpinum* 5m Similar to Common Laburnum, but the twigs are hairy only for a short time when young, the leaflets are hairless and slightly glossy, and the racemes are up to 40cm long but look more slender and dense. The pod is less than 5cm long and slightly winged on one edge, and the seeds are brown, not black. A native of the mountains of central, S and SE Europe, but planted and naturalized elsewhere, where it may grow to 10m in sheltered sites.

Voss's Laburnum *L. × watereri* 11m A hybrid between Common Laburnum and Scotch Laburnum which shows the early-opening flowers of the first and the longer, more densely packed racemes of the second. Where laburnums are planted for ornament they are likely to be of this type, which has good hybrid vigour and makes a finer, longer-lived tree.

Robinia or Locust Tree or False Acacia
Robinia pseudoacacia 30m

A medium-sized deciduous tree with a fairly erect habit, an open crown and a short trunk with spirally ridged bark. There are sometimes several trunks in old trees, and the species suckers freely if grown in open situations on light soils. The alternate leaves are up to 20cm long, pinnate, comprising 3–10 pairs of oval yellowish-green leaflets; the petiole has 2 woody stipules at the base, and each leaflet also has a small stipule at the base of its petiole.

Reproductive parts The fragrant, pea-like flowers, which open in June, are white and grow in dense, pendulous clusters up to 20cm long. The pods are up to 10cm long, smooth, and remain on the tree long after the leaves have fallen.

Habitat and distribution A native of the Appalachian Mountains, USA but naturalized over a wider area of N America and also now very common in Europe as a garden and street tree and in the countryside, where it has also become naturalized in places.

Comments The timber is attractive and durable, although not often used in Europe. The early settlers in New England made good use of it for everything from tool-handles and kitchen spoons to furniture, fence-posts and firewood.

Similar species
R. pseudoacacia 'Frisia' 15m A smaller tree, with attractive golden-yellow foliage in summer which turns orange in autumn. It is very popular in smaller gardens and is becoming a common sight in towns.

Clammy Locust *R. viscosa* Very similar to *R. pseudoacacia*, but the flowers are pink and the hairy pods are sticky to touch. Native to the south-eastern USA.

Voss's Laburnum

Common Laburnum, seeds

Locust Tree 'Frisia'

Locust Tree 'Frisia'

Clammy Locust

CITRUS FRUIT FAMILY, Rutaceae

CITRUS A family of small trees with simple alternate, usually thin and leathery leaves, a winged petiole and a joint at the meeting of the blade. The flowers are solitary or in small spikes in the leaf axils and are usually white and fragrant. The fruit is a large, succulent, juice-filled berry with a colourful leathery skin. Many are of great commercial importance for their edible fruits and are widely cultivated: they are far more likely to be encountered in groves and orchards than in the wild state.

Lemon
Citrus limon 10m

A small, rounded tree with thorny branches and twigs and alternate glossy leaves, up to 10cm long, with minutely toothed margins and narrowly winged petioles. The bark is greyish with paler vertical stripes and mostly smooth.

Reproductive parts The white, sweet-scented flowers are mostly solitary or in small clusters in the leaf axils. The fruit is green at first, growing to a diameter of up to 12.5cm and ripening to yellow. The lemon is the only citrus fruit with a distinct protruding apex. The skin is thick and waxy, and aromatic when broken. Both fruits and flowers can be present on the tree at the same time, although most fruits ripen in the winter.

Habitat and distribution Probably a native of China or SE Asia, but long cultivated in the Middle East and then the Mediterranean, where it is now common and frequently seen in gardens, courtyards and groves of other *Citrus* species. Of great commercial importance to many Mediterranean countries. Not tolerant of frosts, so restricted to the warmer south of Europe.

Similar species

Citron *C. medica* A small tree with much larger lemon- or orange-coloured fruits, up to 25cm in diameter. The Sweet Lime *C. limetta* has a shorter, more rounded, greenish-yellow fruit which is more palatable when fresh than the lemon.

Sweet Orange
Citrus sinensis 10m

A small, rounded tree with alternate, elliptical, waxy leaves up to 10cm long on a short, winged petiole. The youngest twigs often bear spines.

Reproductive parts The white flowers are mostly solitary and very fragrant, growing in the leaf axils, and the petals surround numerous protruding stamens. The fruit is the familiar orange, usually around 7.5cm in diameter with an orange, aromatic skin, and sweet, very juicy flesh. The flowers are mostly seen in May, and the fruits ripen in the winter but, as in the Lemon, both fruits and flowers can be present at any time.

Habitat and distribution Grown in gardens, citrus groves and even naturalized in a few places. There are a number of cultivars, differing in size and shape of fruit and thickness of skin.

Similar species

Seville Orange *C. aurantium* Looks very similar, but the flowers may be even more fragrant and the fruit is palatable only when cooked or sweetened. The most popular fruit for making marmalade.

Tangerine *C. deliciosa* 8m A small, spreading tree, armed with spines. The leaves are elliptical and rather narrow and the flowers are smaller than Orange flowers. The fruits are smaller, usually up to 7.5cm in diameter with a thin, freely peeling orange rind.

Grapefruit *C. paradisi* 12m A larger, more densely branched and leafier tree than most other *Citrus* species. The leaves are up to 15cm long and elliptical to oval, growing on broadly winged petioles. The white flowers are larger than those of most other *Citrus* species and the fruit is also larger, at up to 15cm diameter, and rounded with a thick yellow skin.

Lemon

Sweet Orange

Sweet Orange

Sweet Orange

Tangerine

QUASSIA FAMILY, Simaroubaceae

A mainly tropical and sub-tropical family of about 20 genera and 150 species of trees and shrubs. Leaves are alternate and usually pinnate and the flowers are small and 5-petalled. The fruit is either winged or a capsule.

Tree of Heaven
Ailanthus altissima 20m (30m)

A vigorous deciduous tree which grows rapidly, developing a high and somewhat spreading crown. Its straight bole is often surrounded by suckers, some of them as far as 20m from the base of the tree. Young trees have a smooth, grey bark, and older trees have a paler and more scaly bark. The branches are thick and mostly ascending. The twigs are also thick and smooth, showing obvious leaf scars, and they terminate in tiny, ovoid scarlet buds. The alternate leaves are pinnate, and may reach a length of 60cm, comprising up to 25 7–12cm-long, pointed leaflets with irregularly heart-shaped bases. When first open the leaves are deep red, but they then become shiny green for the rest of the summer, falling early in the autumn without any significant colour change. Crushed leaves have a sour, 'catty' smell.

Reproductive parts The greenish flowers, which open in July, are strong-smelling and borne in fairly open spikes, usually all of the same sex, with males on one tree and females on another, although occasionally hermaphrodite flowers are produced. The fruits are in the form of reddish winged and twisted seeds about 3cm long.

Habitat and distribution A native of China, widely planted in Britain, Europe and the USA as a street tree and in parks, and in more southern areas as a shade tree in town squares or for soil conservation. It is often seen naturalized, either by its long-rooted suckers or by seed, produced prolifically in warmer climates.

MAHOGANY FAMILY, Meliaceae

A largely tropical family of about 600 species of trees and shrubs which may be deciduous or evergreen, but most have alternate pinnate leaves. The flowers are usually small and borne in clusters and the fruit is a dry capsule. Some of the trees produce the valuable hardwood, mahogany, and through exploitation are becoming very scarce.

Indian Bead Tree or Persian Lilac
Melia azedarach 15m

A graceful, small deciduous tree, usually quite short-lived, with a spreading, open habit. The bole is usually short and covered with dark grey, slightly furrowed bark. The twigs are slightly hairy. The alternate leaves are bipinnate, up to 90cm long and composed of many small, oval,

Indian Bead Tree

glossy leaflets, each one up to 5cm long, pointed at the tip and toothed or slightly lobed on the margins.

Reproductive parts The lilac-coloured, scented flowers are composed of 5 or 6 narrow, divergent petals and a tube-like group of stamens, and they usually open in June. The fruits are rounded and yellow, about 18mm long, and contain one seed.

Habitat and distribution A native of SE Asia, usually occurring in drier, hilly habitats. Planted in the Balkans and S Europe for ornament and sometimes as a shade tree.

Tree of Heaven

Tree of Heaven

Indian Bead Tree, in flower

Indian Bead Tree, fruit

CASHEW FAMILY, Anacardiaceae

A large family of more than 800 species of trees, shrubs and climbers found mainly in warm climates. They may be deciduous or evergreen, but most have alternate leaves which can be simple or pinnate, and many, such as poison ivy, have an irritant resin in the leaves which can damage human skin. The flowers are small and the sexes are often on different plants.

Stag's-horn Sumach
Rhus typhina 10m

A small, spreading deciduous tree with downy, forked branches and twigs. The crown is usually rounded and the tree may have more than one trunk arising from suckers. The alternate leaves are pinnate, with up to 29 leaflets, each leaflet up to 12cm long, coarsely toothed and sometimes shallowly lobed at the base. The leaves produce a splendid display of fiery autumn colours, and when they fall the fruiting heads are an attractive feature.

Reproductive parts The very small flowers are of separate sexes; male flowers are greenish and female flowers are red, both are borne in dense conical clusters up to 20cm long at the tips of twigs, with the sexes separated on different trees. The fruits resemble small nuts, about 4mm long, and are borne in dense reddish heads which persist through the winter.

Habitat and distribution Native to eastern N America and common in many open habitats there, but also very common in gardens in Europe, and becoming naturalized in places.

Similar species

Common Sumach *R. coriaria* 3m Never more than a shrub, with semi-evergreen leaves, white flowers and a brown fruiting head. A native of S Europe, occurring in dry, rocky places and growing amongst scrub.

Varnish Tree *R. verniciflua* 14m A larger deciduous tree with a domed habit and aromatic leaves, clusters of yellow flowers and poisonous pale-brown fruits. A native of Japan, planted in Europe as an ornamental species.

Pepper Tree *Schinus molle* 12m A pendulous evergreen tree with long, trailing clusters of tiny white flowers and shiny-pink fruits. The alternate pinnate leaves are composed of up to 13 pairs of leaflets up to 6cm long and smelling of pepper if crushed. A native of central and S America, growing mainly in mountains, and introduced into S Europe where it is sometimes naturalized, from Portugal to

Pepper Tree

Greece. The **Brazilian Pepper Tree** *S. terebrinthifolia* is very similar, but without the pendulous foliage. The fruits are bright red.

Stag's-horn Sumach, flower

Stag's-horn Sumach

Pepper Tree, fruit

Stag's-horn Sumach, winter

Brazilian Pepper Tree

Mastic Tree
Pistacia lentiscus 8m

A bushy, often rather untidy-looking evergreen tree with very aromatic leaves and fruits. The twigs are hairless, but have a rough feel because of the prominent lenticels. The dark-green leaves are alternate and divided into 3–6 pairs of small, leathery, spine-tipped oval leaflets, each one no more than 5cm long.

Reproductive parts The flowers, which open in April, grow in dense, conical heads up to 5cm long; there are no petals, but the anthers and styles are colourful and vary from yellow through red to purplish-red. The fruits are about 4mm long, rounded with a pointed tip and aromatic, ripening from red to black.

Habitat and distribution A widespread and common native of the Mediterranean from Portugal to Turkey, occurring on dry, rocky slopes and woodland edges.

Pistachio
Pistacia vera 6m

Usually little more than a large deciduous shrub, with rough, ridged bark and grey twigs. The grey-green leaves can be simple or pinnate, with rarely more than 3 ovate, rather thin leaflets, each one up to 9cm long. Young leaves are downy, but become smoother with age. The petiole remains downy and the central rachis has slender wings.

Reproductive parts The small green flowers are borne in open spikes about 10cm long and give rise to ovoid edible seeds covered with a reddish skin and encased in a hard outer shell.

Habitat and distribution A native of W Asia, widely cultivated around much of the Mediterranean for its edible pistachio nuts which are an important cash crop in some areas. Naturalized in some places.

Turpentine Tree
Pistacia terebrinthus 10m

A small tree or, more often, a sprawling shrub, with resinous leaves and twigs and a sticky texture. Resembles Mastic Tree, but the pinnate leaves are larger at up to 8.5cm and there may be as many as 9 leaflets on a cylindrical, not winged, leaf axis.

Reproductive parts The greenish or purple-tinged flowers, which open in March or April, have no petals and are borne in long, rather lax clusters, with male and female flowers on separate trees. Small ovoid, pointed fruits are produced in summer, starting off a shiny-red colour, but becoming purple-brown when ripe.

Habitat and distribution A common species of scrub and sparse woodland on dry calcareous soils across most of the Mediterranean region from Portugal to SW Asia.

Similar species

P. atlantica Seems to be incorrectly named as it occurs only in the E Mediterranean region from Greece to the Crimea, and not anywhere near the Atlantic coasts. It has narrow leaflets with blunt tips, hairy petioles (view through a hand-lens) and narrow wings on the leaf axes.

Mastic Tree, fruit

Mastic Tree

Pistachio, nuts

Turpentine Tree

Turpentine Tree

MAPLE FAMILY, Aceraceae

A family of about 100 species of trees and shrubs, some evergreen, some deciduous, mostly occurring in northern temperate regions. Leaves are opposite and nearly always lobed, and sometimes divided into leaflets. Flowers are small, and the seeds are winged, in 2 halves. Many have beautiful autumn colours and are popular garden trees, and some are important timber-producing trees.

Field Maple
Acer campestre 26m

A medium-sized deciduous tree with a rounded crown and a twisted bole. The bark is grey-brown and fissured and the shoots are brown, sometimes covered with fine hairs and often developing wings, especially in trees regularly pruned back in hedgerows. Rather variable in appearance, much depending on its habitat. The opposite leaves are up to 12cm long and usually strongly 3-lobed, and the lobes themselves often have lobed margins and tufts of hair in the axils of the veins on the underside. Newly opened leaves have a pinkish tinge at first, becoming dark green and rather leathery later. They turn bright yellow in autumn, producing an excellent splash of colour in hedgerows.

Reproductive parts The yellowish-green flowers are borne in small, open, erect clusters; there are 5 sepals and 5 petals, and male and female flowers occur together, opening at about the same time as the leaves in April–May. The winged fruits grow in bunches of 4; the wings are horizontal and greenish tinged with varying amounts of red. The hard seeds are at the base.

Habitat and distribution A widespread and common native tree in N Europe, occurring in woods and hedgerows, and also planted for its beautiful autumn colours.

Sycamore
Acer pseudoplatanus 35m

A fast-growing and vigorous deciduous tree with a very spreading habit and a broadly domed crown. The greyish bark is broken up by numerous fissures into irregular patches which sometimes fall away, leaving more orange-coloured areas beneath. The branches are usually quite thick near the main bole, terminating in grey-green twigs with pale lenticels and reddish buds. The opposite leaves are up to 15cm long, and divided into 5 toothed lobes; immature and fast-growing trees have deeply cut leaves and long scarlet petioles, whereas older, slow-growing and more senile trees have smaller leaves with shallower lobes and shorter pink or green petioles. The leaves produce a cheerful bright-green display when first open in spring.

Sycamore,
male flower

Reproductive parts Flowers are normally produced prolifically in slender, pendulous, yellow clusters up to 12cm long, opening at about the same time as the leaves in April–May. The paired fruits ripen in late summer and reach a length of 6cm, starting off green, then becoming redder and finally brown and dried.

Habitat and distribution A native species of the hills and uplands of central and S Europe, but widely planted and naturalized abundantly elsewhere. Very invasive and can dominate some woodlands to the exclusion of all else.

Sycamore,
female flower

Field Maple, autumn

Field Maple, autumn

Field Maple

Sycamore, flowers

Sycamore 'Prinz Handjery'

Sycamore, seeds

Norway Maple
Acer platanoides 30m

A tall and spreading deciduous tree with a relatively short bole and a high, domed crown. The smooth grey bark is sometimes slightly ridged. The branches are less crowded and thinner than those of the Sycamore and the twigs are green, sometimes tinged with red. The bright-green, smooth leaves are up to 15cm long with 5–7 toothed and sharply pointed

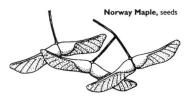

Norway Maple, seeds

lobes. The lowest pair of lobes are smaller than the others, and there are white hairs in the axils of the veins on the paler underside of the leaf.

Reproductive parts The greenish-yellow flowers are borne in compact erect clusters of 30–40, opening before the leaves in March–April; males and females are separate. The paired, yellowish fruits are up to 10cm across.

Habitat and distribution A native tree of the forests of much of Europe but not Britain, where it is introduced and naturalized, and found only at higher altitudes in the south. Widely planted as an ornamental tree in towns, gardens and parks, and often used as a street tree. The cultivar A. *platanoides* 'Crimson King' has dark-red foliage and is a popular tree for municipal plantings.

Comments Many large maples, including Sycamore and Norway Maple, produce hard, light-coloured wood, ideal for wood-turning and making kitchenware. The best bread-boards are made out of sycamore.

Montpelier Maple
Acer monspessulanum 15m

A small deciduous tree with a neatly domed crown and blackish or grey fissured bark. The smooth twigs are thin and brown, terminating in small, ovoid orange-brown buds. The leathery leaves are up to 8cm long, with 3 spreading lobes, entire margins, a shiny dark-green upper surface and a bluish underside with a few tufts of hairs in the axils of the lower veins. The petiole is about the same length as the leaf and orange-tinted. The leaves are a fresh green in the spring, but look very tough and dark in summer, and remain on the tree until well into the autumn.

Reproductive parts The yellowish-green flowers, which open after the leaves, are borne in small clusters on long, slender pedicels which are upright at first but become pendent later. The red-tinged fruits are about 1.2cm long, with parallel or overlapping wings.

Habitat and distribution A native of S Europe, mostly from warmer, drier hilly areas, but planted as an ornamental species elsewhere, including Britain.

Heldreich's Maple
Acer heldreichii 25m

A medium-sized deciduous tree with smooth grey, sometimes pink-tinged and slightly fissured bark, ascending branches, red-brown twigs terminating in sharp-pointed dark red-brown buds, and a high domed crown. The leaves are up to 17cm long, with 3–5 deep lobes; the middle lobe is cut away to the base and coarsely toothed on the margin. The leaves are usually a fresh green above, and bluish green below with hairs on the lower veins.

Reproductive parts The yellowish flowers, opening with the leaves, are borne in mostly erect clusters, but are rather sparsely scattered over the tree. The fruits are up to 5cm long with incurved reddish wings and greenish seeds.

Habitat and distribution A native of the mountains of the Balkans, occasionally planted elsewhere in Europe as an ornamental, and mostly seen in specialist collections.

Norway Spruce

Norway Maple, fallen autumn leaves

Norway Maple, seeds

Norway Maple, winter

Montpelier Maple, young tree

Montpelier Maple

Balkan Maple
Acer hyrcanum 16m

A small deciduous tree with ascending branches and a domed crown. The bark is grey-brown, breaking up into squarish plates in older trees. The buds are covered with red-brown scales with greyer margins. The 3–5 lobed opposite leaves are up to 10cm long on a long, slender, pinkish (sometimes yellow) petiole. The lobes are usually parallel-sided and cut about half-way to the base, with a few teeth on the margins. The upper surface is green and smooth and the lower surface is paler with some hairs on the veins. **Reproductive parts** The yellowish flowers are rather sparse, opening before the leaves, on short slender pedicels. Male and female flowers are separate. The fruit is up to 1.5cm long with parallel, sometimes diverging wings, growing in clusters of 6–8 on thin greenish pedicels. **Habitat and distribution** A native of the woods of the Balkans and the Caucasus, but infrequently planted elsewhere, mostly as an ornamental species.

Similar species
Acer granatense Very much like Balkan Maple, but the leaves are smaller, reaching a length of only 7cm, and the leaf undersides, young petioles and young twigs are hairy. A rare species restricted to S Spain, Majorca and N Africa.

Cretan Maple
Acer sempervirens 12m

Sometimes little more than a shrub, but occasionally a small, compact evergreen tree with tangled, twisted branches and shiny-brown twigs. The smooth bark is grey with a few lighter patches in places. The opposite leaves are up to 5cm long and often 3-lobed, but occasionally irregular or simple with untoothed margins. **Reproductive parts** The greenish flowers, which open in April, are borne in small erect clusters and are rather sparse. The fruits are green or red-winged, with the wings either parallel or slightly divergent. **Habitat and distribution** A native of Crete and Greece, occasionally seen elsewhere as an ornamental tree, although not hardy in very cold areas where it may cease to be an evergreen.

Italian Maple
Acer opalus 20m

A small deciduous tree, but occasionally a large shrub, with a broad domed crown, low spreading branches and brown twigs marked with pale lenticels. The smooth, dark-green leaves are up to 10cm long with 3–5 lobes, hairy on the underside in young leaves, and on the veins only in older leaves. The petiole is shorter than the leaf and is red on the upper surface, green below. The leaves turn yellow in autumn. **Reproductive parts** The large pale-yellow flowers are pendulous, on yellow petioles, and thinly distributed over the tree, opening just before the first leaves in April, making the tree an attractive and conspicuous specimen in a mixed woodland. The small parallel-winged fruits are about 2.5cm long in clusters of 8–16; the wings are greenish, becoming pinker, and the seeds are red or brown when ripe. **Habitat and distribution** A native of the hills and mountains of the W Mediterranean and Alps, and occasionally found elsewhere in parks and gardens.

Similar species
The very similar *A. obtusatum* has larger leaves, up to 12cm long with 5, or more rarely 3, broad rounded lobes and a very hairy underside and petiole. Native to Italy and the W Balkan region.

Italian Maple, flowers and seeds

Acer obtusatum, in flower

Box Elder or Ash-leaved Maple
Acer negundo 20m

A small but vigorous deciduous tree with numerous shoots growing from the bole and the main branches, giving it a rather crowded and untidy appearance. The smooth bark of young trees is replaced by darker, shallowly fissured bark in older trees. The small buds have only 2 whitish scales. The pinnate leaves are up to 15cm long with 3 or sometimes up to 7 irregularly toothed oval leaflets.

Box Elder

Reproductive parts The male and female flowers occur separately, opening in March before the leaves. There are no petals on either; the male flowers are greenish with prominent red anthers, and the female flowers are greenish-yellow and pendent. The brown fruits are about 2cm long with the wings slightly spreading, remaining on the tree after the leaves have fallen.

Habitat and distribution A native of eastern N America, commonly planted as an ornamental tree, and sometimes for shelter. Becoming naturalized in some areas.

The cultivar 'Variegatum' is now a common street and town park tree, best recognized by its green and yellow variegated leaves, although it does sometimes revert to the plain green colour of the original tree. The variegated form bears only female flowers.

Smooth Japanese Maple
Acer palmatum 16m

A small deciduous tree with a very short and usually twisted bole, and a domed crown. Young trees have a smooth brown bark with paler patches, but these tend to disappear as the tree ages. There are numerous spreading branches which end in thin reddish twigs with green undersides. The leaves are up to 9cm long, with 5–7, sometimes 11, toothed lobes divided at least half-way to the base of the leaf.

Reproductive parts The dark purple-red flowers are borne in upright clusters of 12–15 on thin green or red 4cm-long pedicels, usually opening in April–May. The reddish fruits usually hang in clusters, each fruit being about 2cm across with the 2 wings diverging widely.

Habitat and distribution A native of the woodlands of both the lowlands and the mountain slopes of Japan, introduced into Europe for its compact shape, interesting foliage and fine autumn colours. Two cultivars are commonly planted in parks and gardens; 'Atropurpureum' has fine purple leaves through the season, and 'Osakazuki' has brilliant scarlet autumn leaves and fruits.

Similar species
Downy Japanese Maple *A. japonicum* 14m Similar in habit to Smooth Japanese Maple, but the bole may be even shorter, and the leaves are hairy when young, with the veins remaining hairy through the season. The leaves are lobed, but divided less than half-way to the base, with forward-pointing teeth on the margins. The purple flowers grow in long-stalked, pendulous clusters, opening just before the leaves. The paired, winged fruits are up to 5cm across with the wings diverging widely, and the margins are hairy at first. The cultivar *A. japonicum* 'Vitifolium' is popular for its bright-red autumn colours.

Box Elder

Smooth Japanese Maple

Smooth Japanese Maple
Downy Japanese Maple 'Vitifolium'

Smooth Japanese Maple 'Atropurpureum'
Downy Japanese Maple

Sugar Maple or Rock Maple
Acer saccharum 26m

Can be overlooked as a Norway Maple, but the bark has large fissures and falls away in shreds in older trees. The 13cm-long leaves are lobed, but the teeth on the lobes are rounded, not drawn out into a fine point as in the Norway Maple, and there are hairs in the vein axils on the underside.

Reproductive parts The pendulous yellow-green flowers are small and lack petals, opening in spring with the leaves.

Habitat and distribution A native of deciduous woodlands in eastern N America, introduced into Europe for its autumn colours, although specimens in gardens do not always fulfil the promise of wild trees. **Comments** The sap is collected and made into maple syrup.

Silver Maple
Acer saccharinum 30m

A broadly columnar deciduous tree with a spreading crown and many slender ascending branches with pendulous brownish twigs. The smooth greyish bark becomes scaly as the tree ages, and numerous suckers emerge from various parts of the bole. The leaves are up to 16cm long, deeply divided into 5 lobes with irregularly toothed margins, orange or red-tinted when first open, becoming green above later, but with a silvery appearance below due to a thick covering of hairs. The thin petiole is usually pink-tinged.

Reproductive parts The yellowish-green flowers are borne in small short-stalked clusters of separate sexes in spring; there are no petals. The green, then brown, fruits are about 6cm long, with diverging wings and prominent veins. It rarely ripens in Britain, usually being shed in late spring.

Habitat and distribution A native of eastern N America, usually growing in damper soils such as along riverbanks, but introduced into Europe as an ornamental tree, especially in towns. The cultivar *A. saccharinum* 'Laciniatum' is frequently seen in city squares and other municipal plantings.

Red Maple
Acer rubrum 23m

A fast-growing and vigorous deciduous tree with a rather spreading habit and an irregular crown. The branches are mostly ascending, but arch outwards. The grey bark is mostly smooth. The leaves are up to 10cm long and almost as wide, with 3–5 toothed lobes which are less than half the width of the leaf. They are red-tinged above when first open, becoming greener later, and are silvery on the underside, with a red petiole. In autumn they turn a variety of shades of red and yellow.

Reproductive parts The small red flowers are borne in dense clusters on thin pedicels, opening in spring before the leaves. Males and females are separate, and as they mature the pedicels grow longer, with the female flower stalk ending up the longest. The bright-red winged fruits are about 1cm long, the wings diverging at a narrow angle.

Habitat and distribution A native of eastern N America, usually growing in damp habitats, and often seen elsewhere as an ornamental tree, especially for its multi-coloured autumn foliage, but its red spring colours are also attractive.

Tartar Maple
Acer tartaricum 10m

A small deciduous tree, with a smooth, brown, lightly striped bark. The opposite leaves are up to 10cm long, often entire, but sometimes divided into 3–5 shallow lobes with a finely toothed margin. The leaf base is usually heart-shaped and the white or red-tinged petiole is up to 3.5cm long.

Reproductive parts The greenish-white flowers are borne in upright spikes of about 20–30, the sexes being separate, normally opening after the leaves in May. The red fruits are about 2.5cm long, with a green edge to the wings, and are hairy at first, becoming smooth when ripe. **Habitat and distribution** A native of S and central Europe to the Crimea.

Sugar Maple

Sugar Maple, autumn

Silver Maple

Red Maple, fallen autumn leaves

Red Maple

Red Maple, autumn
Tartar Maple, in flower

Nikko Maple

Acer nikoense 15m (20m)

A broadly spreading deciduous tree with greyish-brown, smooth bark and small, blunt, blackish buds which have grey hairs on the scales. The compound leaves are made up of 3 leaflets, the central one up to 10cm long, the other 2 smaller and unequal at the base. They are mostly green and smooth on the upper surface, but bluish-white below with a covering of soft hairs. They turn a bright fiery red in the autumn.

Reproductive parts The small yellow flowers are borne in pendulous clusters of 3, on hairy stalks, opening at about the same time as the leaves. The green, winged fruits are about 5cm long, and the wings spread widely, but the seeds are rarely fertile or fully formed.

Habitat and distribution A native of wet ground and streamsides in Japan, and now popular in Europe as an ornamental tree, mostly for its fine autumn colours.

Similar species

Paper-bark Maple *A. griseum* 15m The most distinctive feature is the reddish-brown bark which peels off in thin papery scales. The pinnate leaves are divided into 3 blunt-toothed leaflets and the yellow-green flowers are small, growing in drooping clusters. The pale-green winged fruits are about 3cm long. A native of central China, not common elsewhere except in gardens and parks.

Rough-barked Maple *A. triflorum* 12m Best recognized by its pale, grey-brown bark which peels in vertical strips. The pinnate leaves are composed of 3 sparsely toothed, bristly-hairy leaflets which turn a bright orange or red in the autumn. A native of mountain woodlands in NE China and Korea, popular in gardens in Europe for its autumn colours.

Moosewood

Acer pennsylvanicum 14m

One of the 'snakebark maples' with attractive green, vertically striped bark: the stripes are usually reddish-brown or white, and the bark becomes greyer as the tree ages. The leaves are up to 15cm long and about the same width with 3 triangular forward-pointing lobes which taper to slender points, the central lobe being the longest. In summer the leaves are a rich yellow-green with a smooth upper surface and a hairy lower surface when first open. In autumn they turn a deep yellow but do not remain on the tree for long. As in other snakebarks, the buds are stalked.

Reproductive parts The small yellow-green flowers hang in pendulous racemes, appearing in spring at about the same time as the leaves. The greenish fruits are about 2.5cm long and have downcurved wings.

Habitat and distribution A native of N America, occurring mainly in lowland woods on damper soils, but now a very popular garden tree because of its attractive bark (seen well in winter), its rich autumn colours, and its compact size and shape.

Comments The name 'Moosewood' originated in N America because in hard winters Moose strip off the bark for food

Similar species

There are several other maples with similarly attractive bark, but they all originate from China and Japan.

Pére David's Maple *A. davidii* 16m The commonest in gardens, in a variety of cultivars, some of which show poor autumn colours but have fine bark.

Red Snakebark Maple *A. capillipes* 16m Has bright scarlet shoots and leaf stalks and boldly striped bark.

Nikko Maple

Nikko Maple

Paper-bark Maple

Moosewood, flowers
Moosewood

Pére David's Maple

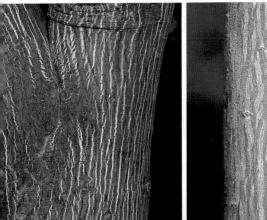

SOAPBERRY FAMILY, Sapindaceae

A very large family of trees, shrubs and climbers, mainly confined to tropical and sub-tropical regions. The leaves are alternate and may be simple or more complex. The flowers are small and 5-petalled and the sexes are separate. The fruit can be winged, a capsule, a nut or a berry.

Pride of India or Golden Rain Tree
Koelreuteria paniculata 15m

A broadly spreading deciduous tree with pale-brown, slightly fissured bark revealing more orange-coloured patches beneath. The youngest shoots are slightly downy. The alternate, dark-green pinnate leaves are up to 40cm long, composed of up to 15 ovate–triangular leaflets, each one 3–8cm long and coarsely toothed or almost lobed. **Reproductive parts** The 4-petalled yellow flowers are borne in large spikes up to 40cm long; each flower is about 1.2cm across and has 8 stamens. The fruits are conical, inflated capsules, about 5.5cm long, divided internally into 3 valves containing black seeds.

Habitat and distribution A native of China and Korea, growing mainly in hot, dry lowland habitats, but widely planted in S and E Europe as a roadside or park tree, and becoming naturalized in places.

HORSE CHESTNUT FAMILY, Hippocastanaceae

A family of 2 genera and 15 species of deciduous trees and shrubs occurring in N America, SE Europe and E Asia. The compound leaves are strongly palmate, and the showy flowers are 4- or 5-petalled, growing in large upright clusters at the ends of the shoots, usually in summer. The fruits are large shiny nuts in a variably prickly husk. The timber is not particularly strong for such a large tree, and is best used for carving and turnery.

Horse Chestnut
Aesculus hippocastanum 25m

A large deciduous tree with a massive, domed crown. The bark is greyish-brown, often flaking away in large scales. The reddish-brown twigs have numerous whitish lenticels. The winter buds are a conspicuous and familiar feature, being shiny-brown and sticky, up to 3.5cm long. The large, long-stalked leaves are composed of up to 7 leaflets up to 25cm long, the central leaflets being the longest, all of them sharply toothed and elongate-oval. The upper surface is mostly smooth,

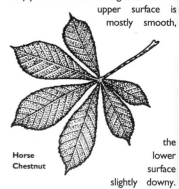

Horse Chestnut

the lower surface slightly downy.

Reproductive parts The flowers are produced prolifically, often covering the tree in a mass of creamy-white panicles. Each panicle is made up of 40 or more 5-petalled, pink-spotted white flowers, and reach a length of 30cm. Fruits are spiny-cased and rounded, reaching a length of about 6cm and containing a single large round seed ('conker'), or occasionally 2 or 3 flattened seeds, each one bearing a large pale scar.

Habitat and distribution Native of the mountains of the Balkans, but widely planted over much of Europe, apart from the far north. Long established in Britain.
Similar species
Red Horse Chestnut *A.* × *carnea* 20m A hybrid between Horse Chestnut and Red Buckeye. Leaves are composed of 5–7 leaflets. Flowers similar to those of Horse Chestnut: creamy-white with yellow blotches, turning pink with red blotches.

Pride of India, in flower

Horse Chestnut, flower
Red Horse Chestnut

Horse Chestnut, in flower

Horse Chestnut, fruit

Horse Chestnut, opening buds

Red Buckeye *Aesculus pavia* 5m
A small, spreading deciduous tree with a domed crown and smooth dark-grey bark. The palmate leaves are composed of 5 lanceolate, pointed, sharply toothed, short-stalked leaflets which are dark glossy green above and turn red in autumn.
Reproductive parts The slender red flowers are about 4cm long with 4 petals, growing in erect spikes in early summer. The fruits are rounded or pear-shaped, with a smooth brown outer skin enclosing one or 2 shiny-brown seeds.
Habitat and distribution A native of woodlands and thickets on rich, damp soils in the south-eastern USA, but seen elsewhere in parks and gardens.

Indian Horse Chestnut
Aesculus indica 30m
A large, broadly columnar tree with ascending branches, but more pendulous twigs and shoots; it resembles Horse Chestnut, but is more graceful, especially in winter outline. The thick trunk has smooth greyish-green or pink-tinged bark. The leaves also resemble those of Horse Chestnut but have much narrower, stalked and finely toothed leaflets up to 25cm long which have a bronze tinge when young, then become green in summer, finally turning yellow or orange in autumn.
Reproductive parts The flowers, which open in midsummer, after the Horse Chestnut's, are white or pale pink with bright-yellow blotches and long stamens extending out of the flower; the yellow blotch becomes red as the flower matures. The erect flower spikes are up to 30cm long. The stalked brown fruits are pear-shaped and scaly on the outside, and contain up to 3 seeds.
Habitat and distribution A native of the forests of the NW Himalayas. Popular as a street tree, or in parks and gardens, elsewhere.
Similar species
Sweet Buckeye *A. flava* 30m A large deciduous tree with a peeling, scaly grey-brown bark and ascending branches. The palmate leaves have 5 leaflets up to 20cm long. The leaves turn red early in the autumn. The 4-petalled yellow flowers are borne in erect spikes about 15cm long, usually opening in late spring or early summer. The smooth rounded fruits are about 6cm across, covered in brown scales on the outside and containing one or 2 seeds. A native of the eastern USA, usually growing in woodlands on rich, damp soils. Planted elsewhere in parks and gardens for its excellent autumn colours.
A. × *neglecta* 15m A hybrid between Sweet Buckeye and *A. sylvatica* with long-stalked, finely toothed and pointed leaflets up to 20cm long and 9cm across with hairs on the upper veins and most of the underside. The leaves are bright pink when first open. The whitish flowers are borne in erect conical spikes, opening in late spring or early summer. A native of the coastal lowlands of the south-eastern USA.

Indian Horse Chestnut

Red Buckeye

Indian Horse Chestnut
Sweet Buckeye

Sweet Buckeye

HOLLY FAMILY, Aquifoliaceae

A large family of evergreen and deciduous trees and shrubs from temperate and tropical regions, most of which are Hollies. Leaves are usually alternate. The male and female flowers are normally small, white or pink-tinged and borne on separate plants. The fruit is usually a colourful berry.

Common Holly

Ilex aquifolium 15m (25m)

A striking evergreen tree with fine, shiny dark-green foliage with very strong prickles. Sometimes only a shrub, but can grow into a handsome conical tree with a smooth silver-grey bark which produces fissures and tubercles with age. The branches sweep downwards but the tips of younger branches turn up. The shoots and buds are green. The alternate leaves are up to 12cm long, tough and leathery with a waxy upper surface and a paler lower surface. The margins are wavy and spiny, although there may be some variation on any one tree, with leaves from the upper branches of a large tree being much flatter and mostly spineless.

Reproductive parts The white flowers are about 6mm across and 4-petalled, growing in small clusters in the leaf axils. The males and females grow on different trees and the male flowers are fragrant. Trees that grow in the shaded understorey of a woodland are usually sterile. The fruit is a bright-red, stalked berry with a thin fleshy layer, up to 12mm long.

Habitat and distribution A native tree of woodlands and more open habitats across most of W and S Europe, and parts of W Asia, and widely planted as an ornamental tree in parks and gardens elsewhere. A common component of the understorey of oak and beechwoods. Hedgerow trees are often mutilated in winter as people gather branches for Christmas decorations.

Comments Woodlands with a deer population often have hollies with few lower branches as the leaves and shoots are a favourite food in mid-winter when little else is green.

Similar species

Highclere Holly *I.* × *altaclarensis* 20m An evergreen tree with a dense columnar habit, spreading branches and a domed crown; the bark is purplish-grey and the twigs are greenish or purple-tinged. The alternate leaves are mostly flat, smaller than those of Common Holly and not as prickly; they may have up to 10 small forward-pointing spines on each side. The small white 5-petalled flowers are sometimes purple-tinged near the base and, like Common Holly, the males and females are on separate trees. The bright-red berries can be up to 12mm long. A hybrid between Common Holly and Canary Holly *Ilex perado*, and very popular as a park and garden tree because of its vigorous habit and resistance to disease and pollution. It grows well in towns and near the sea. There are numerous cultivars, mostly with variegated leaves; some look almost completely gold.

Holly, berries

Holly

Holly, female tree with male behind

Highclere Holly

SPINDLE TREE FAMILY, Celastraceae

A family of almost 100 genera and more than 1,000 species of evergreen and deciduous trees, shrubs and climbers, found in many parts of the world and in many climatic types. The leaves may be opposite or alternate and the greenish flowers are usually small and insignificant.

Common Spindle
Euonymus europaeus 6m
A slender, sometimes spreading and rather twiggy deciduous tree with numerous branches. The smooth grey bark becomes slightly fissured and pink-tinged as the tree ages. The green twigs have an angular feel to them when young but become rounded when older, and they terminate in tiny pointed buds. The ovate leaves are up to 10cm long, with a pointed tip and sharply toothed margins; they turn a rich shade of purple-orange in autumn.
Reproductive parts The yellowish-green 4-petalled flowers are small, growing in clusters in leaf axils, and opening in early summer. Fruits are pink capsules about 1.5cm across and divided into 4 chambers, each containing an orange seed.
Habitat and distribution A native tree in much of Europe except for the extreme north and south, and found mainly in hedgerows and copses, especially on lime-rich soils.
Similar species
Broad-leaved Spindle *E. latifolius* 6m
Very similar to Common Spindle, but the twigs are not as markedly angled and the buds are longer and more pointed. The leaves are up to 16cm long and elliptical with finely toothed margins. The 5-petalled pink flowers grow in lax clusters of 4–12 in the leaf axils. The pink, more sharply angled capsule is divided into 5 chambers, each containing a single orange seed. A common native tree of woods and copses of S, central and SE Europe, but planted elsewhere as an ornamental shrub for gardens.

BOX FAMILY, Buxaceae

A family of about 60 species of evergreen trees and shrubs, with a few herbaceous plants. The leaves are normally opposite and the flowers are tiny, usually growing in clusters.

Box
Buxus sempervirens 6m
A small, very dense or sometimes spreading evergreen tree or large shrub. The young twigs are green and angular with a covering of white hairs, and the bark is smooth and grey, but breaks up into small squares with age. The opposite leaves are ovate to oblong, up to 2.5cm long and 1cm across, with a notched tip; the upper surface is dark green and glossy but the lower surface is paler.
Reproductive parts The flowers are small and green; male flowers have conspicuous yellow anthers and are borne in the same cluster as the female flowers, opening in early spring. The fruit is a small, woody, greenish capsule, about 8mm long, with 3 spreading spines; it ripens to brown, and then splits open to scatter the hard, shiny-black seeds.
Habitat and distribution A scarce native tree of dry, calcareous hills and slopes in SW and W central Europe. There are a number of different cultivars which are mainly used for hedging and topiary, and occasionally for timber.
Similar species
Balearic Box *Buxus balearica* Very similar to Box, but the leaves are a paler green and less glossy, larger at up to 4cm long and 2.5cm wide, and the twigs are stiffer and thicker. The flower clusters are larger and the capsule may be up to 1cm long with longer, more curved spines. A native of the Balearic Islands, Sardinia and S Spain, but found in gardens in many parts of Europe.

Box

Spindle, autumn

Spindle, berries

Box

Box, fruits
Balearic Box, flowers

Box, cultivated

MALLOW FAMILY, Malvaceae

A large family of about 1,500 species found all around the world, except for the coldest regions. There are many herbaceous plants, but some deciduous and evergreen trees and shrubs as well.

Flowering Maple
Corynabutilon vitifolium 9m

A small deciduous tree with a short bole, spreading branches and a domed crown. The young shoots are covered with numerous white hairs and the alternate leaves are also woolly. Each leaf is up to 15cm long, with 3 unequal pointed and toothed lobes, a heart-shaped base and a short petiole. **Reproductive parts** Flowers are long-stalked, growing in small axillary clusters of 3–5, opening in May–July. Individual flowers are 5-petalled, 7cm across, with the pale-blue or whitish rounded petals overlapping slightly. The fruit splits open to reveal single seeds inside separate segments. **Habitat and distribution** A native of coastal Chile, but sometimes seen in gardens and parks in W and S Europe.

BUCKTHORN FAMILY, Rhamnaceae

A family of about 60 genera and 900 species of trees, shrubs and climbers found in most regions of the world. They may be deciduous or evergreen, bear spines on the shoots and branches and have alternate or opposite leaves. The flowers are small and the separate sexes may occur on different plants. A number of species yield useful dyes, and many are poisonous.

Buckthorn
Rhamnus catharticus 10m

A spreading, sometimes rather untidy deciduous tree with slightly spiny shoots and dark orange-brown bark which becomes almost black in older trees, but still reveals orange patches between the numerous fissures. The opposite leaves are ovate or nearly rounded with a short pointed tip, up to 6cm long and 4cm wide, finely toothed around the margin and glossy green above with a pale underside. The leaves have conspicuous veins on the upper surface which converge towards the tip of the leaf. In autumn they turn yellow. **Reproductive parts** The fragrant flowers are very small with 4, or rarely 5, green petals. Male and female flowers are on separate trees and grow in small stalked clusters, or sometimes singly, on 2-year-old shoots. The fruit is black, shiny and berry-like, about 8mm in diameter. **Habitat and distribution** A native of most of Europe, apart from the Mediterranean area, growing in open woods and copses, especially on drier, calcareous soils.

Alder Buckthorn
Frangula alnus (*Rhamnus frangula*) 5m

A small tree with a broadly spreading or sometimes sprawling habit, and smooth grey, vertically furrowed bark. The twigs have numerous small fine hairs and are green at first, becoming grey-brown later, and are opposite, like the branches. The opposite leaves are up to 7cm long, broadly ovate with entire margins and a short-pointed tip. There are up to 9 pairs of veins on the leaf which curve towards the margin. The leaves are glossy-green above and paler below, turning a clear lemon-yellow in autumn, or redder if exposed to bright sunlight. **Reproductive parts** The greenish-white 5-petalled flowers are very small and inconspicuous, rarely more than 3mm across; they grow in small axillary clusters and open in May or June, sometimes later. The berry-like fruits are up to 10mm in diameter and ripen from pale green through yellow to red and finally black. **Habitat and distribution** A native of much of Europe, apart from far north and drier parts of Mediterranean region. Mostly found in marshy woodlands and on acidic soils.

Flowering Maple

Buckthorn, fruit

Alder Buckthorn, young fruit

Alder Buckthorn

Alder Buckthorn, mature fruit

Common Jujube

Zizyphus jujuba 8m

A small, multi-branched, deciduous tree, with flexible green zigzag twigs. Non-flowering shoots have spiny stipules at the nodes, flowering shoots are unarmed. The alternate leaves are up to 7cm long, ovate and bluntly toothed. The upper surface is bright shiny green, the lower surface is paler and slightly hairy, the petiole is short with 2 spiny stipules at the base; one is long and straight, and the other is short and curved.

Common Jujube

Reproductive parts The inconspicuous greenish-yellow flowers are only about 3mm across and grow in short-stalked axillary clusters, opening in mid-summer. The fruit is an ovoid drupe up to 3cm long and reddish-brown or sometimes black when ripe, with a sweet flesh. **Habitat and distribution** A native of Asia, brought to S Europe and cultivated for its edible fruits, and also sometimes found naturalized.

LIME FAMILY, Tiliaceae

A family of more than 700 species of trees, shrubs and herbaceous plants. The majority are found in the tropics but the 30 true limes (*Tilia*), which originated in the cooler regions of the northern hemisphere, are the only trees. The leaves are alternate and may be lobed, and they often have star-like hairs. The flowers are small, frequently fragrant, with 5 petals and sepals and many stamens. The fruit is usually a dry capsule, but it may be hard and woody. The timber is pale and soft and can be used for wood-carving.

Silver Lime

Tilia tomentosa (*T. argentea*) 30m

A broadly domed deciduous tree with grey, intricately ridged bark. The branches are mostly straight and ascending. The young twigs are whitish and woolly, becoming darker as they mature and turning grey-green on top and brighter green below, tipped with downy, greenish-brown ovoid buds up to 8mm long. The leaves are up to 12cm long, and rounded, with an irregularly heart-shaped base, a tapering pointed tip and sharply toothed margins. The upper surface is dark green, hairless and has a wrinkled texture, and the lower surface is white and downy with stellate hairs; the petiole, usually less than half the length of the leaf blade, is also white and woolly.

Reproductive parts The 5–10 off-white, strongly scented flowers are supported by the long leaf-like bract which is yellowish-green and slightly downy; their stalks are about 3cm long. The flowers open in late summer. The fruit is up to 1.2cm long and ovoid with a ridged, slightly warted and downy surface. **Habitat and distribution** A native of the Balkans and E Europe, and SW Asia. Frequently planted elsewhere as a town tree where it thrives.

Comments It has no aphids, mainly because of the woolly leaves, so it is good for city streets, and for sitting under, as there is no rain of 'honeydew'.

Similar species

Weeping Silver Lime *T. petiolaris* 30m Very similar to Silver Lime, but the branches are pendulous at the tips, although ascending near the base. The buds are smaller at only 5mm long, but the leaves are about the same at up to 12cm; the petiole is at least as long as the leaf blade and often markedly heart-shaped at the base. The underside is very white and downy, as is the long petiole. The flowers and fruits are similar, but the fruits are nearly always sterile.

Silver Lime

Weeping Silver Lime

Silver Lime

Weeping Silver Lime

Small-leaved Lime
Tilia cordata 32m

A tall deciduous tree with a dense crown and ascending branches which become downcurved on older trees. Young trees have a neat, almost conical shape, but older trees are more untidy with burrs, sprouts and criss-crossed heavy branches. The bark

Small-leaved Lime, flowers

is smooth and grey on young trees, but becomes darker and cracked in older trees, often breaking away in flakes.

The twigs are smooth and brownish-red above and olive below and the ovoid buds are about 5mm long and dark red. The leaves are up to 9cm long, rounded, with a pointed tip and heart-shaped base and a finely toothed margin. The upper surface is dark shiny green and smooth, and the lower surface is paler and smooth, but with tufts of darker hairs in the vein axils. The petiole is smooth and up to 4cm long.

Reproductive parts The 5-petalled flowers are white or pale yellow and fragrant, growing in clusters of up to 10 on a 10cm-long, green bract. They open in midsummer, and project at all angles from the foliage, making this an attractive tree when in flower. The fruit is rounded and hard, and about 6mm in diameter.

Habitat and distribution A native of Britain, Europe and W Asia, found in woodlands on base-rich soils. Once the dominant woodland tree in much of Britain, but now much reduced in range.

Comments Greenfly usually live on this tree, but not as many as on Common Lime.

Broad-leaved Lime or Large-leaved Lime *Tilia platyphyllos* 40m

A tall and often narrow deciduous tree whose mostly ascending branches have slightly pendent tips. The dark-grey bark has fine fissures in older trees and is sometimes ridged. The bole is normally free of suckers and shoots, distinguishing this species from Common Lime. The twigs are reddish-green and sometimes slightly downy at the tip of the twig, and the ovoid buds are up to 6mm long, dark red and sometimes slightly downy. The leaves are up to 9cm long, sometimes as much as 15cm long, and broadly ovate, with a short tapering point and an irregularly heart-shaped base. The margins are sharply toothed, the upper surface is soft and dark green and the lower surface is paler and sometimes slightly hairy.

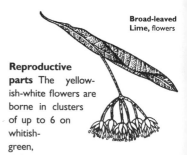

Broad-leaved Lime, flowers

Reproductive parts The yellowish-white flowers are borne in clusters of up to 6 on whitish-green, slightly downy bracts, usually opening in June. The hard, woody fruit is up to 1.8cm long, almost rounded or slightly pear-shaped with 3–5 ridges. A few fruits remain on the lower branches in winter.

Habitat and distribution A native of lime-rich soils in Britain and Europe. Introduced elsewhere, and frequently planted as a street tree and in parks.

Comments Sometimes used as a stock for grafting other *Tilia* species.

Similar species

Red Lime *T. rubra* Very close to Broad-leaved Lime. The smoother, less flexible leaves have teeth which terminate in a fine hair-like point. A native of the Balkans and E Europe.

Small-leaved Lime, *flowers*

Small-leaved Lime, *flowers*

Small-leaved Lime
Broad-leaved Lime

Common Lime *Tilia × europea* (*Tilia × vulgaris*) 46m

A tall tree with a mostly upright habit, but with an irregular crown and a bole frequently covered with burrs and masses of sprouts. The branches are ascending, but arching on older trees, the young twigs are smooth and green, and the ovoid, 7mm-long buds are reddish-brown. The leaves are up to 10cm long and broadly ovate with a short pointed tip, a flattened, heart-shaped base and a toothed margin. The upper surface is dull green and the lower surface is paler with tufts of white hairs in the vein axils.

Reproductive parts The yellowish-white, 5-petalled, fragrant flowers are borne in clusters of up to 10 on a greenish-yellow bract. The fruit is hard, thick-shelled and rounded with slight ridges, and is nearly always sterile.

Habitat and distribution A hybrid between Small-leaved Lime and Broad-leaved Lime, probably arising in the wild where the 2 parents grow together. A very common tree in towns and parks, often more common than either parent.

Comments Always heavily infested with aphids, so there is a constant rain of honeydew from the branches, causing damage to cars if they are parked beneath it. Not a very suitable tree for street planting because of the honeydew, invasive roots, untidy bole and lack of autumn colours. Common Lime is vigorous and long-lived, however, and can grow to a great height in difficult places.

Similar species

Caucasian Lime *T. × euchlora* 20m Similar to Common Lime, but the leaves are dark, shiny green on the upper surface and have reddish hairs in the vein axils on the underside. The flower clusters have 3–7 flowers and the fruits are elliptical and pointed at either end. A hybrid between Small-leaved Lime and *T. dasystyla*, frequently planted as an ornamental species in central Europe.

T. dasystyla Originates from the Crimea, and has downy young twigs and newly opened leaves, with yellowish hairs in the vein axils on the undersides. Through a hand-lens, the style in the centre of each flower can be seen to be slightly downy as well. Rarely seen away from its native range, except in good tree collections.

American Lime or Basswood *Tilia americana* 25m

A broadly columnar deciduous tree with greyish-brown ridged and cracked bark. The branches are mostly ascending and large at the base. The leaves are up to 20cm long and 15cm wide, with short tapering points and a coarsely toothed margin. The upper surface is deep green and the lower surface is slightly paler and more glossy with tufts of brown hairs in the vein axils.

Reproductive parts The fragrant, pale-yellow, 5-petalled flowers are up to 1.5cm across, hanging in clusters of up to 10 from a 10cm-long bract. The fruits are hard and rounded and up to 1cm in diameter.

Habitat and distribution A native of a large area of N America from SE Canada to Arkansas, growing mainly in woodlands on damper soils, but commonly planted as a street tree as far west as the Pacific coast. Also occasionally seen in Britain, but not very successful there.

Common LIme, winter

Common Lime

Common LIme

Common Lime, flowers

American Lime

TUPELO FAMILY,
Nyssaceae

A small family of 7 trees native to E Asia and N America. The male and female flowers are separate but borne on the same tree. The flowers are small and lack petals, but may be conspicuous because of large showy bracts below them. The leaves are alternate.

Black Gum or Tupelo or Pepperidge
Nyssa sylvatica 25m (30m)
A broadly columnar deciduous tree with a stout bole and dark-grey ridged bark which breaks up into squarish plates. The branches are mostly level. The ovate leaves are up to 15cm long and 8cm wide, tapering towards the base, usually with an entire margin, but sometimes slightly toothed, and mostly smooth, except for the midrib and petiole which is up to 2.5cm long and red-tinged.

Black Gum, fruit, male flower and female flower

Reproductive parts Male and female flowers are borne separately; they are up to 1.5cm in diameter and have downy stalks up to 3cm long. Male flowers are in crowded, rounded clusters, and female flowers are in few-flowered clusters of up to 4 flowers. The fruit is about 2cm long, egg-shaped and bluish-black, with a hard stone containing one seed in the centre.
Habitat and distribution A native of eastern N America, growing in damp woodlands and swampy areas such as river valleys. Introduced into Europe for its exciting yellow, orange and red autumn colours. Grows best in warmer and more sheltered areas.

Handkerchief Tree, Dove Tree or Ghost Tree
Davidia involucrata 20m
A slender, conical deciduous tree with orange-brown vertically peeling bark, a stout but tapering bole and thick branches. The shoots are smooth and brown and the buds are red. The leaves are up to 18cm long and heart-shaped with a pointed tip and toothed margin, 5–9 pairs of veins and a 15cm-long pinkish or yellow-green petiole. The upper surface is a dark shiny green, and the lower surface is paler and slightly downy.
Reproductive parts The flowers are small and have no petals, growing in dense clusters of many male flowers with purple anthers and one hermaphrodite flower. They are surrounded by a very large pair of white bracts, one larger than the other at up to 20cm long, making the tree very conspicuous from a distance in late spring when they open at the same time as the leaves. The rounded fruits are up to 2.5cm across, green at first, ripening to purple-brown later.
Habitat and distribution A native of humid, mountainous wooded areas of China, but very popular in parks and gardens in NW Europe. First brought to Europe at the end of the nineteenth century and now very popular in large gardens and tree collections where it makes a good display in summer.

Black Gum, autumn

Handkerchief Tree, flower

EUCRYPHIA FAMILY, Eucryphiaceae

A small family of 5 species in a single genus, but widespread, occurring in Chile and Australasia. The leaves are opposite and may be simple or pinnate, with entire or toothed margins. One is deciduous but the others are evergreen. The flowers, borne in summer, are showy and make these trees popular subjects for large gardens.

Nymans Hybrid Eucryphia
Eucryphia × nymansensis
'Nymansay' 17m
A narrow, columnar evergreen tree with smooth grey bark and dense branches and shoots. The compound leaves are composed of 3 toothed, glossy dark-green leaflets with paler undersides, up to 6cm long.
Reproductive parts The 4-petalled white flowers are up to 7.5cm across and contain many pink-tipped stamens. They grow in the leaf axils, opening in late summer and often covering the tree, especially in older specimens, making a spectacular display in a well-sited tree. The fruit is a small, hard, woody capsule.
Habitat and distribution A hybrid between *E. cordifolia* and *E. glutinosa*, raised in Nymans Garden, Sussex, and the most frequently seen *Eucryphia*. *E. glutinosa* originated in Chile and is deciduous, giving fine autumn colours. *E. cordifolia*, known as Ulmo, is also from Chile, is evergreen, and can reach a height of 40m. Its fragrant white flowers turn pink and then orange.

OLEASTER FAMILY, Elaeagnaceae

A family of about 50 species of evergreen or deciduous shrubs and small trees, found in temperate and cooler regions in the northern hemisphere. The twigs are frequently armed with spines. The leaves have entire margins, may be scaly on the underside and are either opposite or alternate. The flowers are small and lack petals and the sexes may be separated on different plants. Some species produce edible fruits.

Sea Buckthorn
Hippophae rhamnoides 11m
A multi-stemmed and thickly branched shrub or small tree often surrounded by many suckers. The bark is fissured and peeling in older trees, and the thorny twigs are covered with silvery scales, but they look black where the scales are rubbed off. The leaves are long and thin, at up to 6cm long and 1cm wide, although usually less than this, sessile and covered on both sides with silvery or occasionally reddish scales.
Reproductive parts The flowers are minute, usually no more than 3mm in diameter and lacking petals, opening just before the leaves in March or April on 2-year-old twigs. Male and female flowers grow on different trees. The fruits are oval bright orange, shiny berries, up to 8mm long.
Habitat and distribution A native of most of Europe, mainly found on the coast on sandy soils. Does not compete well with larger trees which shade it, but copes well with shifting sand so is often planted to stabilize dunes. Can be invasive in places. Sometimes planted inland as an ornamental shrub.
Comments The orange berries, which remain after the leaves, are a favourite food of birds and are especially important for migrant species which make sea-crossings and arrive hungry on coastal dunes.

Nymans Hybrid Eucryphia, flowers

Sea Buckthorn, fruit

Sea Buckthorn, in fruit

Oleaster
Elaeagnus angustifolia 13m

A deciduous shrub or small tree with spiny branches, silvery young twigs and a short bole. The leaves are up to 8cm long and no more than 2.5cm wide, so always look lanceolate. They have silvery scales on the underside, but are a dull green above.
Reproductive parts The fragrant flowers are up to 1cm long, growing singly or occasionally in pairs in the leaf axils on 2–3mm pedicels, but opening before the leaves in midsummer. The outside of the bell-shaped flower is silvery-white, but the inside is yellow. The juicy oval fruit is up to 1cm long, and yellowish, covered with the same silvery scales as the leaves.
Habitat and distribution A native of W Asia, introduced into Europe as an ornamental tree and now naturalized over much of central and S Europe.
Similar species
Silver Berry *E. commutata* Very similar. This is a N American species which has brown, mealy fruits. It was introduced into Europe for its attractive silvery foliage, and has become naturalized in many places.

TAMARISK FAMILY, Tamaricaceae

A family of small trees and shrubs with tiny, scale-like, clasping alternate leaves and glands which excrete salt. The flowers are small but borne in dense heads. The seeds are wind-dispersed and are good colonizers of disturbed ground. Many grow near the sea.

French Tamarisk
Tamarix gallica 8m

A small, sometimes rather windswept tree with purplish-brown bark and numerous fine branches and shoots. The greenish-blue leaves are minute and scale-like, rarely more than 2mm long, clasping the younger shoots.
Reproductive parts The minute pink, 5-petalled flowers are borne in long tapering racemes up to 2.5cm long. Each petal is no more than 2mm long, but many flowers are grouped into the spike. Each flower has a bract which is shorter than the calyx. The seeds are released from a small capsule and are wind-dispersed, floating away on tiny tufts of hair.
Habitat and distribution A common species of coastal shrub in SW Europe, including Britain. Cultivated and planted as a windbreak, or for soil stabilization. Sometimes found inland as a garden shrub.
Comments Like other *Tamarix* species, this one can secrete salt by way of special glands located on the minute leaves. The closer the plant is to the sea, the more likelihood there is of it taking up salt.
Similar species
African Tamarisk *T. africana* 8m Usually has larger white, not pink, flowers which open in spring, and the larger leaves are up to 4mm long. The bract on the stalkless flowers is at least as long as, and sometimes longer than, the calyx. Found mainly on the coasts of SW Europe as far east as Sicily.
Canary Island Tamarisk *T. canariensis* 10m A large species, with reddish-brown bark and pink flowers. Much more downy than other *Tamarix* species. The petals are very small at only 1.5mm long, and the bract is longer than the petals. Native to the shores of Portugal and the W Mediterranean.

Canary Island Tamarisk, flower

Small-flowered Tamarisk *T. parviflora* 6m Similar to French Tamarisk, but the floral parts are in fours, the flower spikes are about 3–5cm long, and the petals are up to 2mm long with a papery bract. A native of the Balkans and Aegean region, occurring in hedgerows and damp ground along riversides. Cultivated elsewhere for ornament, and naturalized in central and S Europe.

French Tamarisk

Small-flowered Tamarisk, flowers (below)

French Tamarisk, flowers

African Tamarisk, flowers

MYRTLE FAMILY, Myrtaceae

A large family mainly occurring in the southern hemisphere. Only a single representative occurs naturally in Europe (the evergreen shrub Myrtle *Myrtus communis*), and none are known in N America. There are about 4,000 species of mostly evergreen aromatic trees and shrubs. The leaves are generally opposite and the flowers have 4 or 5 petals but many stamens.

Orange-bark Myrtle
Myrtus luma (apiculata) 12m
A broadly spreading evergreen tree with attractive bright-orange flaking bark, which peels away to reveal contrasting white patches beneath. The bole is normally short with numerous ascending and slightly spreading branches, which also show the peeling bark low down. The pointed leaves are elliptical, up to 2.5cm long, with entire margins; the upper surface is glossy dark green, the underside is paler, and the leaves are aromatic.

Reproductive parts The white, 4-petalled flowers are up to 2cm across, and have large numbers of stamens bearing yellow anthers. The solitary flowers grow in the leaf axils, opening in late summer and sometimes continuing in bloom until the autumn. The fleshy fruits are rounded and berry-like, up to 1cm long, turning from red to black through the autumn.

Habitat and distribution A native of the forests of Argentina and Chile, introduced into Europe for ornament and now seen in many parks and gardens.

GUMS OR EUCALYPTS *Eucalyptus* About 500 species occur in Australasia, but not in New Zealand. Many are large aromatic evergreen trees which grow throughout the year, slowing only in very cold weather. The flowers are enclosed in capsules which have a cap which is eventually shed.

Lemon-scented Spotted Gum
Eucalyptus citriodora 40m
A tall and usually slender evergreen with white, or sometimes pink-tinged, bark which peels regularly. The bristly juvenile leaves are opposite and elliptical, up to 15cm long and 6cm wide. The adult leaves are alternate and lanceolate, up to 25cm long and 4cm wide and release a lemon-like scent if crushed.

Reproductive parts The white flowers grow in clusters of 10 in flattened branching spikes; the flower buds are about 1.2cm long with a rounded cap. The fruits are rounded, narrowing at the mouth and containing 3 or 4 internal divisions.

Habitat and distribution A native of Queensland, Australia, introduced into Europe as an ornamental species, and mainly found in Italy, Spain and Portugal. Can cope with thin, poor soils.

Swamp Mahogany
Eucalyptus robusta 30m
A fairly densely foliaged evergreen tree with dark fibrous bark. The juvenile leaves are opposite, up to 11cm long and 7cm wide and thick to the touch. The adult leaves are alternate and lanceolate, up to 18cm long and 4cm wide with pointed tips. The upper surface is shiny and dark green, the lower surface is more dull.

Reproductive parts The white flowers grow in clusters of up to 10 on flattened stalks, and the buds have a pointed cap. The fruits are mostly cylindrical and about 1.5cm long.

Habitat and distribution A native of E Australia, introduced to Europe as an ornamental and shade tree, but also used as a shelter-belt tree; found mainly in Iberia, France, Sardinia and Italy.

Orange-bark Myrtle   Ribbon Gum

Ribbon Gum

Tasmanian Blue Gum
Eucalyptus globulus 45m (65m)

A large and vigorous evergreen with peeling grey-brown bark, often with strips hanging off the bole. The bark is usually persistent at the base of the bole. The juvenile leaves are a bright blue-green colour, opposite, and stem-clasping. They are usually about 16cm long and 9cm wide. The adult leaves are dark green, alternate and much longer (at about 30cm) and narrower (at only 4cm wide); they are sometimes sickle-shaped and pointed, and are always pendent.

Reproductive parts The white, sessile flowers are about 4cm across and mostly solitary, or in groups of 2 or 3. The flower bud is up to 3cm long, with a pointed and warty cap. The fruit is a flattened sphere, or slightly top-shaped, with ribs and a warty skin, and 3–6 chambers inside.

Habitat and distribution A native of Australia and Tasmania, but now very common in much of the Mediterranean region, especially Spain and Portugal where it is an important timber tree. It also provides pulp for the paper industry and an oil from the leaves.

Similar species

Maiden's Gum *E. globulus* ssp *maidenii* 45m A large evergreen tree with smooth, bluish-white bark which peels each year. The juvenile leaves are greyish and ovate, up to 16cm long and opposite. The adult leaves are sickle-shaped and up to 25cm long, and all alternate and pendulous. The white flowers are borne in clusters of 3–7 on flattened stalks up to 15cm long, in the leaf axils. The fruit is up to 1.2cm long and bell-shaped with a waxy surface. A native of SE Australia, but introduced into S Europe as a timber tree.

Snow Gum *E. pauciflora* ssp *niphophila* 15m A smaller eucalyptus with grey-green bark which peels away revealing much whiter patches beneath. The short-stalked fruits are cup-shaped and about 12mm long. A native of mountainous areas of Australia, and therefore tolerant of cooler conditions, so is successful in colder climates, and is planted as an ornamental tree in Britain and parts of W Europe.

Ribbon Gum
Eucalyptus viminalis 50m

A large tree with rough bark which hangs from the bole and branches in long ribbons, revealing smoother, paler patches beneath. The bole is usually straight and unbranching. The juvenile leaves are opposite and oblong, up to 10cm long. The alternate adult leaves are long and tapering, on short petioles, and may be flat or slightly waved in texture, usually reaching a length of 18cm.

Reproductive parts White flowers are normally produced in short-stalked clusters of 3, and the flower buds have distinctive scarlet domed caps. The fruits are rounded, opening to reveal 3 or 4 chambers.

Habitat and distribution A native of S and E Australia, and introduced into Europe as a timber, ornamental and shade tree. It is tolerant of colder conditions so does well in Britain and the north regions.

Red Gum
Eucalyptus camaldulensis 40m

A large and usually spreading evergreen with a short, thick bole and numerous spreading branches. The whitish bark has pink and grey patches, and falls away in large scales. The juvenile leaves are opposite and oval, up to 9cm long and bluish-green. The adult leaves are alternate, long and very narrow, usually 25cm long and only 2cm wide with a long tapering tip.

Reproductive parts The white flowers grow in stalked clusters of 5–10 and the buds are up to 1cm long with a brown conical cap. The fruits are up to 8mm long and rounded, opening to reveal 4 seed-chambers. Flowers are normally borne from December to February.

Habitat and distribution A native of Australia, brought to Europe as a timber tree and found mainly in the Mediterranean region.

Tasmanian Blue Gum

Snow Gum

River Red Gum

Tasmanian Blue Gum

Snow Gum

Red Mahogany
Eucalyptus resinifera 40m

An impressive, large tree with a thick bole and rough, reddish bark which peels away in patches on older trees. The juvenile leaves are opposite and lanceolate to oval, at up to 6cm long and 2.5cm wide, and the adult leaves are alternate and lanceolate, up to 16cm long and 3cm wide, with slightly prominent veins, a dark-green upper surface and a paler-green lower surface.

Reproductive parts The white flowers are borne in small axillary clusters of 5–10 flowers on short flattened stalks. The buds are up to 1.5cm long and short-stalked with a rounded cap. The fruit is small and rounded with 4 projecting valves.

Habitat and distribution A native of Queensland and New South Wales, Australia, which thrives on thin, sandy soils with a high water-table. Introduced into Europe as a timber tree, as it produces a hard and durable timber suitable for a variety of uses, including building houses. Most common in the Mediterranean region, rarer further north.

Cider Gum
Eucalyptus gunnii 30m

A medium-sized eucalyptus with smooth, readily peeling greenish-white or pink-tinged bark. The sessile juvenile leaves are ovate, up to 4cm long, and opposite with slightly heart-shaped bases. The adult leaves are ovate to lanceolate, at up to 7cm long and 3cm wide. They have short petioles and are greener than the juvenile leaves, with veins sometimes prominent.

Reproductive parts The white flowers grow in small clusters of 3 on slightly flattened stalks up to 8mm long. The buds are cylindrical or sometimes bulbous, about 8mm long and with a rounded cap. The fruit is up to 1cm long and bell-shaped, with a slightly concave disc and up to 5 valves.

Habitat and distribution A native of the uplands of Tasmania. Hardy in the British climate, so is much planted in Britain and NW Europe and now is a popular park and garden tree. It can easily be raised from seed.

POMEGRANATE FAMILY, Punicaceae

A small family of only 2 species, one of which is a shrub found only on the island of Socotra. The Pomegranate is characterized by its flower structure and its unique fruit with the large persistent calyx at its apex.

Pomegranate
Punica granatum 8m

A small, spreading deciduous tree with a short bole and many crowded, slender ascending branches and smooth 4-angled twigs which are sometimes spiny. The short-stalked opposite leaves are up to 8cm long and 2.5cm wide, smooth and shiny and with entire margins.

Reproductive parts The flowers are borne on the ends of the shoots and sometimes on small side-shoots. They are often solitary, but sometimes occur in pairs. The 5, sometimes 7, petals are scarlet and are crumpled when first open. They surround many yellowish stamens. The flowers are usually about 4cm in diameter and the sepal tube is funnel-shaped. The short-stalked fruit is up to 8cm in diameter and rounded with a shiny, leathery outer skin which ripens to a brownish-red. It contains several chambers each packed with seeds surrounded by a translucent purplish or clearer white flesh which is acidic at first but ripens to become sweeter.

Habitat and distribution A native of SW Asia, but long cultivated in S Europe for its edible fruit and naturalized in many parts of the Mediterranean. Often found on waste ground and by roadsides.

Comments This is thought by some to be the 'apple' picked by Eve in the Garden of Eden.

Cider Gum

Cider Gum

Cider Gum, flowers

Cider Gum, fruit

Pomegranate

Pomegranate, fruit

DOGWOOD FAMILY,
Cornaceae

A family of about 100 species of ever-green or deciduous shrubs which grow in temperate regions of the northern hemisphere. Leaves are usually opposite and the flowers are small but often surrounded by conspicuous colourful bracts.

Cornelian Cherry
Cornus mas 8m
A small, spreading deciduous tree with an untidy crown and mostly level branches which terminate in numerous greenish-yellow, slightly downy twigs. The opposite, short-stalked leaves are ovate and pointed, and up to 10cm long and 4cm wide with rounded bases. The upper surface is dull green and slightly downy and the margins are entire.

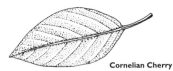

Cornelian Cherry

Reproductive parts The flowers are borne in small stalked flower-heads about 2cm across consisting of up to 25 small yellow flowers, each one about 4mm in diameter. The flowers normally open very early in the year, well before the leaves open. The fruit is a short-stalked, pendulous, bright-red, fleshy berry up to 2cm long and with a pitted apex and an acid taste.

Habitat and distribution A native of scrub and open woodlands in central and SE Europe, introduced elsewhere for its winter flowers and edible fruits. It is naturalized in many places but is most likely to be found in parks and gardens.

Dogwood
Cornus sanguinea 4m
Often little more than a shrub, but may sometimes grow well on a slender bole to

become a small tree. The dark-red winter twigs are distinctive after the leaves have fallen. The opposite leaves are oval and pointed, with entire margins and 3–4 pairs of prominent veins. If a leaf is snapped and the two halves gently pulled apart, stringy latex appears where the veins were broken and connects the 2 halves of the leaf. The leaves are reddish-green above but become a rich, deep red in the autumn.

Reproductive parts The white flowers are small, but they are grouped in large terminal clusters which are an attractive feature in early summer. The fruit is a blackish, rounded berry borne in clusters.

Habitat and distribution A widespread native across most of Europe, but not in the very hottest or coldest places. Prefers calcareous soils, usually growing in thickets, hedgerows and woodland edges. May form large thickets of its own on chalky soils. Sometimes planted as an ornamental shrub on roadsides, and is quick to colonize new ground as birds carry the seeds.

Japanese Strawberry Tree
Cornus kousa 15m
A columnar to pyramidal deciduous tree with reddish-brown bark which peels off in patches in older trees. The leaves are ovate, up to 7.5cm long and 5cm across, with a tapering point and a wavy margin. The upper surface is dark green and the underside is smooth with patches of brown hairs in the vein axils.

Reproductive parts The yellowish-white or greenish flowers are very small and are clustered together in compact rounded heads, which are surrounded by 4 large yellowish-white or pink-tinged bracts. They open in early summer and are followed by a bunch of tiny fruits which collectively look like strawberries. The pendulous fruit cluster is edible.

Habitat and distribution A native of woodlands on mountain slopes in Japan and a garden tree in Britain and Europe.

Cornelian Cherry

Dogwood

Cornelian Cherry, in flower
Japanese Strawberry Tree

Japanese Strawberry Tree, fruit
Japanese Strawberry Tree

Dogwood, fruit
Japanese Strawberry Tree

HEATHER FAMILY, Ericaceae

A large family of 100 genera and about 3,000 species found all around the world. Most are trees or shrubs and may be evergreen or deciduous with alternate leaves. The flowers are variable, but most have 5 petals joined at the base. The roots form an association with a fungus which helps the plant absorb nutrients from the soil.

Strawberry Tree
Arbutus unedo 9m
A small, spreading evergreen tree with a short bole and a dense, domed crown. The reddish bark peels away in shreds which turn brown and hang down the bole obscuring the finer colours beneath. The branches are often ascending and twisted, with many slightly hairy, reddish twigs. The leaves are up to 11cm long and 4cm wide, and may have sharply toothed or almost entire margins, and a prominent midrib. They may be slightly hairy near the base, with a dark glossy-green upper surface and a paler underside, and the 1cm-long petiole is usually red and hairy.

Reproductive parts The flowers are borne in pendulous clusters late in the year at the same time as the fruits from the previous year. Each white flower is up to 9mm long and sometimes tinged pink or green. The fruit is a round berry about 2cm in diameter, with a warty skin which ripens from yellow through orange to deep red; the flesh is acidic.

Habitat and distribution A native of SW Europe and the Mediterranean region, but also occurring naturally in SW Ireland. Usually found in open woods, thickets and on scrub-covered hillsides. Planted as an ornamental tree in gardens in other mild areas of Europe.

Comments The specific name *unedo* means 'I eat one', referring to the fact that the acidity and rich taste of the berry make it difficult to eat any more. The fruits are used in Portugal to make a powerful liqueur.

Similar species
Cyprus Strawberry Tree or **Eastern Strawberry Tree** *A. andrachne* 12m Very similar to the Strawberry Tree *A. unedo*, but can become a larger tree. The smooth red bark peels away to show yellowish or red-tinged underbark. The young twigs are smooth and yellowish green, becoming brown later. The long stalked leaves are up to 10cm long and 6cm wide, usually less than twice as long as they are broad. Young leaves may be toothed, older leaves are entire. The flowers are borne in erect, not drooping clusters, and open in spring. The orange berry is up to 1.2cm in diameter and almost smooth, but with a slightly rough texture when ripe. It is a native of the Aegean and S Crimea, and it does occur on Cyprus. Sometimes seen as a garden tree outside of the native area.

Hybrid Strawberry Tree *A. × andrachnoides* A hybrid between the 2 European species, with brightly coloured bark which peels to reveal paler patches. The leaves have the red petioles of the Strawberry Tree *A. unedo*. The flowers may appear in spring or autumn and the fertile fruits are smaller and smoother than those of the Strawberry Tree. Found in S Europe where both parents occur together.

Madrona *A. menziesii* 40m A native of the west coast of N America, introduced into NW Europe as a garden tree and even growing well in towns. It is much larger than the other species, growing into a fine tall tree. The bark is reddish-brown and peels away in shreds. The leaves are up to 15cm long and elliptic, entire, dark glossy green above and bluish-white below.

Reproductive parts The white flowers are borne in upright clusters and the fruit is a warty orange berry about 1cm in diameter.

Habitat and distribution Occurs in the shade of redwood and oak forests, in deep valleys and on coastal cliffs. The edible fruits are a great attraction to birds

Strawberry Tree, fruits

Strawberry Tree, flowers

Strawberry Tree

Cyprus Strawberry Tree

Madrona, in fruit

Sorrel Tree or Sourwood
Oxydendrum arboreum 20m

A broadly conical deciduous tree with thick, greyish-brown, ridged and furrowed bark, often with scaly areas on the ridges. The branches are mostly ascending and twisted. The leaves are elliptic and tapering, up to 20cm long with a very finely toothed margin. The smooth upper surface is a dark glossy green, and the lower surface is a little paler and slightly hairy; in autumn the leaves turn yellow and red, or even purple. The leaves have an acidic taste, rather like the leaves of sorrel (*Rumex* species).

Reproductive parts The fragrant white flowers are small and flask-shaped and borne in large erect clusters at the ends of shoots, opening in the autumn, often when the leaves have started to turn. The fruits are small brown, slightly woody capsules.

Habitat and distribution A native of woods and streamsides of eastern N America, and introduced into Europe as an ornamental tree, but thrives only on well-drained acid soils.

STORAX FAMILY, Styracaceae

A family of about 150 species of small trees and shrubs found in E Asia, the southern USA, Central and S America, with an isolated species in the Mediterranean. The leaves are simple and alternate, and the flower has a tubular corolla dividing into 5–7 lobes. The fruit is a dryish capsule.

Snowbell Tree
Styrax japonica 12m

A broadly spreading deciduous tree or large shrub with smooth, dark greyish-brown bark which becomes slightly fissured with age, showing orange-brown patches in the grooves. The branches are mostly ascending and the slender shoots have a zigzag appearance with alternate buds, and are purple-tinged or sometimes orange-brown with black speckles. The leaves are elliptic to ovate and up to 10cm long with narrow bases and pointed tips, and a finely toothed margin. They are a deep glossy green above and turn a pleasing yellow or red in the autumn.

Reproductive parts The white, lightly scented, 5-petalled flowers are about 1.5cm long with yellow anthers; they hang singly or in small clusters from the undersides of the branches, opening in midsummer. The fruit is an egg-shaped or rounded grey berry up to 1.5cm long and containing a single seed.

Habitat and distribution A native of China, Japan and Korea, growing on wet ground, usually in open glades and streamsides. Introduced into Europe as a garden tree, for which it is very suitable, and is now becoming more popular.

Similar species

Storax *S. officinale* 7m Usually smaller, often no more than a shrub, and all the parts are hairy, with stellate hairs (check with a hand-lens). The leaves are up to 7cm long and ovate, and hairy on both surfaces. The white flowers grow in small pendulous clusters of 3–6, opening in April–May, and the fruit is a greyish, hairy, berry-like drupe about 1cm long with the remains of the style persisting. A native of woods and thickets, especially on damper ground, in the Mediterranean region from Italy eastwards. Introduced to France where it is now naturalized.

Comments An aromatic gum called storax is extracted from the biggest mature trees by making cuts in the bole and larger branches.

Snowbell Tree

Snowbell Tree, fruit

Storax

OLIVE FAMILY, Oleaceae

A large family of nearly 1,000 species including many sweet-scented flowering shrubs such as Lilac, and numerous large trees like Ash. All trees and shrubs have opposite leaves and the flowers have either 4 petals or none at all.

ASHES *Fraxinus* Members of this genus all have opposite pinnate leaves. Most species have small, wind-pollinated flowers, but a few have scented flowers with petals.

Common Ash
Fraxinus excelsior 40m

A large deciduous tree with a straight bole and a high, open, domed crown. The bark in young trees is smooth and pale grey, but in older trees it becomes vertically fissured, although remaining grey; the true colour is often obscured by large

Common Ash

colonies of lichens which grow well on mature Ash boles in unpolluted areas. The branches are mostly ascending and terminate in grey twigs which are flattened at the nodes and are tipped with conical sooty-black buds. The pinnate leaves are up to 35cm long with a flattened central rachis, which may be hairy, bearing 7–13 ovate-lanceolate, pointed and toothed leaflets, each one up to 12 cm long. The upper surface is usually dark

green and the lower surface is paler with densely hairy midribs. The leaves turn a pale yellow-green for a short time in autumn before falling quickly.

Reproductive parts The very small flowers are purple and borne in clusters near the tips of twigs in spring. Male and female flowers are separate and mostly occur on separate trees, but some trees have both on separate branches. The fruits are single-winged 'keys', hanging in bunches, starting off green and ripening to brown, and usually persisting until after the leaves have fallen.

Habitat and distribution A widespread native of most of Europe, preferring calcareous or base-rich soils. It grows well on limestone uplands, heavy base-rich clays, near the sea and in cities. Woodland trees have the best shape, while hedgerow trees tend to be stunted and misshapen. Widely planted for timber and shelter-belts.

Comments The timber is white, durable and easily worked, and is popular for making farm implements and furniture.

Similar species

Narrow-leaved Ash *F. angustifolia* 25m A medium-sized deciduous tree, resembling Common Ash but with a tall untidy crown, sparse ascending branches and deeply fissured bark which has a warty texture in older trees. The buds are dark brown and hairy and the leaves have much narrower toothed and long-pointed leaflets, especially in older trees. The flowers open before the leaves and are hermaphrodite, and the winged fruits hang in small clusters. A native of S and SE Europe, occasionally seen elsewhere as an ornamental tree.

Caucasian Ash *F. oxycarpa* 25m Very similar to Narrow-leaved Ash, with silvery-grey bark, and glossy leaves which have small patches of white hairs on the base of the midribs beneath. *F. oxycarpa* var. 'Raywood' has a rich purple colour in autumn. A native of the Caucasus, Asia Minor and SE Europe.

Ash, coppiced stool

Ash, flower

Ash, 'keys'

Narrow-leaved Ash

Narrow-leaved Ash
Caucasian Ash

Ash
Caucasian Ash

Manna Ash or Flowering Ash
Fraxinus ornus 24m

A medium-sized deciduous tree with a flattish crown and smooth dark-grey or sometimes almost black bark. The smooth twigs are grey, sometimes yellow-tinged, and terminate in greyish buds with a white-bloomed coating. The opposite leaves are pinnate and up to 30cm long with up to 9 ovate, toothed leaflets, each one up to 10cm long and downy, with white or brown hairs on the veins on the underside.
Reproductive parts The showy, creamy-white, fragrant flowers open at the same time as the leaves. Each flower has 4 petals about 6mm long and they hang in clusters about 20cm across. The narrow-winged fruits are about 2cm long and they hang in dense clusters.
Habitat and distribution A native of woods, thickets and rocky slopes in central and S Europe and SW Asia, and planted elsewhere as a street tree or as an ornamental tree in parks and gardens.
Comments A sticky, sweet edible gum called manna is extracted from this tree.

Red Ash
Fraxinus pennsylvanica 25m

Similar to Common Ash but generally smaller, with a more deeply furrowed reddish-brown bark, stout, hairy twigs and brown winter buds. The opposite, pinnate leaves are up to 22cm long with 7, rarely 9, oval, pointed leaflets. Each leaflet is up to 15cm long, toothed and pointed with the 2 sides of the blade not matching on the petiole, and the undersides are usually hairy.
Reproductive parts The flowers open before the leaves in hairy clusters in the leaf axils, the sexes usually on separate trees. Male flowers are red and female flowers are greenish. Both sexes of flowers lack petals, but the female flowers have 4 sepals. The single-winged fruits are up to 6cm long.
Habitat and distribution A native of eastern N America, introduced into Europe as an ornamental tree, but nowhere very common.

Similar species
White Ash *F. americana* 30m A broadly columnar deciduous tree with grey-brown, intricately ridged bark. The leaflets are smooth above and white beneath and the blades do not continue down the petiole. The autumn colour can be impressive, with purple-bronze leaves standing out among other trees in mixed woodlands. Trees introduced into Europe do not always produce such reliable autumn colours, usually turning yellow or brown instead. The timber is prized for making tool-handles.

Glossy Privet
Ligustrum lucidum 15m

A dense evergreen tree with numerous spreading branches and a broad, domed crown. The bole is short and the grey bark is finely fissured and marked with brownish streaks. The twigs are smooth and straight and spotted with white lenticels. The opposite leaves are up to 12cm long, ovate and pointed with entire margins, and feel thick to the touch. They are dark glossy green above and paler with a matt surface below. When first open the leaves are reddish.
Reproductive parts The small creamy-white fragrant flowers are borne in dense branched panicles up to 20cm long; each flower has a 4-lobed calyx and a 4-lobed corolla narrowing down to a thin tube. The fruit is a small black berry about 1cm long, usually with a grape-like bloom. The flowers are produced in late summer and continue well into autumn or early winter.
Habitat and distribution A native of China, introduced into S Europe as a shade tree in streets and town squares, and also sometimes used for hedging.
Similar species
Common Privet *L. vulgare* A semi-evergreen spreading shrub, or very rarely a small tree, often used as a hedging plant. Found wild in limestone and chalk areas in much of Europe, where it can form a dense scrub. Sometimes used as an ornamental garden plant in one of its variegated forms.

Manna Ash

Glossy Privet

Common Privet

Common Privet

Olive

Olea europaea 15m

A long-lived evergreen tree which usually looks its age with its gnarled and contorted bole and twisted branches. The bole is usually short and the branches are ascending and thick near the base. The bole and larger branches often have many holes in them and the bark is silvery-grey and finely fissured. The twigs are sometimes 4-angled, and normally covered with fine silvery scales. The leaves are up to 8cm long, lanceolate and pointed with a very short petiole. They are greyish-green and smooth above, paler and scaly below. **Reproductive parts** The small, creamy-white, 4-petalled flowers are borne in crowded axillary spikes, opening in mid- to late summer. The fruit is the familiar oil-filled olive which takes a year to develop from green to brownish or almost black when fully ripe. Ripe olives are up to 3.5cm long and usually ovoid; occasionally an ivory-white form is produced. **Habitat and distribution** A native of S Europe, although there is an opinion that it was introduced from further east in ancient times. Now widely cultivated and very common across the Mediterranean region. Usually found in groves, or on stony hillsides. The cultivated olive, *O. europaea* var. *europaea*, is the one most likely to be seen in groves, whilst the wild olive, *O. europaea* var. *sylvestris*, is most likely to be found higher up the hillsides and in scrub; it is smaller and more shrub-like, and the twigs bear spines. **Comments** An extremely important tree over a large area, providing the valuable olives which are a source of food and income for vast numbers of people. Olive groves are an important wildlife habitat, supporting many insects and birds.

Phillyrea

Phillyrea latifolia 15m

A small and compact evergreen tree with a rounded crown and smooth grey bark which becomes ridged in older trees. The branches are mostly ascending in young trees, becoming more spreading later, and terminate in slender, brownish, very hairy twigs. The simple opposite leaves are up to 5cm long and 4cm across, with toothed margins, a glossy dark-green upper surface and a paler, smooth lower surface. On younger trees the leaves are rather variable in both size and shape. **Reproductive parts** The very small greenish-white flowers are borne in dense clusters in the leaf axils, opening in late spring or early summer; they show up when open because the yellow anthers protrude. The fruit is a small rounded berry about 1cm across, and usually a blue-black colour. **Habitat and distribution** A native of shady evergreen woodlands in S Europe and occasionally planted in gardens near the coast in milder regions elsewhere.

Common Lilac

Syringa vulgaris 7m

A small deciduous tree, sometimes little more than a multi-stemmed shrub with a mass of ascending branches, a short bole surrounded by suckers and a rounded crown. The greyish bark is spirally fissured in older trees. The twigs are rounded and shiny greenish-brown. The short-petioled opposite leaves are up to 10cm long, ovate or slightly heart-shaped with entire margins and a slightly leathery feel; they are usually yellowish-green with a smooth surface. **Reproductive parts** The fragrant lilac flowers are borne in dense, paired conical spikes up to 20cm long arising from the apical leaf axils; the flowers are at their best in May and June. Individual flowers are up to 1.2cm long and 4-lobed. The fruit is a pointed ovoid capsule up to 1cm long. **Habitat and distribution** A native of rocky hillsides in the Balkans, growing in open thickets and scrub, but long cultivated in the rest of Europe for its attractive fragrant flowers.

Olive, ancient tree

Olive, flowers

Olive

Phillyrea

Olive, fruits

Common Lilac, in flower

BIGNONIA FAMILY,
Bignoniaceae

A family of many trailing and climbing plants, but the *Catalpa* genus from N America, the W Indies and China contains 11 tree species.

Indian Bean Tree or Southern Catalpa
Catalpa bignonioides 20m
A medium-sized deciduous tree with mostly spreading branches and smooth, stout twigs tipped with very small orange-brown buds. The bark is greyish-brown and scaly and the bole is usually short. The long-stalked leaves are large and broadly ovate at up to 25cm long and 20cm across with heart-shaped bases and short-pointed tips. The margins are untoothed, the upper surface is smooth and the lower surface is downy. The leaves are tinged with purple and downy when young, becoming a lighter, almost transparent green when mature. They are usually very late to open and early to fall.
Reproductive parts The 5cm-long flowers are an open bell shape with 2 lips; the petals are white with purple and yellow spots and they are borne in large showy panicles in midsummer, or sometimes in late summer. The fruit is a long, slender bean-like pod which hangs from the branches long after the leaves have fallen; it can be up to 40cm long. It contains numerous inedible flat, papery seeds about 2.5cm long.
Habitat and distribution A native of the south-eastern USA, growing along streamsides and in river-valley woodlands. It has been introduced into Europe where it is becoming a popular town-park tree, and is quite common in many large cities, including London.
Similar species
Northern Catalpa or **Western Catalpa** *C. speciosa* 40m A large, upright deciduous tree with grey scaly and fissured bark. The long-stalked leaves are ovate and up to 30cm long and 20cm across with a long, tapering pointed tip. When first open the leaves are dark green and downy above, but become smoother as they mature; the undersides remain paler and downy. The flowers are borne in lax spikes in summer; each 5cm-long flower is white and spotted with yellow and purple. The fruit is a slender, hanging, bean-like pod up to 45cm long, which remains on the tree through the winter. A native of the central USA, growing in damp woodlands, swamps and along riverbanks. Occasionally planted elsewhere as an ornamental tree. Survives the British climate quite well, but is not often seen except in well-established gardens.
Yellow Catalpa *C. ovata* 12m Very similar to the Indian Bean Tree, but the dark-green leaves are pentagonal with a short point on each corner; they are quite large, measuring 25cm in each direction, and have a heart-shaped base.
The off-white flowers have a yellow tinge and are red-spotted inside; they are about 2.5cm in diameter and grow in spikes about 25cm long. The pod is about 25cm long. A native of China, introduced into Europe as an ornamental tree and rarely seen outside parks and gardens.
Hybrid Catalpa *C.* × *erubescens* 20m A hybrid between the Indian Bean Tree and the Yellow Catalpa, first seen in Indiana, USA. The very large leaves are up to 38cm long, and sometimes as much as 60cm, and are often much broader than they are long. They may be 3- or 5-pointed with a heart-shaped base. When first open they are purple, but they become a bright green in late summer. The fragrant white flowers are up to 4cm long, grouped together in heads up to 32cm long. The pods contain sterile seeds, so this tree is propagated only by grafting, usually on to a stock of the Indian Bean Tree. Commonly seen as an ornamental tree in parks and gardens in S and W Europe.

Indian Bean Tree

Yellow Catalpa

Indian Bean Tree, autumn

Yellow Catalpa, in flower

EBONY FAMILY, Ebenaceae

A large family of trees found mainly in the tropics and including the African tree which gives the black ebony wood. The Date Plums, *Diospyros* species, producing edible fruits, are mostly hardy in the N European climate.

Date Plum
Diospyros lotus 14m

A small, deciduous, spreading tree with a short bole and grey or pink-tinged bark broken up by fissures into small plates. The leaves are ovate or lanceolate with pointed tips and untoothed margins, dark glossy green above and greyer below; young leaves are downy above, becoming smoother when older, but with hairs on the veins on the underside.

Reproductive parts The male and female flowers are separate and both bell-shaped and salmon-pink or orange-yellow. Male flowers are clustered and smaller than the

Date Plum,
fruit

single female flowers which are about 5mm long, and found on the underside of the shoots. The flowers are produced on separate plants, opening in midsummer. The fruit is a 2cm-long, edible berry which ripens from green, through yellow-brown to blue-black, when it sometimes shows a grape-like bloom.

Habitat and distribution A native of the woods of SW Asia and N Iran where it is frequently cultivated for its edible, if rather insipid, fruits. It has been introduced into N Europe where it grows well and has become naturalized.

FIGWORT FAMILY, Scrophulariaceae

A large family of mainly herbaceous plants such as the familiar foxgloves and speed-wells, but there are about 10 tree species, mainly from China, in the genus *Paulownia*.

Foxglove Tree
Paulownia tomentosa 15m (25m)

A small deciduous tree with an upright habit, smooth grey bark and mostly level branches. The opposite leaves are very broadly ovate with heart-shaped bases and tapering tips, often with forward-pointing side lobes. The upper surface is light green and hairy and the lower surface is grey-green and much more hairy. The petiole is about 15cm long, but may be as much as 45cm long, and is very downy.

Reproductive parts The flowers are borne in lax upright spikes about 30cm long; each flower is brown and downy

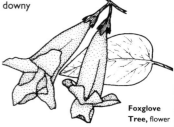

Foxglove Tree, flower

in bud, but opens to become violet, with a yellowish tinge inside the corolla tube. There are 5 spreading lobes and the flower is about 6cm long. The fruit is a short-stalked, ovoid capsule about 5cm long with a tapering tip and glossy-green outer skin; it splits open to release many small, whitish, winged seeds.

Habitat and distribution A native of the mountains of China, brought as an ornamental tree to Europe, where it is often seen in large gardens and some-times as a street tree.

Waterbush

Myoporum tenuifolium 8m

A small domed or conical evergreen tree with a short bole and numerous densely packed branches and pale-green twigs. The alternate leaves are up to 10cm long and oval to lanceolate, with a tapering base and an irregularly toothed or entire margin. The leaves are dark glossy green above and pitted with many paler glands.

Reproductive parts The scented flowers are sometimes solitary, but usually in small axillary clusters, each bell-shaped flower up to 1cm across with 5 white, spreading petals dotted with purple and with curled white hairs on the inside. The purplish-black fleshy fruit is up to 9mm long and ovoid.

Habitat and distribution A native of Australia and New Caledonia, introduced into Europe as a coastal shelter-belt tree, mainly seen in Spain, and naturalized there and elsewhere in S Europe.

HONEYSUCKLE FAMILY, Caprifoliaceae

A family of shrubs and small trees, many with attractive flowers and colourful berries. Found across a range of habitats. A number of species have been taken into cultivation for food or as ornamental plants.

Elder

Sambucus nigra 10m

A small deciduous, often rather untidy tree or large shrub, with numerous spreading, twisted branches. The bole is normally short with deeply grooved and furrowed bark which is greyish-brown and often takes on a corky texture in older specimens. The old bole often has fast-growing young shoots emerging from it. The branches and twigs have a soft white pith in the centre. The opposite leaves are compound and have 5–7 (occasionally 9) pairs of leaflets, each one up to 12cm long, ovate and pointed with a sharply toothed margin and slightly hairy underside. They are green through the summer but can sometimes turn a deep plum-red before falling in the autumn. Crushed leaves have an unpleasant 'catty' smell.

Reproductive parts The sickly-sweet scented flowers are borne in a dense, flat-topped cluster up to 24cm across; individual flowers are small and composed of 3–5 white petals and anthers. The fruit is a rounded, shiny-black berry, often produced in great quantities in pendulous heads.

Habitat and distribution A widespread and common native of woodlands, hedgerows and scrub over much of Europe except the extreme north. Common on waste ground and wherever the soil has a high nitrogen content; seeds are readily dispersed by birds. Treated as a weed and grubbed out in some areas, it is highly prized and even cultivated in others for its edible flowers and fruits.

Similar species

Alpine Elder or **Berry-bearing Elder** *S. racemosa* 4m Very similar to Elder, but generally smaller and easily distinguished in late summer by its attractive red fruits. The twigs have brown pith in the centre and the leaflets are entirely smooth when mature. The yellowish or greenish-tinged white flowers are borne in smaller heads. A native of most of the mountains of Europe from the Pyrenees to the Balkans.

Waterbush

Waterbush

Elder

Elder, fruit

Elder

Alpine Elder

Guelder Rose
Viburnum opulus 4m

A small, sometimes rather spreading deciduous tree with smooth, angular, greyish twigs and sinuous branches if growing in a crowded situation in a wood. The opposite leaves are up to 8cm long with 3–5 irregularly toothed lobes and thread-like stipules. They often turn a deep wine-red in the autumn.

Reproductive parts The white flowers are borne in flat heads, resembling a hydrangea: the large, showy outer flowers are sterile, and the smaller flowers in the centre are fertile. The fruit is a rounded, glistening, translucent red berry which hangs in clusters on the tree after the leaves have fallen.

Habitat and distribution A native of damp woodlands, hedgerows and thickets across much of Europe.

Wayfaring Tree
Viburnum lantana 6m

A small, spreading deciduous tree with rounded, greyish, hairy twigs; through a hand-lens the hairs are seen to be star-shaped. The opposite leaves are up to 14cm long and ovate, rough to the touch and with toothed margins; the undersides are thickly hairy with more stellate hairs.

Reproductive parts The flowers are produced in midsummer in rounded flower heads about 10cm across and containing many small white flowers, all of which are fertile; each flower is about 8mm across with 5 white petals. The fruits

are flattened oval berries about 8mm long which are red at first but ripen to black; this happens at different stages on the same fruiting head, giving a striking mixture of red and black berries side by side.

Habitat and distribution A widespread native of most of Europe except for the extreme north, growing mainly on drier chalky soils at the edges of woods and in hedgerows and scrub patches. Occasionally planted as a roadside tree on suitable soils.

Laurustinus
Viburnum tinus 7m

A small evergreen tree with attractive glossy foliage and flowers produced freely in winter. The twigs are faintly angled and may be slightly hairy. The opposite leaves are up to 10cm long and oval, sometimes lanceolate, with entire margins, a dark-green glossy upper surface and a paler, slightly hairy lower surface.

Reproductive parts The pink and white flowers are borne in branched, rounded clusters up to 9cm across; individual flowers are about 8mm across with 5 petals, pink outside and white inside. The rounded fruits are about 8mm long and steel-blue when ripe.

Habitat and distribution A native of woods and scrub patches in the Mediterranean region, but hardy in colder climates so it is widely planted in much of Europe and is a popular garden shrub or tree, also being used for hedging and shelter.

Guelder Rose, in fruit

Guelder Rose

Laurustinus

Wayfaring Tree

AGAVE FAMILY, Agavaceae

A large family of mostly herbaceous plants from tropical regions, but including one true tree which forms woody trunks: the *Cordyline*, which is hardy in colder climates. Members of this family have only a single growing point from which new leaves and flowers emerge.

Cabbage Palm
Cordyline australis 13m

A superficially palm-like evergreen with tall, bare trunks crowned with dense masses of long, spear-like, parallel-veined leaves up to 90cm long and 8cm wide. The upper leaves are mostly erect, but the lower leaves hang down to cover the top of the trunk. Trees which have flowered have a forked trunk with a crown of foliage on top of each fork. The trunk is covered with a pale brownish-grey ridged and furrowed bark.

Reproductive parts The flowers are produced in midsummer in large spikes up to 1.2m long containing numerous small, fragrant, creamy-white flowers, each one about 1cm across, with 6 lobes and 6 stamens. The fruit is a small rounded bluish-white berry about 6mm in diameter containing several black seeds.

Habitat and distribution A native of New Zealand, brought to Europe as an ornamental tree and now commonly planted in coastal areas of W and S Europe and naturalized in some places. It survives quite far north, as long as there is some protection from severe cold, and tolerates a range of soil types. Often used to create the illusion of sub-tropical conditions in coastal resorts.

Spanish Bayonet
Yucca aloifolia 10m

Rather like the Cabbage Palm, but much more robust with a smoother, thicker trunk and multi-branched crown. The stiff leaves are bluish-green, or sometimes variegated, up to 1m long, with sharply toothed margins and a pointed tip.

Reproductive parts The bell-shaped white flowers are up to 6cm long with 6 purple-tinged lobes, and they are borne in long spikes. The fruits are oval, blackish-purple and edible when ripe.

Habitat and distribution A native of the warmer areas of the south of N America, and the West Indies, often growing in sandy coastal areas and deserts. Introduced into S Europe where it is a popular ornamental plant, and is sometimes naturalized in coastal areas.

Dragon Tree
Dracaena draco 6m (15m)

A curious, much-branched, broadly domed tree with a thick, fluted trunk and dichotomously branching stems. Clusters of leaves are borne at the top of each stem forming a tight, domed canopy. The leaves are bluish-green with a reddish tinge at the base.

Reproductive parts Greenish-white flowers are borne at the top of the canopy, often out of sight, and these produce rounded, orange-red fruits about 1.5cm long.

Habitat and distribution A native of the Canary Islands and Madeira, but commonly planted in Mediterranean countries as a shade tree in streets and parks.

Cabbage Palm, fruiting head

Cabbage Palm

Spanish Bayonet

Dragon Tree

BANANA FAMILY, Musaceae

Not true trees, but large and robust herbaceous plants which form impressive thick stems. Several species occur in tropical regions.

Banana
Musa cavendishii 3m
A robust herbaceous plant with tree-like proportions. The shoots may be 3m tall and bear large leaves. They flower and fruit once only and then die; the plant sends up new suckers each year from a persistent tuberous stock. The leaves grow out from the base and their very long, tough, fibrous sheaths wrap around younger leaves to form a strong false stem. Leaf blades may be up to 2m long and 60cm across. They have blunt tips and entire, but often splitting, margins.
Reproductive parts The flower is a long, pendulous spike up to 1m long and the fruit, the familiar banana, grows from a small green berry to become yellow when ripe and up to 18cm long. The seeds are sterile.
Habitat and distribution A native of tropical Asia, but an important cultivated crop in the Mediterranean where it is grown in small, sheltered but rather untidy-looking plots.

PALM FAMILY, Palmae

A large family from the tropics, adapted to survive in dry weather and often very windy conditions. The unusual form of growth does not enable them to branch, and the trunks do not become thicker as the trees age. Palms have a single terminal growing point from which new leaves and flowers emerge. Some are hardy enough to survive the European climate, growing in southern areas of Britain. Palms are raised from seed.

European Fan Palm
Chamaerops humilis 3m
Usually a short-stemmed palm with a stout grey bole covered with masses of fibres and old leaf bases. The leaves are palmate and up to 1m in diameter, divided almost to the base and very rigid; each segment is narrowly lanceolate and split at the tip. The leaves are held erect and are very rigid; they are usually green or grey-green, sometimes blue-green. The petioles are flattened with sharply toothed edges.
Reproductive parts The flowers are borne in a 35cm-long spike which is often concealed amongst the leaves. The fruits are rounded, yellow or brown, and about 4.5cm in diameter.
Habitat and distribution The only palm native to Europe, growing on dry, sandy ground near the coast in the Mediterranean region. In the wild it is often a low bush, rarely developing the tall bole of trees which are protected from grazing.

Banana

Banana, fruit

European Fan Palm

European Fan Palm

Livistona australis 20m

A much taller palm with a slender bole covered with old leaf bases and straggling brown fibres; only in very old trees do they fall away to leave a smooth bark. The palmate leaves are up to 1.5m in diameter and roughly circular with a short central rib. Each segment is glossy green with a contrasting yellow central nerve which gives an attractive golden-variegated appearance in good light; the tips are soft and drooping and there are threads hanging from the edges of the segments. The petiole is very long and thin, with a spiny-toothed margin.

Reproductive parts Flowers are borne in long, branched clusters and are followed by numerous rounded reddish-brown fruits about 2cm in diameter.

Habitat and distribution A native of E Australia, introduced into S Europe as a street and park tree, and often found along coastal promenades.

Canary Island Date Palm
Phoenix canariensis 20m

A stout-boled tree with a dense crown of large glossy leaves. The bole is covered with old leaf bases, and in old trees it may be up to 1.5m in diameter. The leaves are up to 6m long and grow in a mass of up to 200 on top of the bole, mostly ascending, but with a few of the older leaves hanging down. There are up to 200 pairs of 40–50cm- long leaflets which branch out from the midrib in all directions, the basal leaflets being extremely spiny.

Reproductive parts Flowers are borne in many long clusters, up to 2m long, protected at first by a single enveloping bract. The creamy-yellow male and female flowers grow on different trees, the females eventually giving rise to dense clusters of 2cm-long orange fruits which are inedible.

Habitat and distribution A native of the Canary Islands, but frequently seen elsewhere in the Mediterranean and SW Europe as a street and park tree and especially by the coast.

Similar species

Date Palm *P. dactylifera* 35m Very similar to Canary Island Date Palm, but taller and more slender, with far fewer leaves in the crown. The leaves are shorter, at up to 4m long, and often more upright in the centre but with downcurved leaves near the base. The stem can be massive with accumulated leaf scars, and suckers often arise around the main bole. Best known for its large edible fruits, or dates, which hang in enormous clusters. A very important food species in the Middle East and S Mediterranean, and also planted in other warm areas for ornament.

Chusan Palm or Chinese Windmill Palm
Trachycarpus fortunei 14m

The tall bole is covered with persistent fibrous leaf bases which hide the bole itself. The leaves are palmate and up to 1m in diameter, split almost to the base; the segments are stiff and pointed, usually bluish-green on the underside and dark green above. The petioles are up to 50cm long and toothed on the margins, with the base hidden by dense brown fibres.

Reproductive parts The fragrant yellow flowers are borne on a long, branched spike, with males and females occurring on different trees. Before opening they are protected by enveloping white or brown bracts. There are 6 yellow segments in the flower, the inner 3 being the largest. Large numbers of 2cm-long, 3-lobed, purple-tinged fruits are produced in late summer.

Habitat and distribution A native of China, introduced into Europe as an ornamental tree and common on roadsides and in parks and gardens. One of the hardiest palms, and will survive the British climate, so is also found in many coastal resorts in the milder parts of Britain.

Canary Island Date Palm

Date Palm

Chusan Palm

Chusan Palm

Livistona australis

Canary Island Date Palm

Petticoat Palm
Washingtonia filifera 15m

A vigorous palm with a thick trunk, tapering upwards from a slightly swollen base. The bole has a grey, rough bark, but this is usually hidden by a thick, hanging 'petticoat' of dead leaves. The leaves are up to 2m long and split at least half-way to the base into narrow 2-lobed drooping segments which are connected by thin white threads.

Reproductive parts The flowers are borne in long, thin, branched clusters up to 5m long which curve down from the crown and are protected at first by enveloping papery bracts. The white flowers have 6 segments: the outer 3 form a tube, the inner 3 are very short-lived and fall quickly. Many ovoid blackish fruits up to 6mm long form and hang in large clusters.

Habitat and distribution A native of the deserts of the SW of N America and adjoining regions of Mexico. Introduced into Europe as an ornamental tree, where it is seen most commonly in the Mediterranean region.

Chilean Wine Palm
Jubaea chilensis 30m

A large, slow-growing but long-lived palm with a thick trunk up to 2m in diameter, and smooth grey bark with large diamond-shaped leaf scars. The leaves are up to 4m long, mostly erect and arranged vertically. The leaflets are split at the tips and arranged along the stalk in 2 rows.

Reproductive parts The purple flowers are borne in thick upright clusters about 1.5m long and enclosed by a tough, persistent bract. Male and female flowers grow in the same cluster; male flowers have 3 narrow outer segments, and female flowers have 3 broad outer segments. The fleshy yellow fruits are rounded and up to 5cm in diameter.

Habitat and distribution An uncommon tree in the wild in Chile, but can be found in the Mediterranean region where it is a fairly common ornamental street tree. A hardy palm tree which grows in colder climates than many others and survives well during droughts or long cold spells.

Similar species

Queen Palm *Arecastrum romanzoffianum* 10m A Brazilian species with a slender, smooth bole marked by distinct rings. The leaves are up to 5m long and the leaflets are narrow, less than 3cm wide, and droop from the central stalk. The crown has fewer leaves than the Chilean Wine Palm. The flowers are borne in a drooping spike which hangs down from the crown and is up to 1m long. The flowers are creamy-white and the fruits are yellowish. Mainly seen as a street tree in the Mediterranean.

Sentry Palm *Howeia forsterana* 15m A very slender palm with drooping leaves and a smooth grey bole marked with leaf scars. The pinnate leaves are up to 5m long with widely spaced, flattened leaflets which are green on both surfaces but slightly spotted below; the petiole is up to 1.5m long and ascending. The yellowish flowers are borne in dense spikes and the yellowish-orange ovoid fruits, up to 6cm long, are borne in tightly packed masses. Introduced from Lord Howe Island to the Mediterranean area, where it is now one of the more popular street and garden trees.

Petticoat Palm

Petticoat Palm

Chilean Wine Palm

Index

PHOTOGRAPHIC ACKNOWLEDGEMENTS

The number references are to page numbers and a picture's position on the page. The first number is the page and the second indicates position, reading from left to right and top to bottom.
Nature Photographers: SC Bisserot 67.3, 73.1, 81.1, 85.1, 87.6, 97.1, 101.1, 127.2, 177.3, 197.5, 231.4, 237.2; Frank V Blackburn 107.3, 139.4, 171.3, 181.1, 223.3, 247.4; Brinsley Burbidge 35.4, 47.2, 73.2, 75.1, 107.5, 109.1, 115.2, 145.2, 181.4, 185.5, 227.2, 229.6, 243.5, 245.3, 291.3, 293.5; Robin Bush 163.2; NA Callow 207.4; Kevin Carlson 141.4, 141.5, 207.1, 255.1, 255.2; Andrew Cleave 1, 5, 6, 7.3, 8.1, 8.2, 9, 10, 15.1, 15.2, 15.3, 15.4, 15.5, 15.6, 16, 17, 19.1, 19.2, 19.3, 20.2, 24, 26.2, 26.3, 28, 30, 33.1, 33.2, 33.3, 35.1, 35.2, 35.5, 35.6, 37.1, 37.2, 37.3, 37.4, 39.1, 39.2, 39.3, 39.4, 39.5, 39.6, 39.7, 41.2, 41.3, 41.4, 41.5, 43.2, 43.3, 43.4, 43.6, 45.1, 45.2, 45.3, 45.4, 45.5, 45.6, 47.1, 47.3, 49.2, 49.3, 49.4, 49.5, 49.6, 51.1, 51.2, 51.3, 53.1, 53.2, 53.3, 53.4, 53.5, 55.3, 55.4, 55.5, 57.1, 57.2, 59.1, 59.2, 59.3, 61.1, 61.2, 61.3, 61.4, 61.5, 61.6, 61.7, 61.8, 61.9, 63.1, 63.2, 63.3, 65.1, 65.2, 65.3, 67.1, 67.2, 67.4, 67.5, 69.2, 69.3, 69.4, 69.5, 69.6, 71.1, 71.2, 71.3, 71.4, 71.5, 71.6, 73.3, 75.4, 77.1, 77.2, 77.3, 77.4, 79.1, 79.2, 79.4, 81.2, 83.2, 83.3, 83.4, 83.5, 83.6, 85.2, 85.3, 87.1, 87.2, 87.3, 87.4, 87.5, 89.2, 89.3, 91.3, 91.4, 93.1, 93.2, 93.3, 93.4, 93.5, 93.6, 95.1, 95.3, 95.4, 95.5, 97.2, 97.3, 97.4, 97.5, 97.6, 99.1, 99.2, 99.3, 101.3, 101.5, 101.6, 101.7, 101.8, 103.1, 103.2, 103.3, 103.4, 103.5, 105.3, 105.5, 105.6, 105.7, 107.1, 107.4, 107.6, 107.7, 109.4, 109.5, 111.1, 111.2, 111.3, 111.4, 111.5, 113.1, 113.2, 113.4, 115.3, 115.4, 117.1, 117.2, 117.3, 117.4, 119.1, 119.2, 119.3, 119.4, 121.1, 121.2, 121.3, 121.4, 123.1, 123.2, 123.7, 123.8, 125.1, 125.2, 125.3, 125.4, 125.5, 125.6, 127.1, 127.3, 127.4, 127.5, 129.1, 129.2, 129.3, 129.4, 131.1, 131.2, 131.3, 131.5, 131.6, 133.1, 133.2, 133.3, 133.4, 135.1, 135.3, 135.4, 137.1, 137.2, 137.3, 137.4, 137.5, 139.2, 141.1, 141.3, 141.6, 143.2, 145.1, 145.3, 145.4, 147.1, 147.2, 147.3, 147.4, 149.5, 149.6, 149.7, 151.1, 151.2, 151.3, 151.4, 151.6, 151.7, 153.1, 153.2, 153.3, 153.4, 153.5, 153.6, 153.7, 153.8, 155.1, 155.7, 155.8, 157.1, 157.3, 157.4, 157.5, 159.1, 159.2, 159.3, 159.4, 159.5, 161.1, 161.2, 161.3, 161.4, 161.5, 163.3, 163.4, 165.1, 165.2, 165.3, 165.4, 165.5, 165.6, 167.1, 167.2, 167.3, 169.1, 171.1, 171.2, 171.5, 171.6, 171.7, 173.1, 173.2, 173.3, 173.5, 175.1, 175.2, 175.3, 175.4, 177.1, 177.2, 177.4, 179.1, 179.2, 179.3, 179.4, 179.5, 179.6, 181.2, 181.3, 183.2, 183.3, 185.1, 185.2, 185.3, 185.4, 187.1, 187.3, 187.4, 187.5, 189.4, 191.1, 191.3, 191.4, 191.5, 193.4, 193.5, 193.6, 193.7, 195.1, 195.2, 197.1, 197.2, 197.3, 197.6, 197.7, 199.1, 199.2, 199.4, 199.5, 201.1, 201.5, 203.1, 203.2, 203.3, 203.4, 203.5, 203.6, 205.3, 205.4, 205.5, 207.2, 207.3, 209.1, 209.3, 209.4, 211.1, 211.2, 211.3, 213.1, 213.2, 213.3, 213.4, 213.5, 217.2, 217.3, 217.4, 217.5, 219.1, 219.2, 219.3, 223.1, 223.2, 225.1, 225.2, 225.4, 227.3, 227.4, 227.5, 229.1, 229.2, 229.3, 229.4, 229.5, 231.1, 231.2, 231.3, 231.5, 233.2, 233.3, 235.1, 235.2, 235.3, 235.4, 237.1, 237.3, 237.4, 237.5, 239.1, 239.2, 239.3, 239.4, 239.5, 241.1, 241.2, 243.1, 243.2, 243.3, 245.1, 245.2, 245.4, 245.5, 247.1, 247.5, 249.1, 249.2, 249.3, 249.4, 249.5, 249.6, 253.1, 253.2, 253.3, 253.4, 253.5, 255.3, 255.4, 255.5, 255.6, 257.1, 257.2, 257.3, 257.4, 257.5, 257.6, 259.2, 259.3, 259.4, 259.6, 261.1, 261.2, 261.3, 261.4, 261.5, 263.2, 263.3, 263.4, 265.1, 265.4, 265.5, 265.6, 265.7, 267.2, 267.3, 267.4, 267.5, 269.1, 269.2, 269.3, 269.4, 271.1, 271.2, 271.3, 271.4, 273.1, 273.2, 273.5, 275.1, 275.2, 277.1, 277.3, 279.1, 279.2, 281.1, 281.2, 281.3, 283.1, 283.2, 283.3, 283.5, 285.1, 285.2, 285.3, 285.4, 285.5, 285.6, 287.6, 287.7, 289.1, 289.2, 289.3, 289.4, 291.1, 291.2, 293.1, 293.2, 293.4, 293.7, 293.8, 295.1, 295.3, 297.1, 297.2, 297.3, 297.4, 297.5, 299.1, 299.2, 299.3, 299.4, 301.2, 303.4, 305.1, 305.4, 307.1, 307.2, 307.3, 309.1, 309.2, 309.3, 309.4, 311.2, 311.3, 311.4, 311.5, 311.6, 313.1, 313.3; AK Davies 189.2; Christopher Grey-Wilson 119.5, 193.2, 209.2, 251.2; Jean Hall 107.2, 127.6, 169.2, 189.3, 207.5, 265.2, 307.4, 311.1; K Handford 171.4, 297.6; EA Janes 85.7, 99.4, 221.1, 247.6, 259.5; Charles Palmer 169.3, 193.3, 303.6, David Rae 47.4, 69.1, 135.2, 177.5, 209.5, 225.3, 225.5, 289.5; J Russell 201.3; Tony Schilling 91.1, 95.6, 113.3, 115.1, 233.1, 259.1; Don Smith 75.3; James Sutherland 75.2; Paul Sterry 4, 7.1, 7.2, 12, 19.4, 20.1, 21, 22, 26.1, 31, 35.3, 41.1, 43.1, 43.5, 49.1, 55.1, 55.2, 83.1, 85.4, 85.5, 85.6, 91.2, 101.2, 101.4, 105.1, 105.2, 105.4, 109.2, 109.3, 123.3, 123.4, 123.5, 123.6, 129.5, 131.4, 139.1, 139.3, 139.5, 141.2, 143.1, 143.3, 143.4, 149.1, 149.2, 149.3, 149.4, 151.5, 155.2, 155.3, 155.4, 155.5, 155.6, 157.2, 185.6, 189.1, 195.3, 195.4, 195.5, 197.4, 197.8, 201.2, 201.4, 221.2, 221.4, 221.5, 227.1, 247.2, 247.3, 253.6, 263.1, 265.3, 273.3, 273.4, 277.2, 287.1, 287.2, 287.3, 287.4, 287.5, 293.3, 293.6, 295.4, 303.3, 303.5, 305.2, 305.3, 313.2; Roger Tidman 14, 223.4; J Watson 183.1.
Natural Image: Paul Davies 57.3; Bob Gibbons 79.3, 89.1, 95.2, 163.1, 173.4, 191.2, 193.1, 199.3, 205.1, 205.2, 215.1, 215.2, 217.1, 219.4, 221.3, 225.6, 241.3, 241.4, 243.4, 251.1, 255.7, 267.1, 279.3, 279.4, 295.2, 301.1, 303.1, 303.2, Robin Fletcher 187.2; Michael Woods 283.4.